SH   6-00

Kelly
Jean

O

Women and the Blues

Women and the Blues

Passions That Hurt, Passions That Heal

Jennifer James, Ph.D.

HarperSanFrancisco

A Division of HarperCollins*Publishers*

FIRST HARPERCOLLINS PAPERBACK EDITION PUBLISHED IN 1990.

Library of Congress Cataloging-in-Publication Data
James, Jennifer, 1943–
    Women and the blues.

    Includes index.
    1. Women—United States—Life skills guides. 2. Women—Psychology. 3. Stress (Psychology).
    I. Title.
HQ1221.J35 1988   155.6'33   87–45708
ISBN 0-06-254063-7

ISBN 0-06-250412-6 (pbk.)

94 95   CWI   10 9 8

Honor is fully given to the women who have offered me unconditional love and reached out to offer that love to the community:

Lucy Berliner	Char Lee
Charlotte Bottoms	Jody Locke
Cathy Brown	Sandi MacDonald
Laura Brown	Esther Margolis
Geil Browning	Joan Martin
Johnetta Cole	Sylvia Mathews
Joanna Decker	Ellen Michael
Karen Erickson	Dale Douglas Mills
Laura Fraser	Carolyn Preston
Mary Fulton	Alice Rae-Keil
Georgiana Gregor	Marlene Stevens
Melodie Hurlen	Diana Stice
Karil Klingbeil	Alberta Stone
Dale Land	

I wish you love, sisterhood, and the hope that whatever lessons are left to be learned will be easier than some of those we have shared.

Remember to take care of yourselves, all of you, so you can take care of the rest of us.

Contents

Part Two: Sources of Understanding—Strategies for Loving

Part Three: Sources of Passion—Strategies for the Future

Acknowledgments

Mary Fulton helped me every step of the way. Mary is the administrator of our publishing and lecture business, Jennifer James, Inc., and Bronwen Press. *Bronwen* is Welsh for "strong friend." All these people qualify.

Dale Douglas Mills edited the final manuscript when the words wouldn't stop rolling out. She helped create a book instead of an encyclopedia.

Tom Grady was my patient and creative editor at Harper & Row.

Elizabeth Horowitz cheerfully typed the manuscripts. Good cheer is worth a lot.

Marjorie Johnson is my energetic, optimistic mother. Thank you for all the gifts from you I carry in my genes and personality.

Godfrey James was my father. He gave me humor, honor, compassion, passion, and the greatest gift of all—he reminded me, with the loss of his life, to live my own.

Devon James is my son, a man with a generous spirit and unlimited creativity. Robert Royer is my husband. He is the first truly equalitarian man I have known.

Michael James is my brother. He reminds me with his intelligence and depth why I wrote this book. He knows what I am leaving behind and why.

Preface

This book came out of the pain of "white nights," my own. Nights always measure the innermost heart. I wanted to pass on to other women the kind of help that might have made those times a little easier for me. There wasn't a book I could pick up in the middle of the night or day and know I wasn't alone. I did read a lot, but I didn't want a "what's wrong with you" book. I wanted practical survival skills.

I never thought about writing such a book when I was a cultural anthropologist teaching at the University of Washington Medical School. I was doing research on the adaptive strategies of such high-stress populations as prostitutes, criminals, and drug addicts, and I was teaching "Culture and Illness," a basic course for medical students about how the values of your society can make you sick. I was also sharing the pain of my friends in the 1960s and 1970s redefining woman and love.

Slowly I slipped into my own pit of despair. My father's suicide, my divorce, single parenthood, a disastrous love affair, and the recognition that a university professorship could be a jail for the spirit. The day after Christmas of my thirty-third year I barely survived. Like Alice in Wonderland I had bitten too often from the wrong side of the cookie. I kept getting smaller and smaller until a friend called and sensed the danger in the tiny voice that could still make itself heard.

I did my homework. I dug up the minefield of my past so I could plant my own life. Out of the depression, healed by time and counseling, I began to work more and more in the community. I wanted to be in touch with the reality of people living their lives. So though I liked teaching, when I was offered a chance to do a community mental health radio broadcast, I found I loved having the public as my classroom.

The radio program led to a newspaper column I still write for the *Seattle Times*. I have written other books, but this is the one I've been wanting to write. It was always waiting in my heart for the time to be safe and right. What purpose is there for pain if you cannot find a lesson or some good in it for someone?

I have discovered many alternatives to feeling pain. You can smother it, abuse others with it, or abuse yourself. Or you can understand the mechanism of the trap and spring it. Pain is a powerful teacher.

I offer the thoughts on these pages to you—women who feel hurt and frustrated in our culture and want to be safer and stronger. I offer them also, with love, to men who love women and the feminine side of themselves.

I want this book to be a reminder that, if you are drawn to the most intense pages—the "hard times"—I and others have been there too. You are not alone: other women are also thumbing through books wondering if there is anything for them there. It's not that we are hooked on self-help books. We are sensitive and aware. We want to understand the choices we make.

What can a stranger know about your life? I would recognize you if we met. I feel your pain; it is not separate from mine. I resonate to your willingness to find other, better ways. You are not alone. You are known and loved.

Jennifer James
Seattle

Introduction

We are all caught in history, in a time of tremendous change. Such deep cultural changes affect our external life (our job, family, health) before we can catch up internally (image, self-esteem, sexuality). We have many choices, but we don't have the skills to make them, so most of us are paying a price for trying to have it all. We get the blues. We end up thinking that there is something wrong with *us* instead of looking deeper into the culture around us.

I can remember hating the color pink as a little girl. If my mother bought me a pink dress I would hide it under my bed. On Easter Sunday I always felt that the ladies who wore bright pink suits were hideous. I almost didn't buy my first house because its bathroom had pink fixtures. The only way to disguise it was with a jungle motif designed to overpower the pink tile.

Then pink began to sneak into my life. When I was thirty, I found myself at a sale with a pair of pink undies in my hand. Then I developed an overwhelming desire for pink sheets. Pink linens weren't in style then, and I had to go to four stores before I found them. The next step in this slide was towels. After years of disguising my pink bathroom I bought fluffy pink towels. The finale was a bright pink, deep pile, wall-to-wall bathroom carpet. My friends didn't want to use the bathroom.

I was in heaven. I would sit on the floor of the bathroom, clutching my knees, surrounded by pink and feeling at peace. I found myself staying in there for long periods of time. It was bizarre until I realized what was happening. I had grown. I had finally allowed myself to reclaim my history. All the generations of women who had gone before me were symbolized by pink. Yes, the womb!

Pink represented the softness, the nurturing, the gentleness I wanted in my life to balance out the independence. It was finally okay to connect all the women who had found ways to survive in the past with all the possibilities available to women of my generation. I was no longer split between the two. I was one. I could turn homeward. I could love and be loved.

Marilyn French, in *The Woman's Room*, eloquently describes the pain of being caught with choices. Her heroine has escaped a marriage that sucked her dry; she has grown, taken risks, learned to love and be loved, only to face an impossible choice. She can decide to be a home-maker again with her new semi-equalitarian lover and in so doing give up much of her career, or she can take the chance at forty of being alone and herself.

She chooses her own destiny and is left walking alone along a beach on a windswept day wondering about the future. She could not choose to forget what she has learned. She could not put away the conscious-ness she had gained. She cannot lower her awareness. She cannot be less than she is.

Half of my friends hated the ending; it scared them. I loved it—it was the only possible conclusion. Yet each time I think of it, a ripple of pain runs through me. It has become so difficult to define woman, happiness, success.

Women sometimes think they are God. Within each of us are so many women to be. We want to be all to everyone. Many men see God in terms of hierarchy. If a man follows the rules he will be rewarded; he will be close to God. We women believe that if we open our hearts and love with all our being, God will enter into us and we will feel the ecstasy. We want to be all that history has offered us, and we want what new possibilities we can envision and feel.

All of us get the blues, rich or poor, healthy or not. Women have desires that cannot be met in reality. Women have expectations that grow out of the ideals we are raised with—our womanness, our close-ness to new life, our ability to love too much and hurt. Our deepest values set us up for frustration.

I want this book to touch you, to reach deep inside and bring quiet to some of your painful memories and experiences. I want to give you my understanding of what it is that hurts us at this time in history. Knowing why means a certain freedom, a recognition that you are good, only your time and possibilities may sometimes seem compro-mised. I want to touch that well of energy within you that accepts who you are and feels the joy in it. Don't be blue: you are lovable and capable. There is still so much pleasure in looking out into the world and breathing in the light.

How to Use This Book

This book is about making our choices and developing strategies for survival and quality of life while we reconcile the mixed messages in our culture. The aim is practical—to provide direct answers for what to do when something hurts. The aim is also to go deeper within our womanness: I needed to understand myself as a woman before I could decide I deserved to feel better.

There are many ways to use this book, depending on both your mood and your perception of what the source of your depression is. I've assumed that most of us want to deal with a specific problem and work out a practical solution before we dig deeper into understanding our feelings. You may want to reverse this process, however, and read the part on loving before the one on living.

The first section is a short one, "Quick Help." If you are blue at this moment, there are suggestions that might immediately lift your mood. Sometimes just taking action makes a difference. To clear most blues you need understanding, self-value, and the willingness to commit optimistic acts. The trouble is that most of us find it difficult to understand ourselves or others; we find it even harder to give ourselves value, and when we are immobilized by depression an optimistic act seems futile. Small steps are all we can handle.

After the Quick Help list is Part One, "Sources of Depression: Strategies for Living." It tackles thirty-seven problems—from low-level blues (boredom, procrastination, stress, being single) to deep depression (breaking up, infidelity, jealousy, grief, loss of personal value). In addition, I've divided Part One into three sections, depending on whether you handle the problems alone (Section I), or try to work them out with friends and lovers (Section II) or family (Section III). Each chapter defines the problem by how you feel, offers some insight into why, and suggests what you can do about it now and in the future.

One of the most powerful resources you have to keep the blues at bay is your ability to understand what is happening now and to devise new solutions for the dilemmas you face. A good counselor must have a complex and extensive tool bag of alternatives. You need one too.

I've organized the survival strategies on a problem-by-problem basis for practical action, not just more words. The knowledge necessary to take care of ourselves usually comes after we've managed to recognize, confront, and resolve a trouble spot in our lives. Then we are willing to look more deeply into the causes so that we won't have to face the same issues again.

Part Two, "Sources of Understanding: Strategies for Loving," provides the foundation for finding out why you don't take better care of yourself. This part of the book is written from the perspective of an anthropologist who asks where we have been, where we are going, what the differences are between us, and why women in our culture get the blues. In Part Two, I address the issues of self-esteem, childhood, pain, masculine and feminine, and women of high potential. You need to know what you expected, what you want, and what you think you deserve.

Part Three, "Sources of Passion: Strategies for the Future," digs more deeply into what "it all" is—possibilities for bliss, lifetime connections to passion, and the need to touch the Spirit.

The goal of this book is to help you find practical actions, joy, and passion—a strength and openness to get you through hard times, loss, and confusion. Passion does not depend on the cooperation of others, but only on your ability to connect with yourself and the world around you.

Women are intimately entwined with life. We have a unique and special relationship through our ability to nurture another human being. We need to be able to nurture ourselves as well.

Quick Help

You may not want to read further into this book before you feel a lift in your mood. That's fair. Here are some quick helps that may work for you. If they don't, it's time to go deeper.

Make affirmations. This is a long word for a short, upbeat message that reminds you of what you want to feel. Tape them to your bathroom mirror, car dash, desk. Write one on your hand, tuck it in your pocket or purse, pin it to your bra, where the odd feel of it will remind you.

I am lovable and capable.
I can feel good.
I am making the choices.
Happiness requires my action.
I am never upset for the reason I think I am.
I cannot control the thoughts and acts of others.
All I need lies within.
This too will pass.
Very few things are truly important.
(Make up one of your own.)

Smile. I know it sounds drippy, but the minute you move your facial muscles into a smile the rest of your body goes along. Don't worry about pretense; just give your face a chance. Smile at others too; giving them a lift will give you a lift.

Visit the right people. Keep a list of upbeat friends to chat with. Go to an upbeat movie, or read an inspirational story. Go to hear a speaker who will turn you on.

Distract yourself. Read, work, watch television, crochet, paint, do a crossword puzzle, go to a movie, anything that switches your mind into another gear. Stay away from bad news for a while (whether TV radio, or newspapers).

Create quiet in your mind. Breath deeply, meditate, pray or perform any ritual that brings you back in balance.

Exercise. Put this book down, and go for a walk, breathe deeply, or stretch. If you have the time, go for a run or take an exercise class. Make your tension shift gears.

Laugh. Get your perspective back by appreciating the funny or the absurd. Make up your own joke, or borrow someone else's.

Give up on yourself. When we want love and none seems to be coming our way an alternative is to manufacture our own. Call up a friend and listen to his or her troubles, send a letter or a package to someone, visit someone who needs to feel cared for too. Help one of your neighbors— you know their needs. Pick up litter. Offer a little love to the environment. Volunteer at an agency that gives love through service to others (children, the homeless, those who are ill or lonely). You'll find love and respect.

Get back to nature. Get out in the wide open spaces where you can remember the good things of life. The sound of the ocean, the smell of the forest, the quiet, is always there for you.

Eat or drink something that is good for you. Herb tea, raw fruits and vegetables, anything that makes you feel you're taking care of yourself.

Wash it away. Take a warm bath or shower, and let the blues run down the drain.

Hire some touch. Whether it's a massage, facial, or pedicure, the healing touch always brings a little balance.

Improve yourself. Get a haircut or a manicure, sign up for a class, confess your sins, make resolutions, do anything that sends you a message that you're trying to change.

Go for your strengths. What are you good at? Cooking, keeping accounts, laundry, sorting out drawers, shopping—do something you know you can do well.

Change your music. Put on something that is an "upper," even if you resent it at first. Music that makes your feet want to dance will lighten up your mind. Stay away from misery music or music that reminds you of what you may want to forget. Try classical music. It rarely reminds you of sad things; it makes you feel intelligent and powerful.

Touch life. Bring something living into your home. It will help you care and bring energy to your spirit. Dogs, cats, birds, fish, plants all connect us to life.

Redecorate. Make something for your home, move furniture around, dye something another color, or hang up a new picture. Add some pizazz to what's around you—it may be catching.

Learn something new. New information and new skills will open doors for you. Take the first step in signing up for a class, experience, or project. Buy a do-it-yourself book, tape, or video and actually use it.

Create order out of chaos. Clean out your purse or something else. When the external gets more orderly, the emotions sometimes follow.

Touch the earth. Gardening has special rewards when you're in the middle stages of working your way out of a depression. It gets you outside with a purpose—and an optimistic one at that. You can garden by yourself without feeling alone. Digging in the earth is as therapeutic as watching the ocean; it is a return to the mud pies of childhood. Grow whatever you want: one pumpkin, one sunflower, peas, pansies, potatoes. Make brick terraces; put pebbles around your melon mounds. Grow strawberries in a planter. Grow tomatoes on a trellis. Keep the garden very small so it won't get to be another responsibility. Buy flowered garden gloves, sit in the dirt, play.

Perform rituals to clear your mind. Put what's on your mind into a note and send it up the chimney, float it away as a boat, boil it, flush it, mail it to nowhere. Try letting go.

Be your own mother. Curl up with a blanket, teddy bear, heating pad, favorite childhood food. Buy yourself a toy or a little present, the kind a truly loving mother would bring to a hurt child.

Take a vacation. It's fair to escape. Drive somewhere and stay overnight, or check into a favorite place for the weekend. If you can afford it, fly to some sunshine.

Shift to the future. How will this feel in twenty years—or next week? Is it truly important?

Happiness requires action.

Part One:

SOURCES OF DEPRESSION: STRATEGIES FOR LIVING

I. FRUSTRATION, PAIN, DESPAIR, AND DEPRESSION

1. I Never Get Enough Done

Whenever you think of doing something pleasurable you recall all the things you should be doing. You always are a little on edge because you sense you are behind. And you're not behind just today but years behind in your life. Lurking in corners, in drawers, in other people's minds are those things you have been putting off. You can procrastinate about almost anything: paying bills, renewing licenses, doing unpleasant tasks, leaving a job or a relationship, asking someone to pay back a loan, ironing, mending, replacing light bulbs. Some things you've put off have eventually become irrelevant.

The key symptoms are guilt and tension. You either expect too much of yourself (stress) or you are a procrastinator. Putting things off is hard work. It makes you tired.

The cost of procrastination can be high. You feel out of control of your life. It's hard to allow yourself pleasures because you have so many unmet responsibilities. Procrastination can destroy relationships and sabotage careers.

Procrastinators may be either out of control or actually exerting unconscious control. You may have a deep fear that you cannot cope with your life. Or you may be trying to avoid the expectations of others. These strategies can show up in the rationalizations you use. Sometimes understanding the secret payoff in an emotional system like procrastination can make it easier to change. See if any of the following fit you:

- Resistance to being controlled: "I don't have to do it!" Check your family history or current relationships. Are you being dominated or pushed around? Did you resist your parents' expectations or efforts to control you? Are you gritting your teeth while you think about what you're supposed to do? Check your body tension. What are you holding onto or defending yourself against?

- Fear of failure: "I just didn't get to it in time, so it's not my fault." You have a built-in excuse when things are not perfect. After all, you did the best you could. Procrastination and perfectionism often go hand in hand. "I know I cannot do it perfectly so I won't finish it." Check your expectations again. Is it okay with you if things are not done perfectly all the time?

- Fear of success: "Who wants it, anyway?" "It's not safe to succeed, they won't like me." "I don't deserve it." This is a rationalization based on your sense of the amount of success you deserve. If you achieve more, you may find ways to sabotage yourself. Children whose parents compete with them are often afraid to succeed as adults for fear of losing their parents' love.

- Fear of independence: If you are successful you'll have to take care of yourself. Closely related to fear of failure and of success is the fear of being responsible. Some of us don't want to be in charge of our own life. Procrastination may motivate someone else to take care of you. Check your childhood again. Did you learn that your mother would pick up after you? Were you allowed to develop independence? Being irresponsible has a payoff. It ties others to you. They feel you have to be taken care of because you are unable to take care of yourself.

- Ambivalence: "I'm not sure I really want to do it anyway." You may not know what you want, so you don't do anything. Many of us get caught living by what other people want and resisting it all the way. We may change our values but don't change our life or work. Then we lose interest in getting things done but don't understand why.

- Work or relationship dissatisfaction: "I'd be happy if I liked my work, then I could get it all done." This is the old "if only" defense. Things aren't the way I want them to be, so I won't be the way I want to be. Everything depends on someone or something else changing.

- Thrill-seeking: "I got an A and I only studied the night before!" You like the last-minute rush and the feeling that you just got by. If it's a family pattern, life without the "high" might seem boring. Besides, you can always brag that you do better than most with far less effort or interest.

- Revenge: "It drives my spouse crazy!" You can also drive your parents, children, colleagues, and employer crazy if you don't do what you know they want you to do. There is aggression in putting off something that someone else needs you to do. In a control tug-of-war it's a great way to win, because it seems passive and indirect. You win until they give up on you or make your life so unpleasant you capitulate.

Revenge, procrastination, and the need for control are connected to fear for your own security. Sometimes it follows a pattern of childhood abuse or family alcoholism.

- Secret power: If you are overwhelmed by authority, procrastination offers protection. You can just forget to call or forget to do the assignment. Then you can apologize for it and still keep the power in your corner.

- Depression: When you are "down" your energy level shifts and priorities change. Things you once automatically did seem too much, because all your strength is going within to sort out your pain.

- Culture: A cultural element contributes to procrastination, affecting those born after 1950. Before that, self-discipline was the means to survival. When survival became easier for many, the messages changed too, "If it feels good, do it." Songs were written about the ecstasy of being "mellow," and hammocks were purchased all over America. The good life was redefined.

In the 1980s it's clear that mellow is fine sometimes for balance, but it doesn't take you very far, whether you stay curled up in bed or keep yourself distracted by TV or stoned on something.

Happiness requires action—yours. Accept that you may have conflicting cultural messages in your mind, and work on moving the balance toward more activity, just as you would change any other habit that isn't working for you.

What You Can Do

Be realistic about how much time a project will take. Procrastinators and perfectionists often underestimate time and process and add more things to an already crowded calendar.

Don't force yourself to work under conditions that are unnatural for you. Learn your working habits, and work with, not against, your patterns.

Expect interruptions by people and problems. Raise your tolerance level for frustration, so you're not tempted to get angry and quit.

Be assertive about saying no, so you don't get overloaded with obligations.

Learn to use whatever time you have, even if it's in little pieces. You may never get the perfect block of time with no interruptions.

Whatever job is facing you at the moment, break it into very small steps, so small that they seem ludicrous. It eliminates resistance. If you have a difficult letter to write, here is a possible series of steps:

Day 1—find an envelope and address it.

Day 2—Put a stamp on it even if you have to go and buy one.

Day 3—Find a piece of paper, and write a salutation: "Dear So-and-so."

Day 4—Write one paragraph.

Day 5—Complete the middle of the letter.

Day 6—Finish and sign the letter and fold it.

Day 7—Put it in an envelope, and set it out to take to a mailbox.

Day 8—Mail it, and give yourself a nice reward—maybe a double dip ice cream cone or whatever is a treat for you.

Spend some time finding out what is important to you. The most important defense against procrastination is being true to your own concerns and priorities rather than someone else's.

Remember

Assuming you can fix the procrastination habits of someone else, especially a spouse, may get you in trouble. Try to hold on to the quality of your life without being upset at the other person. If you feel you cannot, make your needs known, negotiate, and consider counseling for both of you.

Don't accept procrastination and its pain and frustration as "just the way I am." It is learned behavior based on old survival strategies. It can be unlearned.

Don't think you're a procrastinator because you cannot do everything all the time. That's the superwoman syndrome. Your expectations may be unrealistic.

You are lovable and capable.

2. I'm Bored

You're starting to drag around the house wondering what to do. Like a little child, you're bored! It's easy to recognize—dullness, apathy, loss of interest—life is tiresome, tedious, empty. You are discontented. You are bored with self-help books. "Is this all there is?"

Boredom was once a disease only of royalty or the very wealthy. It was rarely a problem for women. We were too busy scurrying around at everyone's beck and call. Now, some of us are psychologically underemployed.

Boredom often masks something else. Before we tackle boredom as the true problem, we need to eliminate the possibility that it's really one of these other feelings. The most important is depression. Boredom for a few hours or a weekend isn't significant, but boredom that seems to be a regular part of your life is probably a symptom of low-level depression.

Boredom can cover emotions or pain that you prefer not to feel. You may have painful events in your past, or you may have developed a pattern of covering up feelings. Life is always dull for you, but it is preferable to your true emotions.

Boredom also can mask simple fatigue. You won't let yourself rest, but you are too tired to do anything or to generate interest in anything. Try some relaxation techniques (meditation, a warm bath, a nap), and see if your boredom changes.

Burnout is another possibility. You've just pushed yourself too far. There is a loss of your uniqueness as an individual that goes with burnout. If you are not unique, then why bother to be interested in anything.

Frustration also sets you up for boredom. You cannot for some reason (weather, change of plans, uncooperative person, money) do what you want, so you refuse to be interested in anything else. Adolescents often get into this kind of rebellion boredom. If they cannot do what they want, they won't do anything.

When you've "tried on" the above possibilities and plain boredom is what you're feeling, here are solutions that might work:

What You Can Do

Accept it. Sometimes boredom can be a blessing. At least nothing bad is happening. In one "Garfield the Cat" comic strip Garfield wakes up bored. He moans and complains and then walks out the front door. Outside he is attacked by a dog. He comes crawling back into the house bruised and broken and murmurs, "Sometimes boredom is better."

Let yourself float around for a while. Try doing nothing as a meditative exercise. Accept it as a temporary energy loss, and just stare at the wall or sleep. Use the time to reevaluate what you are doing with your life.

Take an inner voyage. Go back in your mind to a time when you felt contented, excited, interested. Why was it different? What opportunities do you have to create that same feeling now?

Help someone else. Reach out to someone who might love the opportunity to be bored. Offer to babysit; take someone to the store; volunteer on a community project; walk a dog. Give your boredom to someone else.

Recognize it's time for a change. We choose boredom by concentrating on things that don't interest us. You may be too comfortable, so take a risk. Pick up the newspaper, and see what's available that you haven't tried before. It doesn't matter whether you end up liking the activity or not—you're bored anyway. Boredom can be a yearning for unrealized parts of yourself. Do something new.

Keep a file. If boredom turns up often enough to bother you but not enough for you to look deeper into the causes, then set up a boredom file. When you are feeling normal put into it all the things you wish you had time for. When you're bored, something in the file may just trigger your interest.

Sometimes boredom is what counselor Alene Moris calls "divine discontent," and you have to learn to live with it awhile. At certain times of our lives we need to stop and do a review. Boredom is a signal to reconsider priorities, check values, figure out what's important and what brings pleasure and passion to your life.

Personal growth always involves struggle, and sometimes boredom is a symptom of your struggle. When you decide to stretch more of yourself than you have been, boredom is rarely a problem.

Remember

Try not to force someone else to be bored with you; misery does love company. Make sure you are joining with someone else, however, not just bringing that person down.

Don't think that boredom is someone else's problem. If everyone around you seems boring, chances are that you are the problem, not them.

Don't create a disaster so you can banish boredom. Starting a fight with someone, making inappropriate demands, or getting drunk won't solve the problem, but it will create more. Some people generate self-destructive situations (they take drugs, have affairs) to prevent boredom.

Don't wait for an idea to strike you and illuminate your problem. You could end up waiting forever.

All you need lies within.

3. I Don't Want to Go Home at the End of the Day

It's the end of the workday, and you're dragging your feet. You don't want to go home. The transition blues: it's a temptation to hang around work, to run errands, maybe stop for a drink with a friend, but somehow to put off that moment when you pull into the driveway or arrive at the front door.

You feel that things are unfinished at work, and you don't want to leave it behind, so you fill your arms or briefcase with bits of the office, store, or classroom to take home. You know you probably won't work on it at home. You'll even feel guilty for not working on it. But you deny yourself a transition to a place of comfort and pleasure. You have these feelings even though you love your home or whoever is waiting for you at home.

Single persons have feelings that may be connected to not having someone to meet at home. The temptation is to keep on working because it's a familiar and comfortable pattern or in order to avoid being alone with yourself.

Parents often dread the chaos they expect to find: problems, demands, and work that you have less control over than those you face on the job.

If you are a full-time homemaker, you find yourself anxious about your spouse's arrival. You look forward to it, but the control and confidence you've felt all day seem to be gone, and you're not sure how the evening will turn out. You have the feeling you will have to manage one more person's needs.

At a lecture a woman told me that no matter what she did she was always the first one home from work. She and her husband both finished work around the same time, but she always got home first even if she tried not to. One evening she decided to wait him out and began driving around the block. Guess who she ran into? Her husband was driving around the block too!

They laughed, and he explained that the first one home had to talk to the baby-sitter, clean up the mess, start dinner, feed the dog, listen to the kids. The second person home got to read the paper. They agreed to alternate nights until the kids were older, and then they would come home together.

Men have told me that equality cost them their home as castle, or at least the illusion that men had a castle to go home to. Women may imagine there are other women putting up their feet and turning on soothing music.

Whether you live alone, are a homemaker, or you and your husband both work it's important to understand transition tension. It takes different emotions and skills to survive in the work world than it does to sustain a home or a relationship. Many workers feel their day should be over at night, but for those who have spent the day at home, especially with small children, it may seem as though it is just beginning when their spouse walks in. Pierre Mornell, in his book *Thank God It's Monday*, describes the problem:

Work and love are almost always opposites. Work is head. Love is heart. Work is rational. Love is irrational. Work is thinking. Love is feeling. Work is mask on and defenses up. Love is mask off and defenses down. Work involves discipline and logic. Love requires play, passion and an absence of logic.

Men may have a fear of connection at the end of a day because to them it means more responsibility, more performance. Women have different fears, based on security issues; they fear separation. So at the end of a day or week women may want to be loved and listened to and men may want quiet and privacy. Having different needs at the same time can set us on edge with each other, and we end up passing each other in the hall on the way to bed.

Men also fear intimacy, and staying at work is a way to avoid it. They feel confident making widgets, talking to clients, or examining patients. They have control. At home they cannot step behind a professional screen; they cannot easily control what people will do, say, or ask of them. You may want to relate and connect deeply to the man in your life at the end of the day, and he may want to work until you're asleep.

What You Can Do

Check out the things you now do between home and work or when you get home that might be attempts at transition (reading, watching

TV, listening to music, exercising, running errands, cleaning, changing clothes, having a drink). Some homemakers take a bath or set the table as a way of shifting gears. I used to hide in the bathroom with the newspaper.

What works for you? Try to imagine the perfect transition. For me it's a quiet place to read the evening newspaper from cover to cover. I can sit in my car or make sure I take the time when I get home.

Mornell suggests that we make conscious the ways we shift gears between work and home.

- List and discuss the specifics with others involved.
- Tell them clearly about your need for privacy and quiet.
- Know you'll have different needs on different nights.
- Realize transitions involve cooperation.
- Consider transition time as a means to more intimacy.
- Minimize passive ways of tuning out. Maximize active transitions.

Barbara Mackoff, author of *Leaving the Office Behind*, suggests using a closing ceremony to shift gears and gain perspective. It can be as simple as preparing a list or a mental image of what you will do at work tomorrow. You can take a brief vacation in your mind that takes you away from work and toward home. Send the day's mistakes and problems off in an imaginary rocket or toss them in the wastebasket. Throw it all in a drawer or locker, and close the door. Put it in the trunk of your car.

Reconnect to your body by exercising after work or going for a walk. Stop, catch the sunset, and think about the beauty of the world you're in. Stop in a church, and say a prayer. Picture the faces of the ones at home waiting for you. Think about what kind of day they had. Remind yourself to ask them. Imagine the best place to be in your home relaxing. Let music waft through your mind. Dredge up some humor, and make a joke about the day that helps you to let it go.

Check the path you travel, physically and psychologically, between your worlds. All of us need to make a transition either before, during transit, or after we get home. It is a powerful shift in our day (or if it's Friday, our week). Plan it, negotiate it, enjoy it.

Remember

Try not to think it's "their" fault that going home isn't the way you want it to be.

Don't set up transition hassles whenever you go to work, go home, or start a vacation.

Don't drown your transition in alcohol so you can put it off until the next morning.

Don't rev up your stress on the freeway so you can grind your teeth hurrying home and be full of tension by the time you put your key in the door.

The shortest emotional distance between two points is not a straight line.

4. I Want Their Money, Status, and Security

I was once asked to speak at a meeting of successful men and their wives. They were corporate presidents in high financial brackets. The subject they wanted me to discuss was "Self-esteem in the Jungle." As I walked into a first-class hotel, past Mercedes, BMWs, and a Rolls Royce, I wondered at the topic.

In the elegant conference room I questioned them. What do you mean by the term *jungle?* They answered, "The corporate jungle." Were there dangers lurking in the hallways, the board room, the elevators, the parking lots? When I think of a jungle I think of danger, wild animals, lack of shelter, not knowing where your next meal is coming from. I don't imagine corporate boardrooms.

Sometimes we are so far removed from real survival issues that we create false ones. We feel threatened; we think we are in danger. When you are more than a generation past poverty you need to create a feeling that you are still in a battle for your life, the constant pursuit of money seems meaningless otherwise. You've lost the connection with your life force. It is so easy to lose track, whether you are a Wall Street broker or feel as though you're just getting by.

Richard Pryor's notorious statement that "Cocaine is God's way of telling you you're earning too much money" fits as well. When we have enough "stuff" but not enough "meaning" in our lives, we are tempted to find escape. We want to create crisis. Some do it with drugs; others with infidelity, competition, elitism, and envy.

When we feel a little lost and our self-esteem is slipping, money and possessions can seem to be the solution. It is important to be able to tell the difference between "things" that truly add quality to your life and "things" that take away quality by creating responsibilities. Take the time to sort out what you really want before envying what you think others have.

Do you own the possessions you have now, or do they own you? Weigh the actual pleasure and meaning you get out of them against the amount of time, anxiety, and effort you spend trying to acquire them, hold on to them, maintain them, and pay for them. Some rich people become the overworked servants of all the toys, gadgets, houses, and social roles they've purchased. They clamp their jaws so hard they have to wear mouth guards to keep from breaking their teeth.

Envy focuses on acquiring and holding on, rather than creating and enjoying. If you find yourself obsessed with greedy thoughts and schemes, look at your personal life and your career to see if you have neglected to build rewarding relationships that would naturally advance your well-being.

Envy is the feeling of wanting what someone has without understanding the process that person went through to get it. You may be yourself a victim of someone else's envy. People may think that you've got something they don't have or you may feel it yourself.

When I was teaching at the university a talented young student informed me one day that she could be doing what I was doing. I agreed with her and suggested she enter graduate school. She said that wasn't fair; she should be able to do it without credentials because she was just as smart as I was. Why should she have to wait when I was already there?

Envy wants what the other person has and wants it now! Envy does not lay out plans for achievement over time. We don't just envy things: we envy feelings. "If only I had . . ." Envy is connected to impatience, low self-esteem, and childhood deprivation.

Dreaming is wonderful; wishing is okay; but "if only" is a way of saying "never." It is an attitude that focuses on what you lack, on what others have, and that makes it difficult to care about yourself as you are.

"If only" thoughts always mean we are a little stuck, not sure where to go next. We just want to have something more.

What You Can Do

If you have worked on your sense of personal security in other ways and are clear that more money and status would significantly add to the quality of your life, then go for it. Decide what you want to earn or do; list the sacrifices you will have to make (time, relationships, other activities, personal change); and make a plan. Read, study, question, and start building capital. Instead of buying something you want but don't need, open an investment fund.

Take time to figure out what you want, what more money will buy, and what your life can give you.

Accept full responsibility for doing it yourself. Don't expect it from men or assume other women are happy taking it from men. Many men think women view them as lifetime meal tickets, and some women do. The earning power of a male has often been an important part of a woman's decision to marry. Many women still have to depend on a man for whatever money they have.

Couples may be sharing money more easily—you may have money of your own—but the only way to avoid power struggles over money, or thinking, "If only I was married or married to someone who makes more money . . .," is to understand that the only clear source of increased income is your own personal effort.

Any money or status that comes through others (male or female) has strings attached and trades that must be made. Women, with the exception of mothers of young children, are no longer automatically entitled to support from men.

Remember

Try not to compare your happiness to that of others. You have no idea how they really feel.

Comparing your life with someone else's never provides satisfaction. Emotional and material competitions are small death wishes. You can only win by having your own standard. Listen to your own rhythm. Measure happiness by your own heartbeat.

Don't give your life to the success of others. Keep it for yourself.

What you are right now is what I love.

5. I Love to Buy Things

Some of us just think about having everything, but you may be one of the women who goes out and buys it, wreaking havoc with your budget and your life. It's a recognized syndrome, with its own support groups, Shopaholics and Spendermenders.

Women are ambivalent about money. Money is power, and women with power may not be seen as feminine. Money is often used as power in a relationship. "I'll control the money," or "I handle money better than you do." Men and women often view money very differently.

Many men see money, like power, as having a value in and of itself. If you spend money you don't have it to save and invest. It's a Scrooge McDuck phenomenon of collecting money for its own sake and therefore never having enough.

Most women think of money in terms of what it will purchase. Some of us may be starting to think of investments for the future, but most of us still put buying quality of life ahead of saving. We think someone will take care of us.

Even when they don't think that way, women are better than men are at being poor. They can rescue quality of life from flour sacks and food stamps. Men find that kind of compromise very difficult.

When you want a new refrigerator you're thinking of quality of life. Your husband may be thinking of that $750 invested at 10 percent over ten years. If he spends it, it's gone. What does he have to show for it? There are exceptions, such as money spent on demonstrations of power, in particular, automobiles.

Whoever overspends, the cause is usually ambivalence about money or powerlessness over money. When it comes to buying almost anything, the overspender is out of control. He or she gets a high from shopping, then anxiety and guilt take over, and only another purchase stops the depression.

What You Can Do

Write it down. Keep a record, every day, of what you spend, and carry it with you.

Know your weak times. When something has hurt you, when you're tired, have fought with a friend, or survived a difficult project at work, you are vulnerable; the urge to give yourself something is overwhelming. Check out the alternatives—what else could give you the same feeling? Clean something so it seems new? Go through your closet and organize, press, and mend your wardrobe? Rearrange the furniture, or make something? Take a warm bath for comfort. Write a nasty letter for revenge but don't send it.

Use a list. If you cannot keep from shopping, stick to a careful list of what you need. Don't go out of the house without a list, even if the items on it are frivolous. Be as specific as you can be about each item so you don't end up with something you don't want.

Take a friend. A friend will slow you down and provide some comfort. He or she might even provide an alternative to shopping, change your mood, or help you be more careful about purchases.

Evaluate your purchase. Many stores have coffee bars, places to sit. Ask the clerk to hold your selection while you think about it.

Cancel your credit cards. This will take nerve but offer you a little control. You might have to give up a checkbook as well and pay bills by money order. Never have more than one general credit card, so you're not tempted to run up to the limit on them all.

Ask yourself why when you spend on children. We are always guilty about our children and vulnerable to pleasing them with things. Children know when you buy things because you cannot give in other ways.

Learn about money. Men will buy a house to resell. Women will buy a house to live in. Try to put aside what may be a female bias and learn how to budget and invest.

Watch out for holidays. We confuse good feelings with good presents. Slow down, and don't make up for the blues by spending.

What You Can Do with Your Partner

If you are part of an economic relationship, you need to know what is happening to the money you share. Women no longer can refuse financial responsibility or information, nor can they claim that their earnings can be kept separate as "pin" money.

Agree on priorities. Work out a budget, and make a list of what you want to purchase or save for. If you cannot agree (new car versus vacation) then work out a system of alternating preferences or saving for both at the same time.

Communicate regularly. Share financial information on a weekly basis. Consider a brief ritual on Saturday afternoon where you talk over shared and independent financial circumstances.

Recognize different money skills and interests. If one of you is better at handling money, then that person should do it but continue to share information. The other person should always keep an independent bank account; neither should have to ask for handouts.

Consult on purchases over a certain amount. Your income level will determine what you consider a purchase that has to be cleared by the partnership.

Learn together about investment. Our discomfort with money makes it hard for us to treat it as we would any other skill that requires education.

Money can be the biggest source of conflict in our life and relationships or it can be a tool we use as we choose to. Money is a neutral force; you yourself give it positive or negative power.

Remember

Make sure you can survive alone. Dependence always brings conflict and manipulation because of the fears of the dependent person. Make sure that you can survive a breakup fairly and with your own resources.

Very few things are truly important.

6. Stress Is My Way of Life

You know how it feels. Your body is tense; your neck and shoulders ache; you feel jumpy. Your mind and emotions are irritated and tense. Sometimes you feel tired all over even though you haven't accomplished much. Stress is a major source of depression. These are symptoms when your stress is out of control.

PHYSICAL
- increased heart rate
- shallow, rapid breathing
- clenching or grinding of teeth
- high blood pressure
- dizziness
- sweat
- aches and pains
- skin breakouts
- frequent colds
- illness
- abnormal eating habits

EMOTIONAL
- nothing seems right
- feelings that you're working harder than others
- depression
- restlessness
- feelings of worthlessness
- irritability

BEHAVIORAL
- You think that microwave ovens are slow.
- It is hard for you to wait at red lights.
- You finish other people's sentences.
- You are often impatient.
- You can do at least two things at once and often try three.
- When talking to someone you can think about something else.

- Slow lines, unequal lines, traffic, all irritate you.
- It's too much trouble to sort out change, so you pay with paper.
- You do everything rapidly; relaxing is hard for you.
- Adding things to your busy schedule is easier than removing them.
- You hang up the telephone after only three rings.

Stress is a bodily response to physical or emotional demands. You need a certain amount of stress to be able to stand up. When you have no stress you're dead. It's a question of balance. If you refuse to listen to your body, it will do something to get your attention. Constant stress becomes a silent killer. You may adjust to it, accept it, never understanding the cost.

Stress doesn't just kill you or make you more susceptible to disease, it can ruin your life in other ways first. When your health is undermined your work, pleasure, and relationships suffer.

Stress impairs your friendships and your sex life because you are too irritated, busy, or unhappy to make love or to be lovable. You make mistakes, have accidents, and feel depressed.

You know all this, so why don't you do something about it?

Because you want to stay stressed: You like the feeling. It makes you seem important. It means you are working very hard and getting lots done, and it impresses people. Wrong!

Because you can avoid responsibilities at work and home: Anyone can see that you just couldn't cope with any more work.

Because you can avoid relationships, play the martyr, and be irritable: What else could anyone possibly expect from someone as busy as you are?

Because you convince yourself that your needs and your time are more valuable than anyone else's.

Very few people will miss you when you're gone.

There are many more options competing for our time and attention now than at any other time in history. There is a glut of information and choices. Women want to do everything, even at the cost of their health and well-being. We need to learn to cope with multiple options, or we'll end up with mental gridlock.

The most common cause of feeling exhausted is just trying to do too much. You expect far more of yourself than is possible: the superwoman syndrome. You are trying to be the traditional woman and the new woman. You cannot even define a successful woman, so you do it all.

Try a quick review of a few women's magazines. What kind of model are they setting up for you to imitate? Yikes!

"Well it's true I'm busy but I'm so happy. I get up at five in the morning to write poetry, before thirty minutes of aerobics. Then I make a real, home-cooked breakfast for my family and watch the news so I will be informed.

"I toss a load in the washer, work out the menu for dinner, drop the kids off at school, and begin my work as a corporate attorney. There is usually a volunteer meeting on my lunch hour, or I stop to have my nails extended or pick up the latest fashion.

"It's such fun to attend the kids' after-school activities before I pick up a few things for dinner and change into something special for my sweetie. There's lots of time then for listening to the kids problems, cleaning the house, and reading the latest books.

"I love to cook something special—actually gourmet, but of course quick—for dinner and to set a nice table, always with fresh flowers. Then it's off to class, a meeting, catching up with work or correspondence, and a long romantic evening with my man.

"On the weekends I catch up loose ends, meet with friends, have a dinner party or two, sew, garden, paint, remodel the kitchen, and see a play or film. It's a wonderful life."

This may be a caricature, but it's not that far from some of the expectations you have in your mind for yourself. It leaves you feeling you aren't doing enough. Many women find themselves doing dishes or mopping floors after eleven at night. They assume that being tired is the price they have to pay for the good life or that somehow other women are better organized than they are.

There is a lot of dishonesty in the images in the media and also in what friends and acquaintances may portray to each other. What you don't see are the women screaming in their cars with the windows rolled up or crying in the shower. Check your level of competitiveness and your capacity for martyrdom. How often do you pretend you're just fine, even to yourself? A lot of women are afraid to admit how tired they are.

The keys to keeping a reasonable stress balance are knowledge, management, and prevention. You need to know how high your stress level is, what you can cope with before hurting yourself, how to lower stress, and how to prevent stress. Check your stress level:

Level One

Physical symptoms: Your body gives you signals. You may decide that it's normal to feel this way and not respond. Some people don't like to relax because they feel turned off; they like the high excitement of stress. Symptoms include fatigue, frequent illness, headaches, back pain, overeating, sleep problems, drug taking, drinking.

Level Two

Social symptoms: People get in your way. You are irritable and harsh. Eventually you have no time for people at all, so you put them off.

Highly stressed executives find ways to avoid people. They don't look up when people pass their offices, because making eye contact leads to conversation. Walking down the street a stressed-out woman will see a friend coming and turn the other way to avoid having an unplanned chat.

Level Three

Mental or intellectual symptoms: You can't concentrate on projects. You drive home and cannot remember how you got there. Life seems boring; you procrastinate. Minor problems and disappointments throw you off. There is less pleasure in everything.

Level Four

Emotional symptoms: Things just don't seem worthwhile to you anymore. The world is not fair. You focus on your inadequacies and everyone else's. You suspect others aren't doing as much as you are. You feel alienated from people and hide from them more frequently. You look for flaws in everyone, including yourself.

Level Five

Spiritual symptoms: This is the most severe level. You sense your loss of uniqueness as an individual. You are just a cog in a system, in a rut. Nothing matters, because you just don't care. "I don't matter, and life doesn't matter." You feel trapped. You may be seriously depressed.

It is possible to get so detached from your body that you don't know how you feel. People deny stress or assume they can cope even when they reach level five. Can you measure yourself?

How do you feel?

How long have you felt this way?

How aware are you of the sources of stress you face in your environment? These include such things as weather, noise, travel, working conditions, safety, neighbors, smoke, dirt, light intensity, barometric pressure, menacing behavior, smells, world and local events.

What makes you feel stressed? Expecting too much of yourself and others is one stressor; others include change, the unpredictability of events, lack of control over a situation, and personal conflict.

What You Can Do

Examine your life, and list the sources of your stress, from minor changes to major problems that you might be dealing with or worrying about. Include every possible source of tension. Arrange the list from most severe to least, so you know what you are dealing with. Become familiar with your stress system.

What are you willing to do to reduce your stress level? How creative are you with difficult-to-change stressors (small children, money worries, illness)? Have you checked out new strategies? Are you looking for a solution, or are you just stuck? Here is a list of tips from the experts:

Reduce or eliminate caffeine.

Stop smoking.

Exercise.

Do relaxation exercises.

Limit sugar.

Drink more water.

Limit alcohol.

Talk it out.

Work off anger.

Take one thing at a time.

Reduce your responsibilities.

Take vacations.

Schedule recreation.

Ease up on criticism.

Keep your sense of humor.

Check your priorities.

Eat breakfast.

Get plenty of sleep.

Take vitamins.
Use visualizations.
Get a massage.
Apply heat.

Even though we know these things would help, we still set up barriers. See if any of these belief systems fit you:

- Competitive: You are so concerned about your score that you will ruin your own life to look good.

- Workaholic: Work, work, and more work is the only way. We used to celebrate people who worked themselves to death. Now we think they are fools. Researchers have discovered that workaholics don't get more done; they just like to be busy. If they spend all their time with widgets, patients, paper, or clients, they can avoid emotions and intimacy with others. When they go home they have to deal with relationships. They prefer a high-stress style to the threat they feel in an intimate relationship.

- Perfectionistic: Everything has to be perfect, and you cannot relax until it is. Since perfection is an illusion, you never relax, and no one around you can either.

- Martyr: You prefer to suffer and feel it will pay off in the end. Before coming into the house at night you adopt a worn-out, hangdog, look-what-the-world-did-to-me expression, so that everyone will want to help you. Once home, you sacrifice so they will feel guilty, see how stressed you are, and take care of you. "They will notice if I collapse. They'll be sorry." If you aren't stressed, how will you ever get any attention?

  Women often confuse sacrifice with femininity. They think they are more of a woman when they have exhausted themselves serving everyone else. They have listened too many times to the song "MOTHER" ("M is for the . . ."). Submission to stress was once a survival technique whereby women proved their value to the family. Now we can contribute more by being balanced.

- Waiting for others to change: There is nothing I can do until the children grow up, my spouse changes, I get a new job, or something else. You will wait forever.

- Negotiation: The only way you can win in this world is if the other person loses. Therefore you are always in danger of losing. If you win and make them say "uncle" they will be so angry they will work at sabotaging your win. If you lose you'll make sure that they lose too. Compromise is not easy for you, but stress is.

- Unrealistic expectations: You think you can do far more than is reasonable. Therefore you overwork constantly and criticize yourself for not being able to do more. You treat others, especially children, the same way.

- Waiting for justice: The world is supposed to be fair, and my version of justice should prevail. When it doesn't I go through the roof.

- Old strategies: You repeat the same strategies for solving problems even though they don't work. "If I've told you once, I've told you a thousand times."

- Low self-esteem: I don't deserve to feel better. I'm a mess, and messes are stressed.

- Ambivalence: You don't know what you want, so always feel you don't have it. When you get something it turns out to be something you don't want.

- Caring about credit: You can get more done, with less stress, if you don't care who gets the credit. The desire to be noticed and rewarded for everything is related to competitiveness and low self-esteem. Let it go, you'll get the credit when it's important and enjoy yourself meanwhile.

- Old messages: I don't deserve to feel better. It will upset someone if I change. I have no choice. It's too late. I'm not able to change.

- Dependence: You think someone else should take care of you. Your mother, father, spouse, sister, or friend should see your problems and take the load off you since you cannot take care of yourself.

If any of these beliefs fit you, try to analyze why you feel that way. Where did the feeling come from? Can you let it go? Then start planning ahead.

Patterns and habits are hard to change unless you look ahead. Once you have too many pots boiling, it seems too late.

Get out your personal calendar. Look over how you spend each week. Develop a sense of your activities. Take one month that you have a daily record for and underline in one color the things that gave you pleasure and in another color the things you didn't like. Leave neutral activities alone. You will then have evidence, in color, of how you are spending your time.

Try to make changes in your schedule to reduce the negative and increase the positive. Can you do it? Do you have an excuse for not eliminating negatives? If it's your job then it may take longer to change than if it's a voluntary activity you just don't like any more.

Look ahead to activities or events that could be sources of stress and plan ahead. Take extra good care of yourself if you know your work load is going to increase. Build up some pleasure to draw on later. Try the stress reducers in the next section.

Stress Busters

If you face a daily traffic jam, turn it into a break. Keep music or talking-book tapes in your car, snacks, a notepad, and a thermos. Have a picnic, plan your next vacation, or enjoy a comedy routine while you stop and start. The traffic "problem" will be over before you want it to be.

Start and end your day on a positive note. Think of something good to wake up to before you go to bed. Have a nighttime and wake-up routine that includes pleasure. Couples sometimes read in bed and chat before they go to sleep and then wake up and share coffee and the paper in bed before the day takes off. Set up a routine that works for you.

Take longer to wake up so you don't have to jump-start your day. Leave time for a good lunch or a relaxed dinner. Plan appointments and driving with extra time for the unpredictable.

Focus on what you are doing; avoid doing two things at once unless it gives you pleasure (for example, crocheting and watching TV). When your mind is making other plans or carrying on other conversations while you try to accomplish something or talk to someone, your stress level goes up.

Ask if what you are upset about is life threatening. I used to get messages from my office that said, "Very important, call ASAP." I would panic, thinking something terrible had happened. If I was in the middle of my radio broadcast I would have to wait to call or the line might be busy. When I made contact it was usually not that important. My secretary now never says "important" unless the house is on fire or someone is dying. The phrase she uses most often when I check in and ask if anything is important is "nothing that can't wait." She's right, and I've relaxed.

Check your attitude. Your reaction, not the situation, determines how much stress you feel. It's your choice. You can choose peace instead of conflict.

You are eating lunch in a restaurant, and the waitress throws the food at you and is unavailable for service. You get angry, take it personally, and steam through the entire meal. An alternative is to assume her husband just ran off with her best friend and she is barely making it. You don't have to tip, but you can be pleasant until the meal is over and then decide whether you want to eat there again.

Keep a list of your past successes in your mind or pocket. When you feel tense remind yourself that you usually do just fine and you'll handle it this time too.

Ask what the worst thing that could happen is and how you would survive it. You are about to give a speech. You freeze and cannot talk. People get up and leave the room (lots of them) while you are talking. You wet your pants. These are not criminal acts. You will survive—and the worst is unlikely to happen anyway. Desensitize yourself with your imagination. Go over and over the disaster until it gets funny.

If you think that you are one step from becoming a bag lady, make a list of what you would have in your cart. You'll need a poncho, a warm comforter, a thermos, and a library card. Be prepared, and at least you'll be a relaxed bag lady. Imagine the worst, cope with it, and feel your stress lift.

Take action. When things seem unfair or in need of change, start a fight. Diplomatically fighting an agency, a bureaucracy, or your family can clear the air, improve the situation, and relieve stress. At least you will feel you're making a difference.

Figure out the few things you can get control over (laundry, files, body hair), and let some of the others go. It's impossible to have a place for everything and everything in its place.

You have to decide what's important to you. Feeling good should be at the top of your list. Clear out your absurd expectations. Set up priorities based on good health, good feelings, good relationships, and let go of the "you can eat off my floor" craziness. If that one is too important, fine—give up something else.

If you have small children, get help. Even if it's a high school student who comes for two afternoons a week and costs ten dollars, do it! If you're broke, arrange a trade with a friend or join a cooperative. The new furniture you save your money for will never replace the lost joy that you passed up because you are too tired to feel.

Give in occasionally. It doesn't hurt to let others win once in a while. They may be surprised and grateful. Let someone else dominate a situation or decide what to do.

When the present is too much, create an alternative. Take a few moments to dream or visualize something wonderful. Take a mini vacation or a longer one. Leave town for a few days, or leave your body for a few minutes. Go into an art gallery, a church, or a greenhouse and find a different atmosphere.

Step outside your own problems, and take on someone else's. You will feel good about helping, put your own troubles back into perspective, and get some new ideas for handling them.

Forget superwoman. That is another term for work-yourself-to-death. The comic book superwoman had no children, no husband; she had special powers and assistants. There is no glory in being superwoman, only exhaustion. Remember, if you try to do everything you are setting a bad example for your children and making other women feel inadequate.

Check out your relationships. Do you feel safe, supported? Reconnect with friendships you have let slide. Be warmer to those you work with or do business with. Smile at strangers as you pass; say good morning to the bus driver.

Shift gears by using your creative side. Join a singing group, play a musical instrument, garden, paint; anything that uses your hands will relax your mind.

Celebrate finishing something before you tackle the next job.

Touch life. It's very reassuring. The laying on of hands can heal. Get a massage or a facial; hug your friends; pet your dog or cat.

Find a way to laugh.

Set up a cue word. Pick a phrase that reminds you to lower your stress level, and repeat it until you feel calm. The one I use is "I am safe." It reminds me not to go back to my childhood.

Find time to be alone. Spend a few minutes alone every day to review what is going on. Spend a day alone whenever possible; schedule a weekend alone at least twice a year to chart your direction and listen to your heart.

Recognize when you need a stress counselor. If the physical and emotional symptoms continue despite your best efforts, it's time to get help. Stress is like any other medical problem.

Remember

Don't learn to live with stress. You deserve to feel better.

Try not to blame your stress on anyone or anything else.

Lift everything from your mind and shoulders at least once a day just so you can remember how good it feels and that you know how to do it.

There is more to life than increasing its speed.

7. I'm Burned Out

Burnout is stress associated with a particular vocation (teaching, counseling, law enforcement, air traffic control, parenting) or with a project.
The feelings are psychological as well as physical. It's as if you've locked
into stress and it's forever. You doubt your own value system and become suspicious of others and their intent toward you. You're sure that
you are working harder than everyone else. You think the only way out
is a drastic change (divorce, new job, moving). You feel like a victim,
but you're not sure what you're a victim of. Ask yourself, Why am I
doing what I'm doing? Why do I have this job?

If the answers don't please you, it's time to do something else that
does. If you answered, "No choice," you are clearly in burnout.

What You Can Do

Ask yourself, Am I burned out, and why don't I take better care of
myself?

I like to suffer.
They make it impossible.
I've lost my judgment.
I'm suspicious when I'm happy.
There isn't time.
I will when I get a chance.
I can't afford it.
It's my job.
If I collapse someone else will have to do it.
The work must get done.
I don't know what else to do.
Who will do it if I don't?

Ask yourself, What am I willing to do about it?

- get some rest
- take a vacation

- exercise
- get help
- improve my self-esteem
- check my perspective
- change my expectations
- change my job
- change my diet

Work bit by bit on your perspective and expectations. Try to take the world off your shoulders by reminding yourself that you are more than the sum of what you produce. Tell yourself over and over, "I cannot change the thoughts and acts of others."

Start investing in the quality of the process, not the goals. Put your energy into the moment, not a reward that is weeks or months away. Evaluate success or failure by internal not external measures.

If the way you're doing something isn't working, don't hang on to it. Let go and try another.

Things will not fall apart just because you are relaxed. Remember that whatever you do, you do for yourself, not for anyone else. You may help people, but you do it because it makes you feel good. Whenever you involve yourself in a project, it's because you want to be involved.

Give some of your compassion and tolerance to yourself. Harmony depends upon your ability to offer yourself love, and your ability to care for others is wholly dependent upon it. Stay in touch with your feelings so you don't end up always squelching your emotions to protect others. Playing the stoic or the martyr leads to certain burnout. Call upon your friends, and listen to the witnesses outside you who have a less subjective perspective on your work.

Accept the ambiguity and paradox in any helping profession relationship or project and in any situation that requires a long gestation period.

Find out why you don't value yourself and work on changing it.

Remember

Dragging yourself everywhere is not normal. Give up feeling guilty because you cannot do everything. Don't decide to just live this way until the kids are older, the house is finished, you're through school, or your job changes.

Don't push yourself to illness or a breakdown so someone else will have to take responsibility for your care.

Don't hope to gain attention by panting, collapsing, or developing an ulcer.

Try not to brag about how burned out you are. It's hard to give up anything we think we're best at.

Listen to your stomach.

8. I Don't Like My Body

Aaggh! Look at this body! Cellulite, lumps, too short, too tall, too small, too big, too white, too black, too straight, too curly—HELP! It's not just the genetics or the exercise that I don't do. Will I ever be happy with my own body and style?

There was a time when fear of conceit led adults to put children down. People in your family criticized your body. "Look at that nose! I hope the rest of her face catches up!"We were taught to reject compliments: "Oh, this old thing!" Kids grew up aware of their negatives and unaware of their positives—or at least ready to dismiss them.

Girls were exposed to other messages, such as smart women are homely and dumb women are more likely to be beautiful or that God doesn't give everything to anyone. Definitions of beauty were narrow and changed with fashion. Petite gave way to tall as an ideal; full breasts and hips went "out" in favor of slender as a reed; blondes were queen until brunettes were deemed sexy. Beautiful hands were hands that were never used, and women weren't supposed to sweat. *Cosmopolitan* magazine once ran an article on how to go about having your sweat glands removed and another on what sexual positions would hide the most flaws—flat on your back or backed up against the wall, never on top because your face would droop. Keep your arms at your sides, so your breasts can't slide into your armpits.

Beauty has for so long been an essential definition of a women's value that few women see beauty within themselves There is always something wrong with us.

How clearly can you see yourself? Are you always looking through the eyes of someone who is critical?

What You Can Do

Stand in front of a full-length mirror with your clothes on. Make a list of all the things about your appearance you don't like and a list of all the things you do like. Double-check that these really are things you do or don't like rather than what you were told as a child. Images do change.

My mousy hair as a child is really a nice, warm blonde.
My feet are no longer too big.
I'm not as tall as they said I was.
The rest of my face caught up with my nose.

Divide your negative list into things you can do something about if you want to (hair color, nose, weight) and things you cannot or that you don't want to pay or suffer to change (height, crooked teeth, warts, chin, varicose veins).

WILL CHANGE	WHAT I LIKE ABOUT ME NOW
Weight	Height
Flexibility	Skin
Neatness	Feet
Diet	Breasts
Muscle tension	Navel
Clothing styles	Smile
	Laugh
CANNOT CHANGE	Neck
Age	Ankles
Fat knees	Nail shape
Eyesight	Hair color
Crooked lips	Ear lobes
Buggy eyes	Voice
Shoe size	
PROBABLY WON'T	
Nose	
Cellulite	
Droopy butt	
Teeth	
Some wrinkles	
Nails/hands	

Look at the change list, and take some action on each one you can or want to change. If you don't do it within a few months, shift that part of you to the "Cannot Change" list.

Here are things I did: I found a new hairstylist, who helped me find a style that looks good despite my lack of hair talent. I went through my closet and learned what is comfortable for me to wear and got help determining what looks best on me. I gave up all my "high maintenance" clothing. I am trying to exercise, control my diet, and relax. People are more attractive when they're relaxed.

Now look at the other list, and come to terms with reality and your choices. I don't do anything with my nails but keep them clean. Polishing my nails just isn't worth the trouble to me, so no more lamenting that my nails are not perfect and fuchsia. I am not going to get my nose fixed, because I would rather spend the money on a vacation—another choice. But I am going to have bags under my eyes removed if they develop. They will make me look a way that I don't feel is me. I'll start saving the money and investigating the possibilities.

Take everything that you are not going to change or cannot change, one part at a time. Stand in front of the mirror and remind each part that it's time to make friends. Why carry enemies with you into the future? Anything you hate should be fixed, or you two should patch up your differences.

"Nose, I love you. Let's be friends, after all, we've got another forty years together. I know people have made remarks about you in the past. I won't allow that anymore. I'll disagree with them. Nose, I love you. Welcome to my face! Now, on to the hips!"

The motivation to accept and take care of your body is best if it comes from within. Sometimes we wait for a health problem, threat of divorce, loss of love, professional demands, or competition for a new love. Any motivation has merit, but it's strongest if it originates in self-love.

It may take a while to quiet the old voices of evaluation. There will still be doubts and mistakes, but greet each one with a reminder that you're the one who has to accept your image so that others can relax and follow your lead. When you make a mistake, just mark it down and get rid of it. Consider getting professional help on color analysis, image, and style. Each year you will be truer to yourself. Start a scrapbook of things and styles that you feel fit *you*, not some ideal. Remind yourself of what you've learned before you go shopping or seeking a new hairstyle. Notice what people mention about you or compliment you on.

Remember that nobody is perfect. We cannot even define what perfect is. Beauty is truly in the eye of the observer. We all have our quirks. It may not be comforting to us when *Vogue* asks beautiful models to reveal their flaws, but there is a worthwhile message. Each model had to decide that thin hair, gaps in teeth, uneven lips, or a unique nose would not stop her. They accepted that the complete image was what they were offering. When you like the way you look, almost everyone will assume you're right.

Watch out for sabotage from friends, family, children, or spouse. They may not want you shifting out of the image they have given you. Sometimes others will feel threatened and competitive. They may pooh-pooh the changes, ask if you're becoming narcissistic, tell you that plain girls should wear beige, not flashy red, or convey in other ways that you should stay the same.

Beware of your own rebellion. "It doesn't matter what I look like. People should like the real me, even if they and I can't figure out who that is." Check out your use of body image to keep people away. Looking masculine, slovenly, soiled, and rumpled may be a way of creating a fortress that no one will want to penetrate. Fat makes a protective shield.

Another part of rebellion is the power of old patterns. "This is the way I've always looked. Take it or leave it." We found something familiar (like jeans and sweatshirts) that got us through hard times, and it became a lifelong uniform. If you've made the right choice (Katharine Hepburn has worn pleated trousers and white shirts most of her life and looked great) that's fine, but if you haven't (I wore overalls for years and still love them, but they're not appropriate for work) you may have created a uniform as a way of not investing in yourself. Have you formed a blind spot rather than creating your own unique style?

For many years I didn't try to look good. I felt if I didn't try then I wouldn't fail. If I tried, and still looked bad, people would know I couldn't look good, and so would I. Not trying was a way of avoiding commitment and creating the illusion that if I "really" wanted to I could. When I finally started developing my own style, it was scary but wonderful.

Make friends with your body in all ways. Exercise is one of the best. You two need to get to know each other.

Sit down and hold a meeting with your body: Imagine six thousand cells, each with human features and wearing a bright sweatshirt. Now explain to the liver cells why you are drinking things that make them sick. They want to know why they have to wear brown sweatshirts when they prefer red.

Talk to the cells in your lungs and explain why they cannot get their shirts clean. Explain to the stomach cells why they need ladders to avoid the fat that's floating around them. Try to convince the muscle and tendon team that they should jump whenever you ring the bell, even if it's only once a month. They refuse to even dress.

Last, but not least, after checking in with all your other cell friends, what about the sex cells? They are promised romance, and they are getting no action at all or no time to prepare their act.

True, this will be a long and difficult meeting, but they have been waiting a long time for you to show interest.

Break down your resistance to exercise by thinking of all the reasons to do it even when you don't want to.

I can eat more.
I'll feel better all over.
I'll be happy even if I'm otherwise not.
I will get sick less.
I'll look better.
I'll feel in control of my life.
I will be able to move with ease all my life.
My body will be more comfortable.
Sex will be better and easier.
I'll be able to run away from trouble faster.
I'll be more successful at work.
I won't yell at the kids.
I will lower my stress level.
Other decisions will be easier.
I'll be stronger.
I'll feel independent.

Fitness lifts depression because you feel in control; you feel less stress, more self-worth and self-mastery. You are not an easily victimized limp noodle. You are a person who cares about herself and her body.

Remember

Don't give up. No matter how many exercise plans have fallen through, it's still worth another try.

When you get behind because of work, vacation, or illness, don't quit. Just start over. It will be easier than the first time.

Don't imitate someone else's look. Your style has to be your own. Start with someone else as a model if it helps, but tailor the model to you. How you look is how you feel about yourself. Other people will take their vision of you from you.

No one can make you feel inferior without your consent.

9. I've Been Alone Too Long

Somehow you've slipped into a pattern of being alone all the time. Even at work you don't really connect with anyone; you just exchange the usual pleasantries. You feel that you are set apart, somehow different. The ads and TV programs describing busy, social lives are for someone else.

A pattern of aloneness can be lifelong, or it can just gradually evolve from broken relationships and hard times.

Don't confuse a desire for solitude with loneliness. In solitude you are with someone you love, enjoy, and can easily entertain. Loneliness is being with someone you don't like and aren't sure what to do with. The key is the person you are with—you.

Some people crave solitude. They have rich inner lives and need lots of time alone. Others were raised in more social cultures or families and find being alone strange and uncomfortable. Think about your family and culture, your life experience, and give yourself a score for solitude or sociability. One end of the scale is very sociable, hating to be alone, even when sleeping. The other end is hermitlike; you have to force yourself to make contact with others.

Your score changes from time to time. How have you handled solitude so far in your life? What is hard about your current circumstances? Are you alone by choice, or do you feel others are making the choices? If this is a new pattern check the following list of factors that contribute to loneliness:

- New in town: It takes a year for most people to settle into a new town and not feel lonely.

- Divorce or breakup: Grief always makes us feel alone. No one can know how much it hurts. We want only the person we've lost, so we feel lonely with anyone else.

- Stress: Our perspective falls apart when we're stressed. We create rejections.

- Violation: If your trust, home, body, any part of your life is attacked in any way you feel unsafe, scared, and very alone. You want someone to take care of you.

- Loss: Any loss, even small ones, produce grief and loneliness.

- Change in pattern: Someone you used to see has moved, or you talk to that person less. Your job schedule shifts, so you have more time to yourself. The cat or dog is at the vet. The kids are gone. Your roommate is on a business trip. It takes time to rebuild interaction routines.

If any of these fit you, then take action to change the pattern. It's also possible to just accept the temporary feelings you have, understand them, be patient with yourself, and muddle through. That's what most of us do.

We are at heart social animals, and we all need some communication with people, pets, plants, weather, and seasons. Only you can determine what fits you.

Evaluate your preferences and patterns. Build a routine that satisfies you. Be prepared for temporary loneliness by recognizing it happens to all of us, noting the probable cause, and setting up a list of quick cures. Here's mine.

Read, and move your mind into another world.

Call a friend and touch base.

Go for a walk.

Go shopping where you can go in and out of weather and stores.

Tackle a project (plants, art, cleaning, sorting, work, balance accounts).

Go to a meeting or public performance.

Exercise at a club.

Talk to your dog.

Write a letter.

Take a bath.

Turn on the TV, and join a show.

Rent a video.

Volunteer at an agency.

Help someone else.

Long-term Aloneness

If your aloneness is a lifetime pattern, if you have never had a close relationship with someone other than your parents, if you are afraid of connecting with other people, then you have adopted a survival strategy to protect yourself from the abuse or arbitrary rejection of others. You turned inward early, or found it impossible to overcome childhood shyness and fears. It may take counseling to create the feeling of safety you need in order to open up doors. Read the self-esteem section.

Some women end up alone and aren't quite sure how it happened. We were once more social. We didn't imagine a life like this or plan it, but somehow here we are. Things just happened. It may have been

Loss of one who was our social link, through death or divorce

Self-destructive behavior (drugs, alcohol)

Economic instability (loss of a job, chronic unemployment, poverty)

Responsibility for others that excludes ourselves (sick parents, young children)

Mental illness that once separated us from reality and makes it hard to return

Rejection by others because we are in some way different (racism, disability, body image, stuttering, shyness)

Membership in an exclusionary religious group that isolates its members from the community

Childhood pain that makes it hard to expect anything for ourselves or from others

Physical trauma, an accident or illness that separates us from the original pattern of our life and may isolate us from others

Personal experience that makes it hard to relate to people who have not shared them (war, loss of a child, imprisonment, witness to tragedy)

There may be others that you have deep within you. If aloneness is a long-standing pattern, even though the event is in the past, consider counseling to unravel the path you have taken to end up alone.

If you sense that you understand what happened and are ready to take small risks to connect with others, here are some possibilities:

What You Can Do

Find a volunteer opportunity that seems safe. Working in a food bank filling bags or helping to clean up or build something. You will meet people who are open to meeting you. You can go at your own pace.

Join a group that you share a common interest with. Make yourself go to the meetings even when you don't want to.

Practice saying "How are you?" to people you do business with outside of work. Linger a little longer when exchanging pleasantries. Learn a little more about the people you are in contact with.

Reach back into the past for a relationship that is lost (relative, high school friend).

Attend public events that have a social component. Art events with a reception, political fund raisers, community meetings.

Join a support group through a local agency (YWCA, Community Mental Health, church) or a counselor.

Smile at your neighbors when you pass and at strangers when it seems appropriate.

Go to the same stores and restaurants until you are familiar with them and they with you.

Surround yourself with life. Each of us has our own favorites, but love everything living, even mold. You can fill your home with birds, plants, animals, moving water, colors, scents, prisms, crystals, mobiles, fish, pictures, needlework, glass paperweights, globes with snow inside when you shake them, kaleidoscopes, books, stained glass, and a few spiders weaving webs.

Move deeper within yourself. Meditation helps, and reading self-help books and novels, counseling in its various forms, workshops and classes.

Stretch your creative side. Build, design, paint, sew, dig around your place. I have a bowl of sand to play in. Music can fill a house, and so can flowers.

Accept your spiritual connection. Explore religion, the meaning in life beyond yourself.

Connect yourself to the world. Give a gift of yourself. Join an organization, be an activist, write letters, contribute money, organize events. Give care to anything living.

Treat yourself as you would want a lover or friend to treat you. It's good practice for when one comes along and a lot of pleasure if one doesn't. We can be perfect lovers to ourselves because we know what we want.

None of these steps will be easy. You will often feel uncomfortable and fear rejection. You can add many more opportunities, but the key is in follow-through. You have become good at avoiding contact with people, and you will have to gradually change. Make a rule that at least once a day you will do something social that you are not now doing and that once a week you will go to a social event. Wean yourself away from the aloneness strategy in small, safe steps.

When you have taken the small risks of making contact, read the section on friendship to take steps towards intimacy with others.

Solitude

If none of these alternatives appeal to you, then you may, in fact, prefer solitude and not know it. Accept that it may be time to cultivate your inner companion. As we grow older even the most energetic extroverts find themselves turning within and loving it.

You will get to know yourself and your values, which will help in making decisions, improving the quality of your life, and finding peace. Solitude helps us to slow down, catch up with ourselves, and think more clearly. We get smarter.

It is easier to control your schedule and what you eat and drink when you are not being sociable. The environment around you will seem richer and more attractive because your vision will become keener and your hearing more acute. Solitude makes all your senses more powerful and more focused.

One of the gifts of age is the wisdom we gather within. Accept solitude; it's a feeling you can draw from for all eternity. Without it age becomes a threat, a time when we will be alone forever. Put some energy now into drawing the warm quilt of solitude around you.

Remember

Don't think there is something wrong with being alone because of all the messages to be social we receive from the culture around us.

You are not the only one alone. Not everyone is out at a party in a silk dress.

Don't accept the continued pain of a temporary loneliness that seems to be becoming permanent.

Try not to accept a life alone unless it is truly what you want and brings you peace. Fight to have what you feel you want.

Don't let a temporary loss or problem grow into a lifetime pattern.

Don't reject yourself or accept rejection by others. There are millions of people available to you.

I am making the choices.

10. I Worry About Everything

Anxiety stirs up your entire body and mind. You may feel short of breath, a pounding heart, stomach upset, nausea, sweating, nervousness, and faintness. There is an unnamed dread, a strong sense that you are not safe. The feelings can be free-floating tension, a sense something is wrong, or a full-blown anxiety attack.

When you have a free moment, do all sorts of worries pop into your head? If you take a nap, sit down for coffee, linger in bed after you wake up, even sit in your yard or read a book, can you just enjoy it? Or, the minute your body is at rest, do little nagging thoughts and anxieties flood in?

The constantly busy woman is often running away from her anxieties. Demons must be faced if she slows down long enough for them to catch up.

Chronic worriers reveal it on their face. They fuss and wait for the worst. The line at the movies will be too long; the restaurant will be full; there will be no sale items left; someone will be late or early. An overwhelming number of little and much bigger worries (like nuclear war) follow them everywhere. It is often all they want to talk about. It becomes a style of life.

Worry often is inherited. A woman may get the message from her mother that worrying makes a good woman. "My mother always worried about us." In other words, she cared. Check the messages you have received about the worrying woman.

Worry is joy for some because it is familiar and it is all they ever have known. Check your family pattern and your own life and see if worry is your lifework. Maybe you have had an experience that has set a worry in motion for a lifetime. The depression scared many into hoarding forever. Missing a ferry or a plane scares some into departure anxiety. Maybe you are imitating someone else's response and emotions and passing it on to your children. Is worrying an essential part of your safety system, a shield to keep real problems at bay?

Check your heritage for martyrdom. Does it tempt you? Does the word *sacrifice* creep into your mind as you fuss through a day? You may hope that by worrying yourself to death you'll get a reward in heaven, or at least that everyone will notice all you've given. They won't.

Worry can be a dominant force in your life; it keeps you busy, connected, gives you constant sources of conversation, binds people to you, fills your mind, and prevents you from really thinking about what may be possible for you. It may release you from real responsibility for your life and from the pressures to be happy.

What You Can Do

Identify your worries. Put your worries into perspective by putting them into order. Set up a file system in a box on your desk or kitchen counter. Organize your worries into categories, using cards for each worry. You will have your own divisions, but here are some options:

- Things that rarely happen: house burning down, terminal illness, nuclear war, meteor hitting the house, child kidnapped or hit by a car.

- Things that cannot be changed: old decisions made long ago (if only we hadn't immigrated to America), height, skin color, first marriage, the baby we didn't have, the education I didn't get in high school, the years I smoked.

- Misinterpreting the feelings of others: Why did he look at me that way (his stomach is upset)? Why hasn't she called (she is overwhelmed with work)? Are they ignoring me?

- Health: I wonder how long I'll live; is that spot or lump malignant; my bowels feel strange; my veins look blue; I'm tired all the time.

- Legitimate concerns: economics, children, marriage, friendship, housekeeping, work, community service, taking good care of myself, diet, exercise.

Keep track of your thoughts and gut reactions and prioritize your worries until you have the top twenty. Put each of these on a separate card in the box, and make a contract with yourself to not worry about the others until you've taken care of the top twenty. If an excluded worry persists, trade it with one of those in your main box. Tuck the others away for later.

Each time you get a new worry, "Should I paint the living room?" decide whether it goes in the main box to replace another or in the auxiliary (I'll worry later) pile.

Set aside a specific time each day for concentrated worry over the top twenty. Shuffle the cards at that time, and choose which ones you want to worry about. Spend the time thinking of possible solutions to your worry, and note them on the card. If you find you've solved the problem, file that card under "No Longer Worry." It is important to keep old cards so you'll have a sense of all you've accomplished and how much you can handle.

Think about your values: what is truly important to you versus what is important to those whose messages may crowd your mind.

Keep the card in your worry box until you feel comfortable with your proposed solution. The key in this work is to put your energy into *doing* instead of *feeling*. Work on a solution during your worry time, not just on free-floating anxiety.

Here is a sample card:

Nuclear War Anxiety: We'll all be blown up.

Solution: I could say good-bye to everyone and just sit and wait.

Solution: I could join a group that is working against nuclear war and help to reduce the possibility it will happen.

Solution: I can pray at least once a day and put positive messages out into the universe.

Solution: I could travel so I get to know this world better and have more understanding of national and personal fears.

Solution: I could get into a career that would put me in government service closer to the decision makers or to the scientists doing weapons research so I could influence them.

Solution: There is no real evidence that we're going to blow ourselves up. We usually just blow up bits and pieces. I don't need to worry until it actually happens. If it doesn't, I'm fine.

Here's another sample card:

Abandonment Anxiety: What if my husband leaves me?

Solution: I could spend night and day being a homemaker who is irreplaceable, a lover of monumental passion, and a perfect spouse. I could read *Fascinating Womanhood* and wear white go-go boots and plastic wrap. I could run his entire social life.

Solution: I could work on my own independence economically, socially, and personally so I would be a valuable person in life and my husband would then not want to leave me. If he did, I would survive.

Solution: I could work out some basic elements of happiness between us such as taking care of myself, treating him with kindness, making love and intimacy a priority, and never taking him for granted.

Solution: I could give up on marriage altogether so I don't have to worry about someone loving me.

Solution: I could make it impossible for him to leave me by tying up our money and possessions, emotionally controlling the children, and making a few other threats.

The rules for making this system work are:

Accept that we all worry.

Concentrate your worry to a certain time each day, creating extra sessions if you need to.

Stop worrying at other times by reminding yourself that you have a specific time to worry later.

Always concentrate on solutions until one finally comes along.

Free-Floating Anxiety

Most of us carry one level of unidentifiable anxiety, feeling that we are not safe. It can be intense or just a twinge that takes the edge off pleasure or relaxation.

When there is no specific object for our anxiety, only the overwhelming feeling of not being safe, it can become a phobia. You may choose a particular object or activity (dogs, flying, heights, water, crowds) to contain the otherwise overwhelming free-floating fear of life itself. It is much easier to focus anxiety on something and to create an avoidance pattern than it is to understand such pervasive insecurity.

Stress is a response to the environment outside of yourself and your perception of it. Anxiety is an effort to control what is stirring deep within you.

It may be impossible to identify the sources of this type of anxiety, because it is so deeply connected to your culture and to your childhood experience. Many cultures instill anxiety, fear of life, in their members through religion or other belief systems.

Personal war zones also produce "nameless dread." Parents or other influential adults can teach children to be afraid of living with constant cautions: "You never know what to expect." "Bad things can happen." "You'll be sorry." It becomes a pattern of thought and physical response with no beginning or end. It becomes part of what it feels like to be alive.

Children who are not allowed to take a few chances as they grow may be anxious. They have a belief within that they cannot quite cope, and that at some point their whole system could collapse.

Intense feelings of unidentified anxiety also stem from more severe abuse by adults. Unpredictable physical and psychological violence creates a realistic view of the world as dangerous. Incest and molestation teach children that they do not have control over even the most intimate parts of themselves. The shadows, the patterns within, remain; there is a deep sense that they still cannot protect themselves.

Check out your family, culture, and life experience. Listen and watch family members, especially your parents, and see if you can recognize worry patterns. Read newspapers from your community when you were ten. What was in the air; what information and experience might have influenced you?

Learn your history. We develop survival strategies early in life based on the environment that surrounds us. Many of us forget to drop the old strategies when circumstances change and we, as adults, have more power to exert control.

An alternative is to learn to live with a degree of free-floating anxiety. Name it, know it, plan for it. Accept that you will never know all the sources of your anxiety. Some of it may even be a useful life force. When you feel it, take action.

Exercise. It always breaks up the patterns of any anxiety.

Cut caffeine. Stay away from stimulants.

Eliminate alcohol. The initial "buzz" is always pierced by an increase in anxiety.

Review on paper or in your mind home, family, friends, and work. Give each a success rating and decide if anything needs to be changed.

Create peace. Visualize a garden; remember a beautiful place; plan a vacation.

Shift worlds. Read a novel, go to a movie, watch TV (nonviolent), listen to music.

Use your hands. Clean, fix something, crochet, dig, sort, build.

Listen to tapes. Books on tape are wonderful, theater just for you.

Talk with a friend. Share the feelings.

Hug pets. Touch life.

Anxiety Attacks

Anxiety and worry can also take the form of panic, the intense fear of literally losing control of ourselves, losing our minds. We don't know what we would do—scream, rip our clothes off, attack someone. The internal physical symptoms are severe.

If you have panic attacks you require counseling to learn techniques for understanding and relieving the particular pressures that affect you. When you find yourself building up feelings of extreme anxiety the following steps may help:

Take a deep breath. When you breathe in shallow gasps your body mobilizes all its forces. Breathing deeply immediately relaxes these signals.

The tension you feel stems from a biochemical buildup, your body's response to the signals you give it. Any type of physical activity (walking, stretching, jumping up and down) will release the tension and discharge the bottled-up energy.

Contact a friend who will give you support, even if it's over the telephone. Panic attacks are short—usually twenty minutes—and a calming person to talk with or touch can slow them down.

If you've had such attacks before, work out a crisis plan and imagine yourself going through it. Work through each step of the attack and recovery until you feel yourself relaxing. Learn anxiety safety and responses just as you would fire safety. Expect the attack, and be prepared for it.

There will always be times of tragedy and grief when worry is part of the natural process. Often it is the middle of the night that produces uncontrollable worry; we are vulnerable when sleeping or near sleep. If you wake up, remind yourself that you are just checking reality. You are safe.

Your sensitivity to safety also can be seen as a heightened awareness. Early in life you learned to pick up signals, evaluate them, and devise survival strategies; your concerns are a measure of your aliveness.

Remember

There is always a temptation to accept that "this is just the way life is" or to keep a destructive defense system or habit because it seems easier. Don't!

Fussing, whining, and worrying can become your only way of communicating. Don't let this be your life. Try to fuss less each hour until it becomes a new attitude.

Don't stop worry with alcohol, drugs, frenetic activity, or sleep. Sooner or later it will catch up with you in the form of illness, stress symptoms, or depression.

I am rarely upset for the reason I think I am.

11. Competition Makes Me Uncomfortable

One of the strange things about the competition blues is that many highly competitive women don't think they are competitive. They don't like the word or the feeling. Women feel direct competition is cold, hard, mean, unfair, and anything but feminine.

For women the traditional competition centered on "catching" the right man. It once pitted women between sixteen and twenty-five against each other for a scarce resource. It was the most important contest of all, because the results determined your social standing and financial class for life. Whatever else you yourself accomplished, your position derived from your husband's success. Once married, the competition shifted to children, home decor, and cooking. There were many limits on women's accomplishments.

It was difficult to maintain a feeling of sisterhood in the face of such direct and vital contests. Thank God, it's changed! But, even though there are now many alternative routes to success and security, some women continue to watch each other. Divorcées feel the lack of trust from some of their married friends. Some women still spar for a marital partner because they think good men are difficult to find.

Highly competitive people often have a skewed view of the world. The idea that "it's a jungle out there" contributes to stress, hostility, irritability, perfectionism, bad temper, and depression.

Here are some of the things we compete for:

- Attention: Just as when we were babies we think our survival depends on commanding more attention than the next baby. We walk into a room wondering who's watching. Some women cultivate a style that pushes others aside, whether through dress, conversation, or control.

- Men: It stretches throughout our lives. Women who still perceive men as the ultimate prize will compromise themselves, their children, and their friendships to be with a man. When you view men this way all other women are potential enemies.

- Best kids: Since our only work, our only profession, once was home and children, it's not surprising there still is a temptation to live our lives through our children, with constant comparison and not-so-silent scorekeeping. "Tell me, is Jason talking yet?" Children who sense this kind of competition will often embarrass you rather than be victimized.

- Work status: Entering the work force with career objectives does not mean playing by men's rules. Many women think it does. They compete for money, status, network, and assignments.

The fear of competition can cause as much grief as a competitive need that's out of balance. You may avoid chances for success in things you care about because of fear that people will misunderstand, you won't be liked, you'll lose friends, you might not win, it's not feminine.

Take time to understand your own behavior and your perception of competition. How you feel colors all your relationships. Review your parent's attitudes and your culture's, do they subscribe to the limited pie view of life, or the unlimited pie view?

The Limited Pie View of Life

People with the limited pie view of life assume there will not be enough for everyone. They panic at department store sales, plan way ahead, and assume they will not get their share. Some of it comes from childhood deprivation and parents who suffered great losses. The world is a limited pie, and you have to protect your slice or risk losing it.

Your best friend Kathy stops by and tells you that this month has been an amazing series of successes.

"You won't believe this," she says. "I just won ten thousand dollars in the lottery. Then I found out that I'm going to get the promotion in the office that we were both working for. I know you'll be happy for me. While all this was going on, my daughter got a full scholarship to Columbia. I lost ten pounds in the excitement, and I met this great new man. Wow! What do you think?"

Well, what do you think? "I'm so happy for you, Kathy." Arggh! You smile while you clutch your stomach. You feel as though you've been kicked. Somehow you've lost something—not just the promotion you wanted, something more. Even when you are not in direct competition, someone else's successes can hurt you. You feel that your piece of the pie is smaller.

Even if you've been happily married for years, you wonder if others have more romance. It's a tight and stressful view of the world. Individual competition can take on many of the characteristics of war.

The Unlimited Pie View of Life

You assume there is enough to go around. It is a perception of abundance instead of a feeling of deprivation. The spokes of the pie are the same, because we are all connected at the hub, but there is no rim. When Kathy announces all her successes her piece expands outward and in no way infringes on yours. We all have potential and possibilities.

Someone else's success teaches us something and gives us energy. "I could do that!" instead of, "Why her and not me?" Those around us become sources of support instead of people whose scores we have to watch.

Once you understand how you feel about competition try measuring your own success. Wealth, beauty, status, popularity, righteousness are external measures that can provide some security, but without other qualities you still end up feeling insecure.

How do I feel about myself, am I a caring person? These are internal measures. Do I have what I truly want? What are the things of value I carry within me? What are my skills? Can I take care of myself and others? What brings me pleasure? Do I allow that pleasure? Am I satisfied? Am I at peace? Am I true to my own values? Does anything about me require comparison to someone else? Can I hold my value alone?

What You Can Do

Admit you're competitive. Most of us are, and it helps to recognize the symptoms in ourselves instead of pointing them out in everyone else. The issue now is to evaluate whether it's a problem.

Accept the fact that no one is ever really number one. There will always be others who are better at this or that. Victory is fleeting.

Compete with your own high standards, not anyone else. Try doing something well that is private, that matters only to you. Get used to pleasing yourself instead of hordes of anonymous others. Doing your best depends only on you.

Stop exaggerating the importance of things. Slow down, and let off the pressure. The best work is often done carefully, over time, with sustained attention and depth. Everything is not an emergency. You are not "behind" in your life.

Put together a list of noncompetitive activities. Reading, fishing, relaxing, sewing, gardening, listening to music, walking, talking with friends or family, traveling, cooking, admiring the environment or others, playing with animals. Resist the desire to turn these into competitions, "Arfy likes me better than you." Just enjoy them for you.

Examine your fears. Work on letting go of the hostility and aggressiveness connected to competition. Check the old messages and insecurities to find out what illusions you're protecting. Are you still competing with a sister your mother preferred or a woman someone you loved left you for? Do your homework.

Learn from your competitors. Whether the situation occurs at work or home you can use competitive feelings for personal growth. Watch what they do, and how they do it. Become a colleague or a friend and learn the skills you admire in others.

Develop a sense of ease when you have to compete. Be prepared and sensitive when others undermine you because of their own problems with competition. Be direct and assertive. Avoid the tempting snide comment.

Check the sources of your definition of success. You may have learned standards from your parents that don't fit you or your place in history. Many women strive for things that turn out to be meaningless to them once achieved. The cost of such competitiveness often is friendship, marriage, children, and even ethics.

I remember the pain of competition for spelling in the third grade. A string was put around the room with paper airplanes pinned to it. Each child had an airplane with his or her name on it. The beginning airport was Spokane; the ending one was New York. Who would get there first by spelling words each Friday was the fuel.

I was somewhere in the middle; some smarty-pants was first; and George was always last. His plane and a few others never even made it to Idaho. One day George took his plane off the line and threw it away.

We can now choose what is worth competing for.

Remember

Don't feel you'll get behind if you stop scrambling up the ladder. You may not want what is at the top. Life isn't a contest with few winners; it is a moment by moment process. It is how you feel all the time, not just at the end.

Try to avoid the competition bait when someone else sets it out. Colleagues, relatives, friends, and employers may try to push you or goad you. Smile and relax when you recognize their problem.

Try not to force competition on your children. Help them to have high personal standards but not to judge their success by comparison. Don't compare them to each other, peers, or you as a child. Reward positive handling of mistakes, losing with grace, and winning with equal attention and respect.

You are far more than the sum of what you produce.

12. Oh, God, It's Another Holiday

Holidays are supposed to be a time of joy and togetherness, so why do we get stressed out and blue? It is the illusion of perfectibility. We are tempted to believe in an ideal; we work toward it, and somehow our preparations, activities, and feelings fall short. We expect so much that we end up a little lost and disappointed. We think, in at least one corner of our hearts, that it is our fault.

Holidays mean family and friends gathered around each other out of love and commitment. There doesn't seem to be room for the ways things are between us the rest of the year. We hope that people will not be themselves for a few days. Some can do it. Most revert back to their usual reality after the first drink.

Now, it is not all disappointment. Sometimes we do get closer to a friend or relative during a shared holiday. Some rituals do bring peace and joy. It is unlikely that all will.

The first step is to accept that there is love and joy in the reality of the way we are. There is no perfect "Norman Rockwell" American family.

Remember that print of the Thanksgiving dinner he painted? Everyone is sitting around, smiling, at a heavily laden table. Mom is bringing in the turkey; the children all have apple cheeks, and none of them is stoned. You can almost feel the normality, the steadiness, of this family and their celebration.

But you can't hear the conversations. "Well Mom, if you had put the turkey in on time Uncle John wouldn't be drunk!" "Tell me, dear, I know you're busy with your new job, but does little Paul still wet the bed?" "Why do you bother with sweet potatoes; nobody likes the way you cook them." "Did you make the pies yourself?"

We all play the same games on holidays that we do at any other time. I remember one Thanksgiving when I had cooked everything from scratch, cleaned and decorated the whole house, tried to create a haven for seventeen relatives, and then collapsed at the dinner table. My mother's first words, as the food was being passed, were, "Jennifer,

I notice there is a ring around the bowl in the upstairs toilet. I've told you before that a little wet and dry sandpaper will get it right out."

What You Can Do

Here are some ideas and rules that might make your next holiday of togetherness easier:

Create a play. If you always fall into old roles in your family that you don't like, then try to watch instead. Be the audience watching a play; detach from the drama enough to enjoy observing it. You can even keep track of how often Dad criticizes or your sister-in-law competes. You also could add up loving gestures.

Remember you have a choice. You could have chosen to be somewhere else. I have spent holidays completely alone, with only friends, with almost strangers, and with family in various combinations. You can learn from how you feel at this holiday what you would prefer to do for the next one. Don't bow to family tradition if it isn't going to work for you; at least work out a compromise.

Lower your expectations of joy. Don't set yourself up for disappointment. Put together in your mind a picture of a holiday you can enjoy that is also within the realm of possibility. Don't count on anyone being able to change except you. Aim for a comfortable holiday, not a wonderful one. If your expectations are reasonable, you and others will be able to relax. You won't be disappointed, and you may have more joy than you expect.

Fantasize the perfect holiday. Let your imagination run away with you, and then choose the part that means the most. Ask each member of your family what element of the holiday is most important to them, if you plan to share it. Then put your energy into the priorities, and let the rest go.

Review the past. What has worked for you and what has not? There is no reason to repeat bad experiences. You may feel the tug of habit, but you can move on.

Create new traditions. Ritual is meaningless if it creates unhappiness or doesn't speak to your heart. You can design and begin your own traditions.

Deal with relatives. They are yours and that makes them special whether you like them or not. They will be there year after year, so find a way to make peace, be civil, or stay away. Decide to accept any new relatives who turn up (in-laws, step-children, second spouses) without creating in-group and out-group. Welcome them all, especially the children.

Slow down. Remember the speed at which the Spirit travels. Do less and enjoy it more. Children, especially, want a relaxed and loving time with you at Christmas instead of hectic activities.

Do something alone. Attend a church service or a concert. Sit in the dark and listen to Pavarotti on your sound system. Walk around town and look at the lights and decorations without buying anything.

Share a meal with a friend. Pick someone special to have a holiday meal with. Express the warmth and love of the season directly.

Make peace with someone. This is the season for it. Pick one person you are frustrated or angry at, and try to resolve your differences.

Find a way to give to your community. You can give money, time, clothes, toys. Do it as a family or a friendship group, but do it. Don't just give to those who don't need it.

Make a gift. Something from your own hand and heart feels real. Bake something, and fill the house with the scent.

Take a smell tour. Smell cookies, evergreens, candles, incense, and perfumes of the season. Bring a friend, and sniff your way through an hour together.

What if the holiday clearly is going to be a bummer? You know the answer. Is it important to you, or just hyped by others? How can you keep the best feelings and rituals and let the others go? Who is making the choices? You are!

Positive

Doing something for you: reading, cleaning, relaxing, bathing, playing.

Listening to music that lifts you up.

Building a fire, popping popcorn, calling or writing a friend.

Deciding what you want to do for the next holiday.

Leaving the holiday environment: go with a friend to the woods— or the Bahamas.

Write a check to a charity.

Negative

Thinking about what everyone else is doing; imagining them very happy.

Listening to music that brings back painful memories.

Going out with someone you don't like.

Thinking about everything you've done wrong.

Thinking of what you wish you could do if he or she were with you.

Remember

I don't know how many perfect or even passable holidays each of us is alloted in a lifetime. I do know that many of them will happen when you are alone.

You can do it your way.

13. I Want Everything to Be Perfect

Frustration, irritation, impatience, anger—the desire for control. We learn as children a terror of being at the mercy of events, situations, and circumstances we cannot control.

Children of alcoholics and abusers have it burned into their soul: the unpredictable grab or slap, the broken glass that becomes a hurricane.

You want it to be different for you. But no matter how you try, how thoughtful you are, you cannot control the spouse, kids, dogs, friends. You seethe with fear and frustration. One snip of the taut wire, and it will all come apart and you'll be a child again—caught.

You dream of a place for everything and everything in its place.

One of the results of constant criticism is a belief that love and approval come only to those who are perfect. The people who believe this end up with an illness called perfectionism. They feel that only when they have established perfect order and control over everything will they be loved. Since perfection is an illusion, they are forever disappointed and frustrated.

The perfectionist wants the house to look as though she moved out or sealed it in plastic. She cannot recognize that life is an ongoing process, that change is constant. She would be happier if the other members of the family would just become neat pieces of furniture to be put on display. The perfectionist also wants the yard perfect, the car perfect, the dog perfect, and everything at work perfect. She feels irritated about the condition of the neighbor's lawn.

You can only be "perfect" by comparison; therefore, perfectionism requires criticizing others. In a marriage, it's like punching holes in the heart of your relationship with a single-hole punch. It takes awhile, but eventually the love falls apart.

Perfectionists care more for order than for people. They establish their worth only through control and score keeping. Their families are part of the score. They hope to show the world and, of course, their never-satisfied parents.

Parents who never seem satisfied with their children's accomplishments raise children who are never satisfied with themselves. They become driven by fear of being unacceptable.

The healthy pursuit of excellence, the genuine pleasure of meeting high standards, is often confused with perfectionism. Perfectionism is based on the painful illusion of personal perfectibility, people measured entirely by production or accomplishment. Excellence, however, is achievable. There is a feeling of gratification when a project is completed that lasts a long time.

What You Can Do

Rediscover yourself. You are more than the sum of your actions and products. What's your true value? What accomplishments give you good feelings about yourself. Recognize perfection is an unattainable illusion, not a possible or even desirable way for human beings to live.

Strive for excellence. When you do a good job recognize it and let yourself enjoy it. Stop long enough to celebrate the completion of something instead of berating yourself for not doing it sooner.

Stress your accomplishments in your mind. Stop listening to your overdemanding, never-satisfied inner judge.

Imagine not doing something perfectly. What are the external consequences (not your internal responses)? If there are none, as is likely, look at the self-destructive nature of your perfectionism. Do some of your demands really matter?

Avoid getting hooked on someone else's standards. If your parents are never content with what you do, recognize that they have a need to be discontented, not that you have never done anything worthwhile.

Refrain from self-criticism. Try to stop any negative self-talk in your mind or out loud. Avoid harsh criticism of others. Don't pretend it's constructive criticism. Try not to pass along your perfectionism to your kids. Practice easing up on them, and you may ease up on yourself.

Laugh. Look at the funny side of life's mistakes, imperfections and absurdities.

If you yourself are not the problem but you live with a perfectionist, you may have to learn to hold onto your own sense of balance around others. Don't let him convince you to be a perfectionist too. When he criticizes, gently suggest he do it himself, hire someone, or relax. Use the techniques in the criticism section.

Offer to keep the things most important to him as close to perfect as you can. Ask him to set his priorities. Be a little silly about being terribly careful, but do your best to compromise where it makes sense.

Let him know you think he is wonderful. Create safety for him. Try to trace back with him the source of the perfectionism. Whenever trouble starts, remind him that you too have different values and needs. Make it clear that you are unwilling to be stressed out to please someone else.

But I Need to Be Right

A close cousin of perfectionism is the need to be right. The need to be right usually is the need to feel you are valuable. Therefore, you are always out to prove your worth at the expense of other people.

The time for decision is here. Do you want to be right or happy? You can only be one. You may ask, "How can I be happy if I'm not right?"

First of all, I am not talking about the need to be right on crucial issues such as the stress factor of a bridge, the contents of a prescription, or whether you shoot someone or not. Those decisions make up only about 2 percent of our lives. I am talking about the other 98 percent, where it is not only unimportant to be right but hard to tell who is and who isn't. But we still fight over it. Check yourself. What do you need to be right about?

Socks

There are people who fight over the right way to roll socks. They are still nibbling at each other after twenty years of different opinions. There are many ways to roll socks. There are rollers, folders, those who turn down the cuff, and those who don't. There are those who tie socks in knots, those who buy fancy socks that snap together, and those who throw them in the drawer. There are even two kinds of throwers: those who throw them in the drawer and spread them around so the drawer will shut and those who just throw them in and force the drawer shut.

Who is right? Well, you were taught by someone, who told you it was the right way. That person was taught the same thing. But there is no right way. There is only your preference, which is based on someone else's preference (whoever you copied).

A friend of mine ran into a terrible dilemma. She was a roller, and her husband a thrower. She had carped for years. Then her mother came to visit—the same mother who had taught her to roll socks, tightly. Her mother was helping to put away the laundry, and she was throwing the socks into the drawer in a pile. When questioned she said, "Oh, I changed years ago!"

Loading the Dishwasher

Have you recently carped at your family about whether the forks go up or down in the dishwasher? There is no evidence to support either up or down, only your preference. If you ask your family to do it right, they will do it wrong just to frustrate you. Instead, say to them, "I sleep better at night when the forks are up in the dishwasher; it's just a preference I have." They will want to please you, and you won't have to hand out any more barbs.

Children

We often confuse our preference as adults, which you're entitled to, with the "right" way. Children are confused by this. We say, "Do it right," and insult them if they don't. Yet, still being open to the world, children see lots of other good ways to do things.

I had a little boy call me when I was on radio, and he was mowing the lawn. His mother said, "Do it right." He was mowing the lawn his way, but she wanted the lawn mowed her way. She said, "Do it the right way," and it started a fight. He said, "There are lots of ways to mow a lawn. You can mow it diagonally; you can start outside and mow in; you can mow it in chunks. There are lots of ways to mow a lawn." His brain hadn't yet been squeezed into a system that says there's only one right way to do everything.

Now if his mother had said instead, "John, I want you to mow the lawn this way because it's the way my father used to mow it, and it makes me feel secure," he would have been glad to comply. But she said, "Do it right," and that offended his sense of logic. Insist on your preferences if you want to. You don't even have to explain why. But don't insist on being right.

Mistakes

How many mistakes did you make this week? A full life requires thousands of mistakes if you plan to live up to your creative potential.

Check how open you are to mistakes. Can you stand it? Can you laugh? Do you shy away from things you might not do well? Do you laugh at people who seem clumsy or naive? Do you grit your teeth when someone you love makes a mistake? Are you under the illusion that everyone is watching you and keeping score?

Start counting your mistakes on a daily basis, and try to increase them by 10 percent. That will require you to stretch and grow. Take risks: be tolerant of yourself and others.

Congratulate others on the risks they take. Admire their courage. You'll have more pleasure, and be much closer to what you want to be. Mistakes are the dues of a good and full life.

You cannot stretch, have adventures, or grow if you need too much control over the outcome. Practice letting others be right. Find out why you feel insecure and must be right to feel safe. It's possible to have cleanliness, order, and high standards without perfectionism.

Remember

Try not to spend your life fighting over trivial things.

Don't devote your energy to moving around inanimate objects for your own needs or someone else's.

You can be right—or happy.

14. I'm Living Single in a Double World

"My life would be so much better if I were married or at least in a serious relationship with someone."

"I need to love and be loved."

"I am lonely. Everything seems to be for couples. I'm tired of taking care of myself; I want someone to take care of me, someone to lean on."

"I want to share my life and the world with one special person I can call mine."

"I will not be complete, nor will my life be successful if I don't find that special, lifetime relationship."

We still perceive single as different; regular people are married. It is a myth. Forty percent of adult women in America are unmarried (widowed, divorced, never married, lesbian). You are caught in history. Reproduction and economics made marriage essential for so much of our history that we created marriage as an ideal state for women and avoided looking too closely at the reality.

Single status actually seems to be healthier, and happier for many women. Single women top all the health scales, followed by married men, married women, and at the bottom single men. Married women report as much loneliness as single women, no difference on life satisfaction scores and happiness scales.

The key differences between marriage and single are not economic or health or social issues; they are how we think others perceive us and how we perceive ourselves.

Single women sometimes think the choice has been made for them, but actually you have decided to be single. We could always find a husband for you (remember, the Reverend Moon arranges marriages), but you might not accept our choice.

What You Can Do

Check your comfort level—How do you really feel about your choice? Some of us are hurt much more by the image of single than the reality.

- Add up positives: I can make all the choices; my time is my own; I can live, eat, clean, sleep the way I want to. I can make friends, travel, work, without financial or time obligations to someone else. I do not have to share parenting, at least within my own home. I can accept me the way I am. I can have the bathroom and the television to myself. I'm not responsible for someone else's socks and social life.

- Add up negatives: When I want someone to be here, there may not be anyone; when I'm sick who will take care of me? If I lose my job, who will support me? What if I get disabled, or old, or ugly? I don't have a man to be a companion or a lover. I'm afraid of the dark. What will people think?

Review each item on your negative list. See if there is a solution short of marriage. Remember you can always get married (compromise, join a cult, move to another country). Ask your closest married friends to be honest with you about their married life.

What if I'm sick and home alone? Set up an exchange with a close friend. When she's sick you'll visit and bring juice and magazines; when you're sick she'll do the same. Put money in a special account and use it for delivery services or to hire a cleaning person when you don't feel well. Buy disability insurance; find a support group; join a small church congregation. Make sure you have some younger friends. There are many ways to set up social contracts that are as reliable as marriage.

Make a list of who you could marry or could have married: Would they have eliminated all these negatives, or would there potentially have been more? Wait, what about passion? You have probably had more passion in your life already than many married women.

Consider talking it over with a counselor—for a session or two in order to understand what your position is and what you want it to be in relation to another person and a permanent commitment.

The important difference between marriage and being single is that single women are responsible for the quality of their own life. Married women often turn that responsibility over to their husband and children. They create life for others but not always for themselves. Independence means you live your own life and avoid the temptation to let someone else live it for you.

Wait, I still want to marry Mr. Wonderful. Okay, I wish you great success. Marriage can be good too. If you want to get married start taking care of yourself.

You've heard it before: if you do not love yourself you will not be attracted to those who could love you. If you are not pleased with yourself, others will be aware of your feeling and be uncomfortable around you and afraid to love you. Men think of unhappy single women as "hunters" and they stay away from them.

I still remember the spring day I fell in love with myself. It had been a long, hard winter of failed love and debilitating depression. I had worked on taking better care of myself; I had become far more introspective; I had accepted that I would probably be alone, that I would not love like that again.

I was sitting in my garden, having recently begun to work in it again. It was a beautiful day; the flowers were responding; and I suddenly realized, with a powerful wave of emotion, that I was worth loving, that I could live with myself, in this world, and have a good and happy life. I no longer felt compromised. I lost the feeling that I would just make do, make arrangements, but somehow have less. I felt complete happiness roll over me, and it has never left me.

I married five years later, but the knowledge that I was a whole person alone is with me. There will be a time when I am single again. I know I can survive almost any loss. Perhaps it was that strength that attracted my husband and gave me the belief that I could love again.

Remember

Your life is not compromised because you aren't living the traditional life. Many talented women throughout history have chosen to live alone.

You will not have less love in your life. You may end up with more.

Love is something you do.

15. We're All Getting Older

I used to lie in my bed at Girl Scout camp on Lake Coeur d'Alene and figure that I'd know what was going on by the time I was twenty-one.

Certainly, I thought when I was twenty-one, I'd have life understood by twenty-five. That was old; I'd be a fool not to know by then.

At thirty I said, "So this is it." Well, I think I understand.

At thirty-three, I kept singing, painfully, the lines from the song. "What's it all about, Alfie?"

I felt settled at thirty-five; this must be it. But I found myself at thirty-nine revising all I thought I knew.

Now, almost forty, I'm sure I know when I'll understand it all. It will be at the last moment, well into my nineties, when I draw my last breaths and say to myself, "Oh, that was it."

I will be forty this week—almost halfway physically, just starting philosophically and spiritually. At peace personally until next week changes me. Just starting to figure it all out.

Maybe by fifty?

It is painful to age. There are rewards and trade-offs, but there is also loss. Pretending it's not there can leave us unexpectedly depressed. Ours is a culture that rewards youth and beauty, and it is unlikely to change anytime soon.

Having laid out that truth, I can counter it by reminding you of the incredible pleasures that come with the deepening of self that is part of long life experience: self-knowledge, stronger values, a sense of personal honor, awareness of one's competence, independence, freedom from competition, an identity separate from men and family are all wonders of getting older.

Research on happiness indicates that if health remains good, women report their happiest years are their sixties and seventies. There are many reasons cited, but the one that stands out in the surveys is there is no one left to push them around anymore. Some women reach sixty before they feel they can truly run their own life.

The key is in just that—running your own life. If you continue to live by others' expectations for you or your culture's definition of your worth, aging will be hell. "Old age is not for sissies."

What You Can Do

Do an extensive life review each decade. Remember where you've been and chart where you want to go. When you create an image of yourself ten years into the future it becomes a decade filled with possibilities instead of losses.

Each year near your birthday spend the day alone considering where you are now and answering a series of questions. In ten years

What do you want to look like?
Where do you want to be living?
Who do you want to be living with?
What do you want to be doing?
How do you want to feel?

The answers to these questions require you to create a feeling and image that satisfies you. Then list all the steps you need to take now to reach the goals you've set.

I want to be slender, well-groomed, healthy, and dressed in slacks and a shirt and sweater. I have little interest in jewelry, but I love high-quality, natural fabrics. I'll have a style of my own. I can see myself clearly, and I like what I see. It requires me to lose a pound a year, take good care of myself physically, reduce stress, and learn more about the fine points of grooming. All these are possible; I'll make them probable.

I want to live in Seattle. I love this city, with its beauty and its seasons. I'd like a month off in a warmer climate when it rains too much. My present home satisfies me, and I can imagine the gardens becoming older and richer. Old gardens have a special patina.

My relationships are good. I can see us together in ten years, maybe with more time to talk and share. That means taking care of our love now, so it will be there then. It would be nice to see our children and take care of grandchildren. That means treating them with love and respect and offering unconditional friendship to whomever they live with and love. Raffers, the dog, might be gone, but I can see a new puppy.

I'd like to be working on community projects from the vantage point of age as wisdom and with more patience. That means staying in close contact with my community now so they will want to work with me then. Writing is a joy for me, so it will remain a part of my work always.

I want to feel strong and at peace. The decisions I make now about values, my place in the world, my relationships, and financial security will determine my options in the future. I'll try to keep thinking in both the short term (enjoying the present) and the long term. I feel safe.

This seems like such a simple list, a simple review. Try it, and you will discover what you need to know about yourself and your future. When you are charting the course, the unknowns of age become less fearsome. The rewards become obvious.

You must also plan for the unknown to the degree that it is possible. How would your image change and what would you do if any of the following happened:

You do not marry or live with someone.
Your husband leaves you or dies.
Your children decide not to be friends with you.
There are no grandchildren.
You end up without enough money for your plans.
Your health is not good.
You lose your home.
You have to move to another city or country.

Put together a reasonable plan for any contingency. It will give you strength, remind you of your inherent resiliency, and get you through the hard times. Many of us settle deep into a path after fifty, unprepared for it to be blocked. The pain, confusion, and depression are often overwhelming if you don't see alternatives.

This is the best time in history to become a "senior" if you take full responsibility for your life. Seniors are the fastest growing and the largest population group in America. There will be many options for all of us because of that fact. We will be healthier, more secure, and happier than any previous group.

Here is a list of what you can do that makes the difference between loss and gain after sixty:

Take responsibility for your own life. If you are of a generation that always expected to be surrounded by family and neighbors, this will be a hard step. What can you do if you do not know your neighbors and your family lives three thousand miles away? You can move to be closer to them, or you can build a life around your own interests and friends. Most of us try for something in between.

Plan now, in terms of your interests and talents, for the life you want to live then. Make your own living arrangements, and clearly lay out to your children what you want. Think very carefully before you assign any of the responsibility for your life over to adult children or anyone else. I intend to stay in my own home with care. I intend to make it clear that if I am moved before I absolutely have to be moved, my estate will go to my favorite charity.

Figure out what is best for you. Make the arrangements, and be tough. Never depend on your adult children to rescue you or to invite you to live with them. They might, it might be wonderful; but you need a choice. Learn about all the resources available now (maybe through helping your parents), insurance, social security, senior centers.

Stay physically fit. Try to stay active until you die. Exercise, good nutrition, preventive care, are all yours at any age. We cannot control everything about our bodies, but we can do a lot more than we do. If your health is deteriorating, try not to dwell on it. Some people construct their entire life around their illness. Answer direct questions, but don't tell people all the details. Try to shift the subject to something more optimistic.

Organize a support system. You need to be surrounded by friends you have given to and who want to return the generosity. You need professional support (a doctor, lawyer, accountant, helper) you can trust.

The church you belong to, other organizations you have contributed time to, will remember your gifts and want to return them. The generous older women I have known have always been surrounded by caring people. Plan ahead.

Plan for financial security. Whatever your circumstances now, don't count on anyone but yourself to pay the bills. Don't assume that social security or a pension fund will take care of you. Actively pursue investment in your retirement years; investigate medical care; plan for possible emergencies. Reassurances by others that everything is taken care of can be a weak support system if something goes wrong.

Protect your personal safety. At any age we have to take responsibility for our safety, but it is harder when we do not feel as strong. Keep aware of home safety (locks, alarms, accident prevention). Learn about bunco games and scams so you cannot be taken advantage of. Listen to the advice of the police about purses, carrying money, and traveling alone.

Figure out how to have a good time. Keep a golden years file of all the things you want to do. There are places to travel, projects to build, things to write, places to give service to, and books to read. Learn to do well alone, but remember you have alternatives. Keep your sense of humor and your perspective. Enjoy yourself. A funny old lady is the best kind. My friends all plan to be eccentrics.

Learn to be mortal. You will die. We all do. It's a chilling thought, but the knowledge can free you. Let's figure out how long you have left. On a line, put to the left the year you were born. On the right create a number by adding the age your longest-lived blood relative died and adding five years for new technology. That is how long you will live $(83 + 5 = 88)$.

1948 .... 40 2036

Now figure out on the line where you are at this moment. I'm 40, close to halfway on the example given. What do I no longer have time for? Fighting, working at jobs I hate, being with people I feel uncomfortable around, getting my feelings hurt. What should I squeeze in quickly before I get too old? Playing basketball, backpacking, talking with my mother. What are your answers?

The advantage of learning to be mortal is that you then take the time you have more seriously. You give it a greater value. You stop putting off the things you love; you heal relationships, pursue your own interests. It's the game of, What if you only had a day to live, a month, a year? What would you do?

The only fear we have of dying is the fear that maybe we have never really lived.

Remember

Fight bitterness. It is the biggest handicap of all.
Don't wait quietly for the end. Enjoy yourself instead.

Success is not a destination: it's the quality of the journey.

16. I Need to Sleep

It's often difficult to sleep when you have the blues.

There is no question that you need sleep, but just as important is the belief that you *can* sleep. When you want to rest and cannot, fear sets in. Your body suffers; you become exhausted; and you lose faith in the most restorative resource in life. It is impossible to *make* yourself sleep.

You are not alone. Many women suffer from an inability to get to sleep, or they wake up in the middle of the night or have intermittent sleep problems.

Before you decide how serious your problem is, check out the following possibilities:

- Stress: Your body and mind are restless, poised to respond. The moment you lie down to rest, thoughts may enter your mind that you've kept at bay by being busy.

- Tension: Muscle tension might result from too much activity too close to bedtime. Take time to wind down.

- Nutrition: Caffeine, alcohol, a too-full or an empty stomach, chocolate, or a stomach twitching from spicy food may keep you awake.

- Trauma: If you have been the victim of a crime, your sense of safety has been violated. Rape, burglary, assault, domestic violence can affect for months, even years, your ability to feel safe and able to sleep.

- Drugs: Many prescription drugs have an impact on sleep, and your physician may not be aware of your particular responses. Over-the-counter drugs also can affect your ability to sleep. Mixing any drug with alcohol can change the intended response. Cigarettes, or any smoked substance, can interfere with sleep.

- Menopause: Research substantiates what many women have said for years. Insomnia often is a significant side effect of the hormonal changes associated with change of life.

- Age: Our sleep needs change as we age, usually in the direction of needing less sleep. Trying to stick to old sleep patterns may lead to feelings of insomnia.

- Illness: Seek treatment from a specialist in sleep disorders, not a general practitioner. This is a difficult field, and the experience of your physician could be important. There are a number of diseases that affect sleep. In addition, many illnesses can affect your ability to sleep even though they may not be characterized as sleep disorders.

We are not always able to determine why we cannot sleep, but it is worth the effort, especially if sleeplessness is of long standing. Persistent sleep disorders almost always have a neurological cause. Temporary disorders are usually connected to psychological strain.

What You Can Do

There are many aids suggested for sleep problems, from counting sheep to drinking hot milk. One of these or a combination may work for you:

Don't use your bed for anything but sleeping or making love. Your mind needs to associate the room and bed with successful sleep. Paying bills, arguing, or eating set up a different pattern.

Create a bedroom that offers solace. Soft colors, soft fabrics, serene art, gentle light, noise-proofing. You can create a feeling that wraps around you. Make sure the bed is comfortable and the temperature right for you. Most people sleep better in a cool room.

Use sleep aids like "white noise" machines, earplugs, sleep masks, and shades on the windows if they help you control your sleeping environment.

Calm yourself in the hour before you prepare to sleep. Don't watch television. News, drama, commercials, will make you feel tense. Even boring television can be stimulating as it switches from program to commercials to news inserts and back again. Consider taking the television set out of the bedroom.

If you exercise in the evening give yourself an hour to quiet down before you go to bed.

Set up bedtime rituals to prepare your mind for sleep. Remember the ones we used to like as children: teddy bears, a glass of water, tucking in, prayers, whatever feels good to you.

Sleep alone. Cuddling is wonderful, but sharing a bed often interferes with sleep. If your partner is restless or snores, you may have problems.

Use relaxation techniques once you are in bed. Slowly stretching each part of your body is one. Imagining a wonderful calm scene or planning a garden or vacation can create positive emotions. Counting sheep or marshmallows may work. Monotonous activity slows you down.

Warm baths, massage, books, soft music, hugging your dog, herb tea, all are good possibilities for helping you relax.

Avoid naps during the day. There is a temptation to try to catch up lost sleep when you can, but it just prolongs the no-night-sleep cycle.

Try not to fuss about your sleep problem once you are in bed. Never go to bed unless you already feel sleepy. When you cannot sleep after twenty minutes, get out of bed and do something else (jigsaw puzzles, knitting, sorting drawers).

Set up a schedule. Keep the rest of your activities structured so you do the same things at the same time in the same way. This gives your body and mind a chance to catch up, to feel in control. Predictability creates feelings of safety.

Always have something good to get out of bed for in the morning. Your favorite coffee and biscotti, a newspaper to read, a news show to watch, a place to go, something to do. It's easier to sleep at night when you anticipate something positive in the morning.

Try listing the sources of your wakefulness. Think of the smallest possible step you can take toward a solution, and decide to do it when you wake up. Some steps can be done before you go back to bed, such as writing a letter or completing a project.

Something may be nagging at you that you are unaware is important to your peace of mind. Survey your life, and see if you are at peace. Keep track of the tension in your stomach for clues.

Talk things over with a trusted friend to see if he or she has any insight. Consider seeing a counselor to find some guidance into your own mind. Most large cities have sleep disorder centers. Call your community information line to find one.

In the Middle of the Night

When you wake up, instead of assuming you should sleep, accept that you probably won't and plan for it. Don't fight the pain of your insomnia, go with it for a while. It is impossible to force sleep. Slow down your life intentionally so you will not panic at the fear of being tired in the morning.

During a depression that lasted for months I lost my ability to sleep. I spent many hours in the middle of the night sorting out the contents of drawers, boxes, and shelves. I cleaned house and mended clothes. I puttered until I was able to drop off to sleep again. The end result was a very clean house. The order around me helped soothe the disorder within me. Now when I see a messy drawer I remind myself it means I'm not depressed.

The middle of the night, the hours before dawn, have unique meaning for us. Some call it "the hour of the wolf" when danger lurks everywhere. One's mind is off guard and all thoughts can gain entrance. You may be in a growth stage philosophically, spiritually, that has disturbed your equilibrium. It will help to read what others have written in the areas you are exploring; it will remind you that you are stretching yourself, that it can be hard and that you are not alone.

Reassure yourself that the body will eventually insist on sleep if you give in to your thoughts and refuse to substitute naps or drugs for the natural rhythm.

Remember

Except for temporary assistance or medical circumstances, stay away from drugs as sleep aids. They interfere with your natural cycle and cut off indefinitely your chance for normal, restorative sleep.

Don't try to force yourself to sleep: it's not possible. When you're tossing and turning get up—do something else.

If you want peace you must give up conflict.

17. I Want to Understand Why I Cry

I cry at the drop of a hat.
You're too sentimental.
Don't be a crybaby.
You're too sensitive.
I never cry.
There, there, don't cry.
I feel like I will cry forever.
I'm going to end up a puddle on the floor.
I'm so happy, I could cry.

We are so ambivalent about tears. Crying can be either winning or losing, good or bad. We're told to let go. We're told to hold on. We are afraid of tears, except in small children, because we are afraid of emotions.

Tears express deep feelings that we cannot put into words. They are a form of communication with others and ourselves. Our willingness to cry and our comfort with tears depends on family patterns and cultural acceptance. Some cultures are more expressive than others. We expect Italians to laugh and cry openly; we are surprised when Russians do.

We have different feelings about men and women crying. Since women are supposed to love, feel, and nurture, tears are feminine and soft. Men are supposed to protect and discipline, and tears get in the way. They are to be strong and hard. You cannot cry while you are shooting an antelope. You have to concentrate. Men have to be prepared to protect all of us by controlling anything that would interfere with their response to danger.

There are hormonal reasons for the difference in male and female crying patterns. Emotional tears contain concentrations of three stress-related hormones. It is likely that crying washes away the chemical by-product of stress. One of these hormones, prolactin, also stimulates milk production in new mothers. Women have more of this hormone than men, so it is reasonable to expect them to cry more.

For both men and women it is a combination of culture, family, depth of feeling, and the hormone balance, not emotional weakness, that brings on tears.

If you cry at sad movies or for joy, accept that your emotions are close to the surface. That is positive. It means more passion, more connectedness with life. If it bothers those around you, joke with them that this is your way of handling the overflow of feelings, and they are not worry. Even your kids will learn to say, "There goes Mom's faucet again." They will grow up thinking it is okay to display feelings.

Honest emotional tears cleanse your soul and body. They relieve stress. Manipulative tears do not. If you use tears to stop a discussion or to create sympathy, you may lose touch with what you really feel as well as create resentment in those around you. A "crybaby" is often resented because people feel they are being hustled by the power of tears.

Check your own crying habits and those of the people you are close to. Try to be honest with yourself. If you are the one being manipulated learn to continue talking, even if the other person cries or walks away.

How do you feel when people cry in your presence? What about men's tears? Women both fear and desire men's tears. If you want to be truly loved, find a man who can cry when his heart is touched.

When a man cries, banish your old prejudices. You can take care of yourself, so he does not need to pretend he doesn't feel. When necessary you two can take turns taking care of each other.

Tears don't work on the job. Business is by nature logical and material-oriented. Feelings are fine, but they cannot dominate unless the issue is ethics. Train yourself to keep your perspective at work so you are not overwhelmed by rejections, mistakes, or stress. Set up safe outlets when emotions run too high. Breathe deeply, exercise, take a walk, take a break. Give yourself permission to cry later. If you need to cry, go where you can be alone or with a friend you feel safe with.

What You Can Do

Learn about yourself. Find out what emotions or situations are most likely to bring on tears; keep a record. Have a notebook handy, and write down what is happening when you get a lump in your throat or tears in your eyes.

At the end of a few weeks look for patterns. Does time of day affect you, who you are with, menstrual changes? Does anger or love make you cry? Do people make you cry or does music? What makes you cry may be what you want to know more about or show feelings about.

We cry when we hurt, physically or psychologically, when we are tired, when our memories or sensitivities are touched. Nostalgia, sentiment, passion, humiliation, empathy all bring on tears. When you know some of the reasons you cry you can feel free to let the tears flow. Let the lump in your throat become real tears. You will learn to feel more deeply, and it will be safe and wonderful. We are sometimes afraid to cry all our tears because we think if we start we will never stop. You will always stop, to rest or because you are beginning to heal. Crying is a catharsis necessary to growth.

Let it be okay. When friends try to stop you, remind them it's okay. When the setting is safe, go over your losses and let the tears flow. Holding them back will only hold you back. Get as much rest as you can, bathe yourself frequently to remove the residue of the tears you have shed.

We cry when we have an overwhelming feeling of hurt. We grieve at being treated unfairly. We feel the loss of self-esteem. We feel in danger. We cannot control our world. We cry to heal our fear.

I was teaching a fifth-grade class once, and I asked them to tell me what they thought were important differences between boys and girls. One girl said, "Boys don't cry." A boy in the class quickly answered, "They do if they're okay. When my little brother died we all cried, but my daddy didn't. We got better, but my dad got worse, until he got sick. He finally learned to cry, and then he got better too."

Get help. If you find yourself crying constantly over a period of weeks, don't try to be a stoic or withdraw from contact with friends. The desire to hide is a signal to get help. Do it.

If, by your own judgment, you cry inappropriately and frequently, don't just put up with it. Seek counseling, read about stress, worry, and self-esteem, and talk to someone.

Remember

Your tears are a measure of your depth. They are the voice of your heart.

"Every problem has a gift for you in its hands."

—*Richard Bach*

18. Too Much Grief

An important life skill, the skill of a philosopher, is the ability to separate oneself from the moment.

When depression, grief or stress hits, don't think it's the way life is. It's not.

The moment will pass.

Grief is the natural response to great loss. We reject it because the pain seems unnatural; it is hard to feel the healing within. Grief catches us unaware, we try to keep it at bay and then we are overwhelmed.

It has all the physical symptoms of stress and illness: exhaustion, shortness of breath, inability to eat or sleep; your throat tightens, your face aches, your eyes are swollen, your head hurts, your whole body aches, and it seems that it will last forever.

Almost any loss will lead to a grief process. The intensity depends on the event and your commitment. The loss of a job, friend, piece of property, pet, part of you (psychological or physical), home, country, spouse, child, lover, all precipitate the same grief process. The difference is in the depth and breadth of the loss.

One summer a Cambodian began to work with me in the garden. He had escaped in a boat and lost everything. He spoke little English and had numbers and letters tattooed on his arms. He told me with his eyes of the pain of losing his family, his country, and his language. This did not surprise me. Only when he spoke of losing the familiar birds, the foods he had grown up with, the scents in the air, the weather, and the flowers did I begin to understand.

I have a pond with lilies in it, and he told me of missing the lotus that grew wild in his country. I ordered one, and we planted it and together watched it bloom. Some things are replaceable, many others are not.

Stages of Grief

The most intense grief comes with the loss of a spouse, child, or lover. It is most profound when there is no warning, no chance to prepare for tragedy. You are caught in mid-flight with plans still waiting to be carried out. There is no chance to make peace, to say good-bye.

Even when there is warning, we feel remorse as well as grief. What could we have done, have said? There is always the feeling that some change in your action, some shift of fate, could have prevented the death.

We feel so alone and so isolated that we are sure no one in the world has felt this way before. We feel that our life is forever compromised. Yet there is comfort in knowing you are not alone and that you will move through this process and one day feel well again. It is still possible to be happy. The grief process will add depth to your life. Pain, as always, is a great teacher.

These are the stages of grief as outlined by Elizabeth Kübler-Ross and others:

- Denial: It is automatic for the mind and heart to avoid pain by trying to change reality. We will go through familiar rituals to pretend that nothing is out of order. Try to go and see the body, if that is appropriate, touch the person, and say what you wanted to say when he or she was alive.

  Other cultures let members of the family wash and dress the body as a way of facing the death and making the last loving gestures. We tend to separate ourselves from the reality of death. It makes it easier to deny that there has really been a loss. The first step in healing is to recognize the loss. It is real.

- Anger: Loss brings fear, and fear brings anger. We are angry at being hurt so much. We ask why? We want to make sense of the loss, when it may be unexplainable. We look for someone to blame, for some sign that might have foretold it. We come up with nothing, but that is the way it is. We are chosen for loss, and we will never know why.

  Sometimes we turn in anger to others we think could have died instead, or we blame the person who has died. Why couldn't he or she have been more careful? We warn our children of the grief they will leave us if they are not careful.

  Release your anger in whatever way you can. Smash something; scream at someone; exercise until you are exhausted. Release your anger at yourself, and forgive yourself for whatever regrets you have. Sometimes you can hold a conversation or write a letter to the person who died. Say everything you want to and then send it up the chimney or out on the wind.

- Bargaining: As the reality of the loss becomes harder to avoid, you may be tempted to bargain. "Take me instead." If you know your loved one is very ill you may ask that he or she live until Christmas or your daughter's graduation. You will offer your soul to keep a loved one from dying. The dying one may ask you to make promises.

- Acceptance: The full impact of the death and loss is at some point unavoidable. This stage may hit you within hours, weeks, or even years of the moment you know that someone is dead. Finally, there is no avoiding the awareness and the pain. This time is the beginning of the true grieving—and ultimately healing—process.

  There is a discomfort with grieving in our culture. Other cultures feel that wailing is essential to free the soul. Let yourself feel all your feelings. You will not cry forever. Let the pain flow over you in waves; your heart will feel as if it is breaking, but you will survive. The pain is a release.

  Others may try to comfort you or distract you from your grief. There will be a time when this is good, and you will know it. Now may be the time to cry regardless of their discomfort or to find private places to reminisce and feel as deeply as you can. There is beauty in sadness.

  Grief can feel frustrating because so many impulses, actions, and habits are now stymied. You start to do something, and it no longer makes sense. Accept the pain, feel the hurt; you will not find it endless.

- Rebuilding: You will notice that for moments you feel happy. It will surprise you, and you will wonder if it is okay. You will begin to think a little bit in the future and to make small plans. Little bits of you will wake up slowly to taste, smell, and feel again. You are not alone. We have all lost.

What You Can Do

There is a special small book available. Carry it with you: *How to Survive the Loss of a Love*, by Melba Colgrove, Harold H. Bloomfield, and Peter McWilliams. The first six of these thoughts stem from this book.

Believe that you will survive. Nature is on your side, and nature is a powerful ally. You will get better, no doubt about it.

Give yourself time to heal. The greater the loss, the more time it will take. The healing will happen. You will not heal in a straight progression.

There will be many great leaps and frightening backslides. The process is under way.

Get as much rest as you can. Be gentle with yourself. Don't rush around. Your body needs energy for repair.

Keep structure in your life. Keep your work going. Set up a schedule; alternate rest and activity. Keep a sense of order. You need something to hold on to.

Let yourself heal fully. Don't become involved with projects or relationships to block out the pain. Let the healing process run it's full course.

Anticipate a positive outcome. There are powerful lessons in this grief. Remaining distraught is no proof of love.

Expect setbacks. There will be many times as you recover when you seem to drop back into the same pit of depression. Memories will surprise you and catch you defenseless. Special days and special places will be hard for a few years.

Write a letter or make an audio tape. Say all the things you wish you could have said to the person you lost. Create a dialogue to bring you both peace. Let go of any guilt you may feel for things said or unsaid. Recovery from the loss of a loved one is often directly related to the amount of guilt you feel.

Give yourself time to love again. You need at least two years of grieving and healing after the loss of a love before you will be able to bring someone else into your life as a new individual and not a replacement. If you allow a shorter time, you're liable to compare the new person with the one you lost. The new person may fail, and you will have the additional grief of thinking that you have made a mistake.

Avoid blame. Stop any thought that begins "If only." Let go of the need to blame anyone for what was or wasn't done. The need is for forgiveness.

Remember that fear and grief intermingle for women left alone. Often you must return to work, care for children and pretend you are stronger than you feel. You become an "extra" person if most of your friends are couples, and that is a painful reminder of your loss.

Understand your anger. You are angry at being left and feel guilty that somehow you are still alive. As long as you hold on to the guilt and are unable to forgive him or yourself, you will postpone reentry, taking responsibility for the rest of your life. That may be what you are avoiding by constant recriminations about what you didn't or did do.

Avoid fantasies. Another way to put yourself in a time warp is to idealize your lost man. He becomes the perfect man, the only man for you, the love of a lifetime, instead of the companion you made so many compromises with. If you describe him as a saint you are left with a lifetime of illusion. No other man will have a chance, and other women will get tired of listening to your fantasy.

Let go of his interests, hobbies, and clothes unless you were equally enthusiastic about them. Find your own goals to break the old habits that you will try to hold on to.

Create your own identity. If much of your identity was established through your husband's work or status, be prepared to be left alone. Someone else will quickly fill your husband's position, and you will be forgotten by almost all of the people he was involved with. There is nothing you can do except see it as an opportunity to become your own person at last.

Protect yourself. Watch out for the husbands of your friends, who will suddenly turn up offering to comfort you sexually. There are still many myths around about grateful widows. Be careful about any intimacy until you are less vulnerable. Loose sex will leave you far more depressed than celibacy.

Remember

Ask for help from friends or professionals. It's okay to receive. There are many support groups to help you through your grief process or that of someone you care about. Compassionate Friends is particularly helpful in the terrible grief that follows the loss of a child.

Women, by their heritage, love deeply. It is a combination of our experience nurturing children and gardens, feeding life, and our traditional need for safety, someone or something to depend on.

Cherish the depth and passion of your emotions, build independence, and give yourself credit for being someone who can truly care, whatever the cost. You are a better person because you can love.

The patches on our hearts make us stronger.

19. This Pain Feels as Though It Will Last Forever: Depression

It's such a hunger—wanting to be loved. When it doesn't come early (from parents or peers) we think it never will. There is a hollow, an emptiness that penetrates unexpectedly and leaves us catching our breath.

The hollow inside is made by the illusion of unconditional love and the inability to accept the love that's available, the attempt to replace the irreplaceable.

Remember, when you are hurting, the stages of grief: grieve for what never was, and build love into your life now. It's all that's available. It's enough.

You are not alone. Everyone gets depressed, and many people spend significant amounts of their lives depressed to one degree or another. Depressed people are capable of deep feelings, and these are sometimes sad and sometimes wonderful. If you are feeling depressed you are a person of real emotions, a person who cares deeply and responds accordingly.

This may be small comfort if you are in great pain. Many of us have offered to feel less in all of life if only there could be less pain. Don't make the trade. Instead, understand the sources of your depression and what you can do to ease it. Sometimes pain is the only way we learn what we have to learn to achieve peace.

Try to keep these thoughts with you.

We create psychological pain within ourselves.
We can change it.
There is a choice.
We can create an alternative.
Nature is waiting to help us.
Love and personal worth are connected.

The difference between depression and the frustrations, blues, and grief I am describing in this book is one of degree. Depression is a fundamental feeling of sadness and loss. It can be tied to a specific loss or it can be free-floating. The pain is internal and can stretch from a twinge to being almost unable to breathe. Most of us know when we are depressed and sense when it is serious. How long it lasts is, of course, a key to understanding. I have divided degrees of depression into ordinary, tough, and severe. It is arbitrary but a place to begin.

Ordinary

self-pity
sadness
loss of self-confidence
trouble getting up in the morning
fatigue
inability to be productive
aches and pains
loss of creativity and initiative
extensive daydreaming
apathy, lack of direction
anger, resentment, conflict, and frustration
difficulties in relationships with family, friends, and co-workers
sexual problems

Tough

loss of self-esteem
poor appetite
sleep difficulties
loss of sexual desire
self-destructive behavior (involving food, drugs, relationships)
preoccupation with physical functions
loss of ability to concentrate
restlessness, nervousness, agitation
tears
inability to make decisions
anxiety, fear of the future
fear of being alone
feelings of revenge
confusion about dependence and independence
conflict in relationships with family, friends, and co-workers
unexpected life crises that seem overwhelming

Severe

(The key here is moods that are extreme, recurrent, and difficult to change.)

feeling outside yourself (watching)

self-neglect (cleanliness, grooming)

addictions (uncontrollable habits)

inability to eat

inability to sleep (waking up at 4:00 A.M.)

inability to connect to environment (household objects, outside weather)

unwillingness to have any pleasures (reading, watching TV, social activities)

isolation (inability to relate to others)

allowing humiliation

hopelessness

helplessness

feelings of going crazy

fear of hurting someone else

developing phobias (fear of traveling, driving, using the telephone)

feeling overwhelming guilt

giving possessions away

clearing and ending business affairs

feeling consumed with a sense of rejection and worthlessness

heavy use of drugs (alcohol, prescribed, illicit)

having strange feelings of loss of self ("I kept getting smaller." "I felt like a pane of glass, transparent and about to shatter.")

crying and screaming with pain and loss

premonitions of suicide

developing a plan for suicide

making suicide attempts

ATTENTION! SEVERE DEPRESSION AND SUICIDE

If you have any of the symptoms listed under severe depression, please get help now. You do not have to hurt this much. There are alternatives. Your pain is a signal, a cry of your mind and body for help. Ask for help, *now*. It is the loving and reasonable step to take. *Your life has value.*

If it is the middle of the night and you feel that you cannot continue in such pain, do one of the following until you get help and are no longer alone:

- Call and ask a friend to come and stay with you or pick you up. Tell your friend you are afraid of hurting yourself.
- Call your counselor (if you have one) and ask for immediate help. Counselors want to be there for you in emergencies. Don't refuse to call because you are embarrassed at your need.
- Call a crisis line. Look in your telephone book white pages under "crisis" or "suicide." The number is there because so many of us need just that kind of help in the middle of the night. *You are not the only one.* Many of the people who answer crisis lines have been in this same spot themselves. If the person who answers isn't helpful, call back and ask to speak to someone else. This resource is there for you. Do not keep your suicide thoughts secret.
- Call a taxi and go to the emergency room of your hospital. Tell them you are unable to protect yourself from the pain you feel. Tell them you do not want to be committed, just helped to cope with the way you feel. If commitment is suggested refuse to sign until you have rested and talked to counselor you feel trust for.

Keep calling until you have passed the crisis or someone else is taking responsibility for you.

- Do not take any more drugs or alcohol, you will lose awareness and control.
- Do not assume this pain will last forever—it won't!
- Do not assume you are alone. You are not! I have been there. I care about you. These feelings change. You *will* survive the night.
- Take steps to get help. Do not take steps toward more pain by gathering anything that would help you hurt yourself (drugs, weapons, poison, car keys).
- Do not leave the protection of your home unless you are with someone you trust. *You will not feel like this forever.* When you have made it through the night, make immediate plans, with the help of a friend or a crisis line, to see a counselor.

Decide with your counselor whether you can safely protect yourself or whether you should stay with friends or relatives or consider hospitalization. Let the counselor take charge for now. Make a plan, including how to handle the next crisis whenever it occurs. Then, when you are safer, try to understand what happened.

Thoughts of suicide are a form of aggression against yourself. You are frustrated and hurt from enormous personal stress, and you see the cause of the problem within yourself. The desire is to destroy the perceived cause, self, instead of working out the problems. You fantasize peace and freedom while you are courting death. Peace and freedom require consciousness: death is an end to consciousness.

You may also just want relief from pain rather than to actually die. The desire for relief can confuse you into making a tragic mistake.

When I slipped into the deepest part of my depression, I was facing the most fundamental abandonment: the desire to abandon self. I had been rejected in various ways by my parents. I had been rejected by my lover, and now I was trying to reject myself. I felt absolutely worthless and completely out of control.

I still am not sure what pulled me back when I hit bottom: (1) the inclination for life, (2) responsibility for my child, or (3) an awareness I had faced the worst. I somehow began to take small steps toward control. I got help. I cleaned myself; I cleaned my home; I straightened out my responsibilities and business. Then bit by bit I let myself feel my own identity again. I was a survivor.

I kept a diary during the depression to increase my sense of control of what was happening to me. These excerpts reveal how much feelings change.

January

I have had a long, hard climb up from the bottom. Sometime last year I had begun to disappear. I could not write. I became smaller and smaller until I almost disappeared. There were times when I thought I would die from the pain. Nights when I couldn't sleep, I cried like an animal caught in a trap. I moved around the top of my bed on hands and knees. I thought my tears were endless. I promised myself I would not lose another summer, that I would be well by Spring. I'll plant a garden this year. Last year was lost.

April

I fell in love with myself tonight. Actually, it turns out I've been practicing falling in love with myself for quite a while. Now, if you think falling in love with someone else is great, this is better. Wow, is it better!

What You Can Do

You can always choose suicide, but right now there are many other options. When you feel you have a little control over your feelings and some professional support, you may find these suggestions helpful.

- Ritual: Put together a structure for success by setting up a limited daily routine you can control. Have breakfast; do one small job. Give yourself credit for your accomplishments at the end of the day. You are alive!

- Food: Stick to healthy foods (herb teas, whole grains, yogurt). They create a feeling that you care about yourself.

- Sleep: Accept that you will often wake up early, and plan for it. Don't try to force sleep.

- Environment: It will be hard to take care of yourself and your home, so aim for small accomplishments.

    Dress in clean, comfortable outfits like sweatsuits in bright colors.

    Don't do much around the house except water plants (that was my goal each day: to shower and take care of the plants so they wouldn't die).

    Get help if you can possibly afford it, or ask a friend (I had someone come in two afternoons a week for two hours to restore order, be a living presence for me, and bring food).

    Once a day go outside and walk around the block.

- Pleasure: Aim just to survive, but don't deny yourself little feelings of pleasure if they sneak in. Sometimes if we are mourning someone we think it is wrong to feel good for even a minute. In a sense you may be mourning yourself, the pain you had to feel.

    Make a scrapbook for the future, or a file (fashions cut out of magazines, home improvements, garden designs) of other possibilities for when you feel better.

    Keep a journal so you can see that you are feeling better each day or at least different on some days.

    Try simple pleasures like painting with watercolors or making designs with a felt pen (crochet, knit, do puzzles).

    Hug your pet if you have one.

    Look for favorite shows on TV.

    Reread books you know you love.

    Try to plan one outing a day even if it's just to a store.

- Isolation: Make one outing a week to a place where you will make contact with people.

    Consider whether you feel up to taking care of a pet if you don't have one.

    Call the friends you feel safest with.

    Use a telephone talk line just to practice.

    Write letters.

- Hopelessness: Repeat to yourself as a litany, an affirmation, "These feelings will pass," "I will feel better." If you are worried about the past or the future, deal, for this period of time, only with the present.

Keep your protective alternatives handy (a friend who can stay with you or whom you can stay with, hospitalization, day care).

Eliminate any temptation to let go again (drugs, etc.).

Remember, you are not alone.

- Helplessness: You feel out of control of your life and unable to do anything about it. This will not last. You can take back control by very small steps. Just dressing yourself today is one. As you recover you will be stronger, more independent, and more able to control the emotional direction of your life than you have ever been.

  You are tired because of the enormous amount of emotional work going on inside. Externally you think you are accomplishing nothing; you feel guilty at your apathy. Remember, you are doing some of the most important work you will ever do. It does not matter if others cannot sense it, as long as you can.

- Craziness: You are crazy when you *don't* feel. You are aware when you do. Crazy is not the issue here. Growing, stretching, confusion, and ambivalence are normal. You're going to make it.

- Guilt, self-worth: Decent people seem to feel the most guilt. Remember forgiveness. You are worth forgiving; you would quickly forgive someone else. One of the key sources of pain in depression is loss of self-value.

  Make a list of your good qualities; don't list the bad. Pick things you'd like to be, and say them to yourself. "I am lovable and capable."

  Find a volunteer activity you think you can handle (perhaps bagging groceries at a food bank) and help someone else.

  Think of yourself as a cupboard that has been stripped bare, you need to gently put items back on the shelf.

  Avoid people who hurt you or criticize you or in any way are threats to your sense of self. Save them for when you are stronger.

- Safety: Be careful, depression slows you down. Your reaction time will be impaired. Avoid driving, or be extremely cautious.

- Crying: You can wail and scream. We all do.

When you are feeling better be prepared for a sudden recurrence of the desire for suicide.

There is a postpartum effect when we have survived a major attempt at aggression against ourselves. You may feel euphoric for a while, the relief at having survived. You may feel "over the hump." Be careful, sometimes the up produces a down without warning. It will be short, but you need to guard against it. It's as though you suddenly have energy to do to yourself what you were too depressed to do before.

We all have stories to tell about our parents. They may not be accurate but they come from the deepest parts of our emotions. I cannot write about nor truly help myself and others with depression without writing about my father.

My father came from generations of Welsh coal miners. He was a wonderful athlete who played rugby and cricket and boxed in his home county. He went into the mines to work at sixteen and used to show me the coal dust that had settled in pockets underneath his skin. It left blue splotches like tattoo ink.

He was charming, a man's man, a ladies' man, and a wonderful tenor. He was one of the local heroes, polite, generous, and wild. He taught Sunday school and had a powerful streak of violence.

There is not space for an analysis of his family, only that his mother tried to hold onto him and his sisters with an amazing power and determination. He ran away to London at twenty-five. His mother had tried to prevent him playing sports, buried his boxing gloves, and harassed any women he called on.

He had gone to London with the county championship rugby team and met some bobbies in a pub. His charm and amazing ability at darts made him a man they suggested should join the force. After returning to Wales he decided to go back to London to police college. He became a detective stationed at Scotland Yard and eventually middleweight (boxing) champion of the London police force.

My mother was a policewoman of equal charm and appeal; they married, against the objections of both families, for only one compelling reason—passion. Both my parents agree on that. They had nothing in common but immense sexual attraction. She was from a British family of aristocratic lineage with all the pretensions and desires that entails, but no money.

After World War II my mother decided to immigrate to the United States. There was little economic hope in England, and she wanted more. Dad loved his police work and his country but came anyway four months after the rest of us arrived in eastern Washington.

There were many fights, plans to return to England, and a lot of jobs. He was for a while a store detective. He found it humiliating but was unable to apply for police work until he was an American citizen. By the time he was a citizen he was too old.

Dad became a killer on the floor at a meat-packing plant, a steel-worker, and after his hand was crushed in a mill accident, a real estate broker. His charm served him well. People loved to hear him speak, with his accent, his humor, and his wonderful stories of coal mining and police work.

He missed police work and the sense of competence and community it gave him. He became a community leader in lots of small ways. (At his funeral we found out all the people he had helped. I never knew. We never talked.) He said once that one of his dreams was to return to his village in Wales wearing a silk suit.

The money was never there. My mother's jobs often paid the rent, and he knew it. He drank heavily for long periods. As a grade-school child I would find him at night collapsed out in the driveway. He was too big to move, so I would put a pillow under his head and a blanket on top of him. Mom said they were blackouts from an old mine injury. I didn't realize until I was forty that he had passed out from drinking.

Throughout all the years of my growing up we never talked. He sang wonderful songs while my mother played the piano, watched end-less sports on television, especially the Friday night fights, worked, drank, and was sometimes physically violent to all of us. I could never understand the force he represented.

He always seemed much more important than my mother to me. I sensed that he was a deeper character, a more passionate person, more capable of feeling than anyone I knew, but we never talked. Once he came down to visit me at college for a Dad's Day. He charmed all my girlfriends, and they all wished they had a dad like mine. Even then I sensed that it was both a strange joke on us and something I didn't want to deal with.

I drifted away with my own life and problems, and he was an emo-tional shadow to me. He was more successful in his business, tried once to leave my mother, tested out his masculinity in various ways (women, cricket in a local league, violence), joined the church again, and decided to visit Wales.

At fifty-five he went home to his village (his parents were both dead) in a silk suit. It was the first time he had traveled any distance by himself. He seemed to feel fine about the trip, although we didn't talk about it.

I didn't know it at the time, but after his return he was increasingly violent. In desperation my mother had gotten his doctor to give him sodium pentathol in hopes of discovering something that would help. The doctor said all he talked about was his mother. He refused to see a counselor of any sort. Sometimes my mother had to stay at a friend's house or the YWCA because it was too dangerous to be at home with him.

One night, late, he called me from a bar. He was extremely depressed. He said that he had lived his whole life for other people's expectations, not for his own. "I don't know who I am or what I want, and now it's too late." I didn't know what to say. He was fifteen hundred miles away, and I was barely surviving myself. I didn't know how to take care of him. I told him it was not too late, that he could still choose to live his life his way. He said he wished he'd never left England. We talked about Winston Churchill. Dad was fifty-six.

He went home after we talked; my mother was staying at the YWCA because he had threatened to kill her. He collected all the pictures of himself in the house, put them in the fireplace, and burned them.

Dad put on his pajamas, took all the tranquilizers the doctor had prescribed for him, drank a fifth of scotch, and died. My mother found him when she returned to dress for work.

He was from another time, another generation. He didn't believe in talking about feelings or about yourself. He felt therapists were kooks and people who went to them crazy. He didn't see any alternatives in life, only living out whatever you had started.

It took me years to realize both the legacy and the gift he gave me. The legacy was one of passion and pain. I realized, after my own depression, that I would have to be careful or I would follow in his footsteps—not his life-style but his suicide. I also knew that he had given me some of his charm, a bit of his sense of honor, his caring about the community, his humor, his passion and depth, and the brown eyes that only he and I, in the family, shared.

The gift took longer to understand. It changed my life and led to my leaving my career at the university. I realized that if I didn't follow my heart and find out what I truly wanted I might someday call up one of my children late at night and break his or her heart.

I hadn't known what to say to him. I would make sure I could answer the questions for myself. I am trying to remind you to ask the questions and listen to the answers that come from deep within.

Find out what you want.
Give it to yourself.

You deserve it.

You deserve support—ASK FOR HELP.

Remember

Keep the agreements you made with yourself when you were most depressed. Keep pushing through the pain to the other side.

You will not feel like this forever.

20. I Need More Help: What Is Depression, What Can I Do?

There are many sources of depression. Each of us is affected in different ways depending on our unique physiology and personality. Three areas to check are organic/physical causes, maladaptive/stress causes, and reactive/grief causes.

Organic/Physical Depression

Various organic conditions can affect the brain's functioning and contribute to emotional states that lead to depression and thoughts of suicide. Most of these states are temporary. Some involve a long pattern of mental distress. The symptoms range from a feeling of emptiness, a sense that something is wrong with you, to complete detachment from reality and inability to control your body.

Hormonal imbalance due to prescription or illicit drugs, birth control pills, illness, postpartum changes, infection, postoperative stress

Fatigue resulting from stress, illness, injury, infection, drug use or abuse

Menopause and all the physical and mental changes that may accompany it

Premenstrual syndrome (PMS)

Nutritional imbalances (you are what you eat)

Disturbances of the brain or nervous system structure and function from Alzheimer's disease, schizophrenia, alcoholism, drug addiction, manic-depressive illness, or other chronic diseases

Seek help from a physician who is a specialist in organic depression. Very few counselors and physicians fully understand these problems, so you will need to put extra effort into locating one who does.

Make yourself an expert by reading everything you can and interviewing specialists in nutrition, endocrine (hormone) problems, PMS, menopause. Get help from a specialist, but take responsibility for healing yourself or working out strategies that help you adapt to your circumstances.

Treatment with drugs can be helpful for all forms of depression. You need an experienced physician advising you, a psychiatrist trained in the use of psychoactive substances. Do not automatically accept prescriptions. Ask questions about side effects (physical and psychological) and addiction. If you cannot get your questions answered, go somewhere else where you can. Many medical and depression emergencies are related to problems with psychoactive drugs.

Find a women's health center in your city where you can get information, referrals, and counseling about women's health free from what could be traditional prejudices.

Maladaptive/Stress Depression

This form of depression is often related to your personality characteristics. You push yourself beyond your personal defenses and coping skills; you lose resilience and cannot adapt to life's stresses. This is akin to the "nervous breakdown" of another generation.

Physical and emotional exhaustion happen to women overwhelmed by work and responsibilities (caring for small children, financial problems, etc.) and women who demand far too much of themselves. Perfectionists who need control over everything to feel safe and confident end up driving off the road.

These feelings vary in intensity from daily pain and frustration to suicidal gestures. Those of us who feel inadequate, pushed too hard, unable to meet expectations, begin to lose faith in ourselves.

Reactive/Grief Depression

Another form of depression is caused by an event or a loss. It can be a severe loss, such as the death of someone you love, or just the loss of a possibility. Loss of job or promotion, loss of opportunity, rejection under almost any circumstances, abandonment, retirement, loss of country (refugees), separation from family or friends, loss of function, disability, geographic change (which precipitates a loss of the familiar), fire, theft, destruction, loss of justice, unfair treatment—all are sources of reactive depression.

All of us face loss in our lives. We feel for a few hours, or for a lifetime, a sense of emptiness, a feeling of being outside ourselves, that something is missing. We have to accept the pain. Psychological pain, once accepted, may lose its edge. You have reason to grieve. Your blues are appropriate.

What You Can Do

Most of us treat ourselves when we have stress or reactive depression, and that may be enough for you. Start with rest, good nutrition, and the support of friends or others who have shared similar experiences. You can get support and a place to rest in many ways.

You can meet with whomever is involved in the problem and try to talk things out. Just trying to communicate how you feel can make a big difference.

Search out books on the topic that concerns you or general depression. Audio tapes may help. Call a telephone line specializing in the kind of help you feel you need. Most cities have divorce, cancer, widowed, domestic violence, alcohol and drug lifelines.

Try to decide whether this is a temporary inability to adapt or a longer pattern. Just listing stresses and obligations piling up can lighten the load. Keep a close check on your thoughts and your recovery. Ask for more help if you begin to feel hopeless or out of control for more than a few days. You've worked hard to treat your depression, and you deserve to make progress and be healthy.

If you feel you have a repeating pattern, you need to break it. A series of crisis, a number of similar relationships, too many lost or unsatisfactory jobs, too much anger, repeated victimization, long periods of feeling low self-worth require understanding and change. If friends comment on your behavior as inappropriate, try to listen to them. They care about you. The following sources of more intense help and information are available:

Training Groups

Training groups primarily provide information in a supportive setting. Most can be found through schools and social service agencies:

Parent Effectiveness Training
Step-Parenting Training
Assertiveness Training
Marriage Encounter
Engagement Encounter
Relaxation Training

Outward Bound (testing yourself in the wilderness)
Vocational training

You will learn coping strategies, ways to pace yourself and build confidence.

Support Groups

If you have symptoms in the tough or severe range of depression, you need a guide to help you chart a better path. You may find it through a support group or therapist.

There are support groups for particular sources of depression: widowhood, divorce, loss of a child, disease (cancer, MS, Alzheimer's, etc.), surgical loss (mastectomy, colostomy, etc.), being single, domestic violence, victimization (sexual abuse, sexual violence). These groups provide information, practical advice, understanding, and emotional support. They can be located through hospitals, community information lines, crisis centers, and social service agencies. There are specific and general support groups. I've belonged to a friendship group for fifteen years. We meet once a month and just talk things over. It helps to get other perspectives and know that they care about me. Friendship groups can be formed on your own or through women's organization like the YWCA, NOW, and church groups. If you don't have an informal group you can organize one. Do some research until you find a group that fits you. The obligations are minimal; you can quit when you want to; and the support may get you through your depression.

Group Therapy

Therapy groups serve a different purpose because they are led by a therapist. The objective may be to provide support during transition but also to provide a social context for healing and understanding yourself. A therapy or counseling group is arranged through your own therapist or a community mental health program, hospital, or service. Choosing one requires care and effort on your part. The guidelines provided here for choosing a therapist will help.

The bottom line in any group is that you feel supported, cared for, safe, and able to learn and grow through your depression and pain.

Crisis Intervention Centers

Help in a variety of personal crises is available at crisis intervention centers: rape or molestation, suicide, pregnancy, abortion, and domestic violence. They are listed in your telephone book; they can be contacted through your community information line, the police, or any hospital emergency room.

Therapists

You can find therapists in private practice through friends, other health professionals, or the yellow pages. You can find them in social service agencies, publicly funded clinics, or privately supported groups. Make a final list of three names you have had recommended to you, and make interview appointments with them. Many counselors provide this service free or at a reduced rate.

The best therapists will seem confident, warm, thoughtful, and clear in what they say to you. After seeing these three therapists, decide which one gives you the following: a feeling that he or she has a basic desire to help, a sense of trust and respect, a sense that he or she is a person of integrity and gives you a good feeling inside. Be wary of any therapist who seems pushy, promises cures, or discounts what you say.

After a few weeks, evaluate your progress and discuss it with your counselor. Remember that with personal problems things sometimes get worse—as you get in touch with your pain—before they get better.

Your Rights in Therapy

I am including here, because of its importance to the success of your therapy, an adaptation of the Rights of Consumers of Psychotherapy.

You have the right:

To ask questions at any point.

To know if the therapist is available to see you, or if not, how long the waiting period would be.

To ask questions about issues relevant to your therapy, such as therapist's values, background, attitude, and life experiences—and to be provided with thoughtful, respectful answers.

To specify or negotiate therapeutic goals and to renegotiate those goals when necessary.

To know the limits of confidentiality in the therapy setting—with whom will the therapist discuss the case?

To know the extent of record keeping regarding the therapy, both in written or taped forms, and knowledge concerning accessibility of those records.

To know your diagnosis (if the therapist uses such categories).

To know the therapist's estimation of approximate length of therapy to meet your agreed-upon goals.

To understand the specific treatment strategies employed by therapist (talking, body exercises, homework assignments, use of medication).

To choose the format of therapy (individual, family, group).

To refuse to answer questions at any time.

To request that the therapist evaluate the progress of therapy.

To discuss any aspect of your therapy with others outside the therapy situation, including consulting with another therapist.

To require the therapist to send a report regarding services rendered to any qualified therapist or organization upon written authorization by you.

To be provided with copies of written files on you, at your request.

To give or refuse to give permission for the therapist to use aspects of your case for part of a presentation or publication.

To know the fees for therapy and the method of payment (including acceptability of insurance).

To know the therapist's policies on issues such as missed sessions, vacation time, telephone contact outside of therapy, emergency coverage.

To know which ethics code the practitioner subscribes to.

To terminate therapy at any time.

To solicit help from the ethics committee of the appropriate professional organization in the event of doubt or grievance regarding the therapist's conduct.

Problems in Therapy

Often we seek a therapist in the midst of a crisis without going through a selection process. You may then think you have to stay with that person. You realize he or she may not be the best choice for you but you are reluctant to say so or even to admit it to yourself.

You will not have to start over if you shift to a new therapist. It usually takes only one session to catch up. All therapists expect clients to exercise their right to seek a better match if they do not think their first choice was right. Only a problem therapist will try to talk you out of leaving—unless the issue is one covered under "stuck" below.

You will save time, money, and grief by seeking out a therapist you know you can work well with. I spent two years in therapy with a traditional psychiatrist getting increasingly depressed. He provided no feedback and left me hanging over a cliff. A friend finally pushed me into making a change to a more directive therapist, and within three months I was feeling well and able to discontinue counseling.

If you are receiving your counseling through a social service agency they may try to convince you that you have no choice. This is particularly true of Family Court referrals. Trust your own judgment, even if you are in crisis, understand your alternatives, and politely demand the right to interview another counselor.

I'm stuck. There are times in every counseling process when we get stuck. The information surfacing is too painful; we stop wanting to work on the problems; or we are just tired. When you feel this way talk it over with your counselor before you decide to leave. If you remain stuck for more than a month, consider shifting to another counselor whose skills may better enable you to break through.

It's time to leave. Some counselors tell you when it's time to leave and help you make the break. Others will keep you as long as they can for their own purposes. When you sense completion, suggest less frequent visits and talk out the separation.

It costs too much. All counseling is expensive in a budget that never plans for it. Most of us assume we will pay for electricity but not for mental health. Credentials and agency determine fees. A social service agency may charge as little as $5 or as much as $40. Therapists in private practice who are psychiatrists or psychologists range from $40 to $120 an hour. Psychiatric nurses, social workers, and nontraditional counselors charge usually between $30 and $50. Price also depends on the rate scale in your part of the country.

This kind of money is hard to part with, especially when we are in crisis. We may not be sure whether we can hold onto our sources of income. The only answer is not an easy one: without your mental health you have close to nothing.

Sometimes I would look at my old furniture and realize that I could have something concrete like a dining table instead of two months of therapy. Then I realized the dining table could be bought later when I recovered.

My therapist is making sexual advances. Sexual contact between you and your counselor is destructive and unethical in any form. You are putting yourself in great psychological danger if you permit any sexual intimacy. The counselor is well aware that you are in a dependent frame of mind, and his or her advances are tantamount to rape.

Refuse to cooperate; refuse to schedule another appointment; and find the strength to report your therapist to a professional or licensing board. You may be able to protect the next patient who is not able to be as strong as you.

My therapist is sexist. Some therapists, particularly analysts and pastoral counselors, have a strong anti-woman bias. They still adhere to old cultural values that view women in limited terms. Stay away from any counselor you sense does not understand what it means to be a woman now.

There are frightening examples of such sexism and its danger to female patients:

A victim of severe domestic violence is told by her minister to go home, forgive her husband, and try to be a better wife so he won't beat her up again. The violence continues, as does the same advice. She is never told to seek legal protection from assault.

A little girl is told to get on her knees and ask her father's forgiveness for tempting him. She continues to be sexually abused, and the father is never reported to the authorities. The pastoral counselor did not want to upset the family.

A depressed woman who is lonely and devalued at home seeks advice on school and building a career. The male counselor suggests that lots of women her age are frustrated and maybe she could keep herself busy by learning to play tennis.

A rape victim is questioned by a therapist about whether she enjoyed the assault, was she orgasmic, and had she unconsciously attracted her attacker. She becomes a victim of both the rapist and the therapist.

A young woman who has strong lesbian feelings is told to get married, have a baby, and they will go away. What happens to her, her husband, and their children when her unresolved sexuality surfaces?

In marriage counseling, the therapist defers to the husband, agrees with his viewpoint and his version of the conflicts. Whenever the wife discusses her needs, the therapist reminds her of the children.

Usually sexism in therapy is more subtle than these examples. Sometimes it shows up in language—"Honey," "Sweetie," "Have you been a good girl?"—sexual comments about your appearance and attractiveness. You will be able to feel it as a lack of understanding and a lack of support. Change therapists. A woman counselor is not necessarily a guarantee against sexism in the therapy process.

I need a touch-up. Most of us would like to finish therapy and assume we won't have to go back. But life goes on, and we continue to grow, change, and encounter conflict. You may feel the need for another visit every few years. You may prefer to go to another therapist. I sought counseling when I planned to remarry and later when I was getting to know my step-daughter. There will probably be another touch-up in the future. It's a good feeling to know you have a backup. Most counselors are caring individuals who will do everything they can to help you.

When you do nothin, , things rarely improve, although you may become accustomed to a negative situation. When you work on problems, your life gets better and better. The pain of growth is always worth it.

Remember

Don't try to learn to live with pain as a part of life. You deserve to feel better; work at it.

Your circumstances or feelings are not hopeless. You are not alone.

Don't be embarrassed at who you are, what you've done, or how much you cry in therapy. Give yourself credit for having the courage to grow.

If I hurt enough, I'll change.

II. FRIENDS, CRITICS, AND LOVERS

21. I Want a Support System

It is very painful to feel alone. If we were gone, who would care? Where are the legendary wonderful extended families that always took care of everyone? We have movie and television stereotypes of the perfect grandfather, aunt, mother. They may have existed somewhere, but few of us feel we got a complete set.

We each get three families in a lifetime: the one we're born into, the one we use to survive growing up, and the one we build ourselves. Some of the members of these families are blood relatives; some are not. The most important family is the one you build yourself.

The family we're born into sometimes holds together and is supportive, and sometimes not. We don't have much choice about the family we're born into. We will never be able to change the membership of this group or forget that it is part of us. Very few Americans have a complete and loving natal family.

When you first go out into the world you begin to find people you can lean on or be friends with when times are hard. Sometimes they are members of your natal family, but not always. If your first family is not a safe haven you will put more energy into finding others, even as a very young child. You will sense your need for a support group to survive.

Neighbors, teachers, school friends, coaches, children's group leaders, counselors, all are possible members of your second family. It is a transitional family to get you through to independence. Children who have to leave home find support on the street from older kids, street counselors, owners of hamburger joints, shelter staff, and other transients. Some connections are brief; others endure.

When we travel alone we often create transitional support groups by returning to the same café and chatting with the regulars. You'll make an acquaintance of the concierge to feel welcome when you return to your hotel. Friendships develop very quickly when we're in strange territory because the need for a short-term survival group is so strong.

Young people are especially good at meeting someone at a hostel and deciding in one day to travel for weeks together. It's hard to be alone.

Your family, the most important family, is the one you build out of your sense of self and your values, the family you are building now, the one you will contribute to and turn to for the rest of your life. You get to choose the members. It is an important part of your lifework.

This section and the next cover friendship and relatives. This chapter concentrates on evaluating who's in your support group and taking care of your daily network.

What You Can Do

What kind of people do you want in your support group?
Who is in your support group now?

- friends
- relatives
- co-workers
- neighbors
- community
- church
- support services (doctor, dentist, attorney, grocer, cleaner, bookseller, accountant, housekeeper, mechanic)

Are you protected in case of a crisis? Who could you ask for money? Who could you ask to take care of you if you were ill? Who do you interact with every day or every week?

Each of us has our own style, but I prefer to patronize small, stable businesses so I can build a relationship. The grocer smiles when he sees me, tells me the news, cashes my check, orders special items, and would open for me in an emergency.

The local restaurant will deliver dinner to me if I'm not feeling well. The service station attendant always smiles and treats me well. When one quits I make it a point to get to know the next one. Every contact can either be an uplift, a neutral, or a downer. Extra cost in time and money rarely add up to a loss when you feel valued.

Friends can be the center of your support system but not all of it. Cultivate and be concerned about all the other parts. It's like a safety net.

Change doctor, dentist, attorney until you feel you've made a connection with lifetime potential. Don't settle for less. You don't need to pay for technical skill alone when you can get that skill and a supporter too. The same is true of your church. If the church of your denomination near you doesn't provide a community, go elsewhere. Find the neighbors you are compatible with, and don't worry about the rest.

When you lose a member of your support system, notice it and take the time to find a replacement. The extra moments truly connecting with the people you are in contact with will add immeasurable warmth to your life.

You can leave your home in the morning, run errands, work, shop, and return home feeling wonderful because all your business has been transacted in a safe, friendly, supportive environment. It will even out the harsh clerks, abusive drivers, and others that you cannot always avoid. This informal family is as available in an urban center like New York as it is in a rural town.

You can also be part of a more formal support group. There are so many, some based on special interest or circumstance (stamps, widowhood, conservation, disease, backpacking, ethnicity, politics, religion, birds), some on just sociability and community service.

Remember

Don't assume you can go it alone. It may work when you're feeling good, but it will increase your pain when times are hard.

Try to avoid saving money at the expense of support. Pay a little more to get to know your grocer, mechanic, or cleaner—you'll save money and tension in the long run.

On days when you're depressed the temptation is to avoid connecting. Don't try to be anonymous. Take the risk and the smile from someone who knows you. It will help lift the darkest mood, even when being known seems to be the last thing you want.

Take good care of yourself so you can take care of the rest of us.

22. I Have Trouble with Friends

You find yourself wanting to share a moment or plan an event, and you cannot think of anyone to call. The friends you used to call have moved, changed, or died, or you have changed. You wonder, since everyone is supposed to have friends, if there's something wrong with you. You wonder how to make new friends or get closer to the ones you've got.

The ability to build friendships is dependent on making it a high priority in your life. Lots of us like being independent and don't want to be bothered with other people—until suddenly we feel alone. Many people rely on just one other person as a friend (parent, child, spouse) for a lifetime and feel that's enough. It is a risk to be close to only one person, because if you lose that one you are truly alone. You must decide whether you really want friends or, if you want them, whether you deserve friends.

The hardest part is deciding—and feeling—that you are someone special. This may require spending some time thinking about your life and value. If you don't love yourself, you will not be attracted to those who could love you. If you are not pleased with yourself, others will be aware of your feelings and feel uncomfortable.

If you are shy or consider yourself unattractive, work on changing that; try getting involved in volunteer activities where you can learn to be social in a safe environment.

Be available to meet men and women. Join a hiking club or a sports team. Get involved in a cause or political race you could feel committed to (environment, taxes, governor, city council). Take classes. When you're feeling interested and alive, you will attract new friends and learn more about yourself.

The keys to turning an acquaintance into a friend and a friend into a close friend are priority, self-disclosure, touch, affection, loyalty, independence, acceptance, and change.

Friends take time. Are you willing to think of them, to call and set up meetings yourself, to make an effort? Friendship requires the risk of letting someone get to know you. Are you willing to cultivate transparency, to take off some of your masks and let someone see you as you are?

Expressions of friendship as simple as "I like you, I have fun with you" cement acceptance. Being able to touch, to hold a hand, to put an arm around your friend's shoulder builds closeness. Tell your friend you care. Friendship requires loyalty. Avoid saying negative things about your friend to others, stand by a friend who asks for help. Don't break dates or exclude a friend from other parts of your life.

Friendship also needs freedom and independence. Loyalty does not mean someone has to be your only friend and not have other relationships. All friends need time alone. Don't worry if a week or month goes by and you don't make contact. Friendships ebb and flow depending on energy, needs, feelings, and time. Don't try to take over someone else's life. Encourage your friends' other friendships and join in when it's appropriate.

Friendship has to do with acceptance—someone who knows you and still loves you, who listens to you even when you're wrong. Avoid criticism, try not to manipulate so you're always in control. Give as much as you can. Be ready to receive.

Be ready for change. All friendships have ups and downs; all people change. Be open to the choices your friends make and the fact that sometimes you won't be consulted or included.

Build friendships slowly, one step at a time, just as you build your friendship with and acceptance of yourself.

Try to avoid setting up love tests, "You would do it if you liked me."

Don't overwhelm people with gifts and attention; they'll feel they cannot live up to your expectations.

Watch out for competition and envy.

When your life is tough, spread it around. Try not to unload it all, all the time, on one friend—who might give up or wear out.

When you have a fight be willing to let go of "being right" or "justice" because you know the friendship is more important to you than the present argument. Tell your friend that, and negotiate a way around the conflict.

I've Lost a Friend

You and a friend have had a fight that reveals too many conflicts to allow the friendship to continue. You are drifting away from a close friend and the friend from you, or you have made changes in your life or acquired self-knowledge that is ending the friendship. You realize you have different values.

If you were close and very important to each other, the emotions are similar to any loss of love. You begin to feel guilty. Aren't friendships forever? If it's your friend who is drifting away you wonder what you said or did or if something is wrong with you.

Friendships fade or change for many reasons. Try to figure out or ask your friend what happened. The information will help you feel safer, because you'll know what you can do next time.

Here are some of the reasons friends are lost:

- Project connection: You were working on a project together, and it was easy to share lives and events. When the project ended the focus of your friendship was gone. You made promises to continue seeing each other, but it just didn't happen. You didn't have a common interest anymore.

- Geography: You worked in the same building or lived next door to each other. When one of you moved, it seemed too difficult to have that same informal friendship. What once just happened now would have to be planned.

- Fade-out: Your life has changed, or your friend's life has.

- Resentment: Maybe there were conflicts that never made it to the surface. You two may need to fight.

- Marriage/divorce: The friendship was one of couples, and it's harder to socialize now she is single. You are afraid she might attract your husband. She prefers to be with other single people.

- Career change: You don't have time anymore. She doesn't have time. Your job change has put barriers between you.

- Values: You've grown and developed strong values that she or he doesn't share. Growing often means leaving people behind even though it hurts. It's okay to move on.

- Loyalty: One of you was disloyal to the other, and it has broken the trust between you.

- Competition: You are successful in ways that she envies. It becomes uncomfortable to be around you.

- Priority: The friendship is just not high on your priority list.

What You Can Do

Make a decision. You may not be able to pin down what is happening, but you can decide what to do about it.

Decide to leave. If you want to continue to drift away from your friend or use a current conflict to get away, do it gently. Avoid confrontation. Always be civil. Find good things to think about the person you're leaving. You were friends. Just gradually drop out and become interested elsewhere.

Watch out for any tension that could mean you'll avoid all your common friends—unless you want to get away from the whole group. People don't like open rejection, so if you aren't careful you'll end up with enemies when all you wanted was to drift away.

Decide to stay. If you don't want to let go of the friendship and there has been a conflict or you feel guilty, talk to your friend. You may need more information to decide what's going on and to decide what you want to do.

If you want to stop drifting away or want to resolve the conflict, say so and see if there's enough interest on both sides to put the friendship back on track. If you are uncomfortable talking to your friend, then write. Don't use third parties as mediators.

Be ready to fight for the friendship if that is what you want. Express your intent, and set up a confrontation to try to clear the air and find out what is going on.

Accept the loss. If the friendship is gone, take a no-blame posture. There always is a sense of loss in a major change in a relationship. No one is really to blame. Don't say negative things to other people. Don't look for justice. There may be a time in the future for you to become friends again.

Sometimes we lose a friend and never know why. You can come up with all sorts of reasons and even talk with the other person about it, but you still feel confused. The temptation is to blame yourself, and maybe you played a part, but it may be more accurate to just accept the cause as unknown and let it go.

Check out your friendship patterns. Do you choose people who are inferior so you can dominate, the reverse, or equals? Do you have a variety of friends or just people who mirror your values? What conflicts seem to occur, and what's been your history of resolving them? Try to learn from the changes.

I Don't Want to Have Any Enemies

Most women were raised with the notion of being "popular." We worried and struggled with our peers to be thought of as "nice" because for many of us nice and security came in the same package. Women who were not liked or approved of could be ostracized.

When there were two classes of women your whole life might depend on which class you fell into. Your destiny could be controlled not just by social class but by the perceptions of and support of other women.

Good women were taken care of. Bad women were not. Oh, they might have a few good years in the "fast lane," but the community would neglect them when they were old, shun them while they were young, and take their children away with their reputation.

There were dangers then more serious than not getting into the right club if you were an unpopular female. We learned, even as women's roles opened up, to keep our behavior and our opinions within the realm of acceptability. One of the classic contemporary examples is the number of successful, independent women who say, "I am not a feminist." They are feminists to their core but are afraid of not being acceptable.

What this has to do with collecting enemies is that women's independence can free you from being bland, a bowl of oatmeal. If everyone likes you, I guarantee that you are not an interesting person and you are not living up to your full potential.

Life and passion require us to feel strongly and to share (within reason) those feelings. That means you will upset some people, offend others, and take sides. Straddling the fence just means you've decided not to be connected, unless your position truly is in the middle.

People who are afraid of upsetting others let many things go by that ultimately hurt their personal integrity.

- racist, sexist, anti-Semitic remarks
- destructive gossip
- illegal or unethical behavior
- personal criticism
- ideas and policies they care about
- mediocre standards
- disloyalty

I am not suggesting we become judgmental, just reminding you that being an independent and whole person means sticking by strongly held beliefs and making that known. It doesn't mean constant battle but at least spirited dialogue, involvement in change, and passionate opinion.

The key to unhappiness is wanting everyone to like you.

The only way to guarantee that you will be liked by everyone is to stay in bed. Then the only person who will be upset is whoever has to feed you and change the sheets. If you venture out into the world at all, you will make enemies or at least irritate a few people.

I not only advocate the development of people who don't like you, but I also want to suggest they can be great sources of energy and testing of your quality as a person. Think of all the energy you can derive from a new enemy.

Choose good, strong people as enemies. Don't bother with creeps or unethical people. You don't want to exchange energy with people you cannot admire, at least on some level.

Rotate your enemies. Don't keep the same enemy around too long, because he or she loses juice. Try to recycle enemies every year so you can learn new things about yourself. When you've had an enemy around for more than a year (unless it's a relative) invite your enemy out to lunch. You two have a lot in common, or you wouldn't have such strong feelings. Often enemies have personality traits that we most fear in ourselves. Clear out the old ones so you will have room for new, perhaps more interesting enemies.

Limit the number. Don't keep too many enemies going at any one time. It's a sign that you are more than just independent and opinionated. You may have a personality problem that needs working on. Try to limit your list of known (you cannot bother with the unknown) enemies to five. When it gets to six, take one out to lunch.

Learn from the people you upset and those who upset you. What is really happening? Check your defenses and hot buttons. Enjoy and put energy into strong feelings, discussion, different opinions, but save your enemy slots for more important differences.

Remember

Try not to stew and get upset over an enemy; instead, draw energy and information from your feelings.

Don't violate your own integrity to "get" an enemy. That's missing the whole point of having them in the first place. Enemies are a test of our honor, not an excuse for giving it up.

Don't try to turn a friend into everything. He or she may not be the right person to baby-sit your children, get you a bargain, or lend you money.

Try not to give up a friend you care about easily. Be tenacious; give a second and a third chance before you throw in the towel. Friends aren't always forever, but it's wonderful to build and share a history with someone.

It's a lot easier to get your way if you have more than one way.

23. I'm Being Hurt by Gossip

Gossip will be with us forever because it's vicarious fun that we couldn't get any other way. It would be very difficult for any society to get along without exchanging informal information about people and events.

Gossip is a way of building trust and intimacy between friends and learning more about yourself. If we knew only what people wished to reveal directly, our ability to understand them and respond would be much more limited.

That doesn't mean that it can't hurt. The important thing to understand is the difference between good and bad gossip.

Good gossips know a lot but are careful to share only information that feels appropriate. They are rarely indiscreet and regret hurtful mistakes. They can keep a secret. They like to keep up with the news, not dig for the dirt.

Anyone who claims not to gossip is either lying or uninteresting. Don't give it up; just follow the rules.

Don't lie or exaggerate information.
Don't tell someone things you know will hurt that person.
Keep your promises of secrecy.
Don't gossip all the time, with everyone.
Be thoughtful and discreet.
Assume you'll be gossiped about too.

Remember, if no one is talking about you it is because your life is not interesting to them. If lots of people gossip about you, think of all the entertainment you provide and how important you are.

What You Can Do

Rarely does it make sense to try to find the source of a piece of gossip or to fight back. Someone who wants to hurt you can always find another way. It's a grin-and-bear-it situation. You can limit bad gossip about you by either telling everyone everything (my strategy) or sharing very little. A middle ground is to take risks with trusted friends and pay the price if you're wrong. It is probably worth it for the pleasures of sharing. These rules may protect you if you fear being hurt:

Never tell anyone secrets about your involvement in criminal behavior.

Never share questionable tax-reporting practices.

Never share information about your infidelities or anyone else's.

Never tell anyone negative things about your husband's sexual performance.

Don't say hurtful things (even if they are true) about friends and relatives unless you are *sure* your motivation is positive.

Your stomach will tell you what you're doing.

Be very careful with gossip at work. Always assume that someone who is listening will tell the boss.

At the television station where I worked the building was being redecorated for a special visit of the national network anchorman. It was exciting, and many of the upper-level managers were taking it very seriously. I overheard a joke that they were replacing the toilet seats in the men's bathrooms but not in the women's. The theory was that the anchorman would not see our toilets.

I repeated the comment in front of some colleagues, never dreaming that one would report it to the president of the company. I was called on the carpet and told to be more positive. It was hard not to giggle, but I used common sense and kept quiet—the second time.

Someone who has betrayed your confidence before will probably do it again. Ask your friends not to repeat bad gossip about you to you. Tell them you don't need to know. If they tell you anyway, they may not be friends. They may like stirring up trouble between you and others.

A woman I worked with, liked, and trusted, told me for years that another woman didn't like me. She told me a number of stories about this woman sabotaging our plans or saying critical things about my work. For years I hated the woman, even though I hardly knew her. Eventually I decided it was silly and took her out to lunch; we realized that we were both being told negative stories about what the other had said. Our feud was created out of what others saw as a natural competition and gossip. We realized we liked each other, laughed, and agreed not to listen to any more stories.

Remember

Don't let low self-esteem make you accept gossip as a valid indication of what people believe about you. Negative information can make us irrational.

Avoid becoming obsessed with an attack on your integrity or family. If the stress of being gossiped about stays with you more than a few days, get some help to put it in perspective.

Try not to attack whoever you think is the gossip. You could be wrong, and the person may deny it anyway.

I cannot control the thoughts and acts of others.

24. Critics Can Ruin My Day

No matter what you do, it doesn't seem right. You're beginning to doubt your competence and self-worth. You start apologizing for everything. You begin to wait for the next criticism.

You get them everywhere. Waiters criticize what you ordered for dinner. Your best friend points out your flaws. Your lover mentions the weight you've gained and notes that he likes taller women. Your mother calls you to tell you what's wrong with you, and your boss complains. Even your ten-year-old feels free to correct your grammar and suggest a new hairstyle.

My view of criticism is that all those nasty remarks are just "slugs" (a Northwest slimy mollusk you find everywhere) that people are trying to unload. Criticizers may have received so many of the slimy things as a child that they are still trying to get rid of them. They get up every morning with a bucketful of slugs, looking for victims.

I call criticisms "slugs" because they're hard to put down; they stick to you, and if you swallow them, they'll make you sick.

Those who criticize call their remarks "teasing," "kidding," or "constructive." Constructive criticism is just a slug in a tuxedo. The slug carriers don't understand the difference between criticism and encouragement. They mean to hurt, and they do.

You think it's your problem when it's someone else's. People who hand you slugs are so concerned about their own value that they need to put you down just to keep ahead of the competition. It's a way of keeping you under control. Here is some of the slug collection I've developed over the years with the help of friends.

> I like those pants you're wearing, nice color. Too bad you don't have the right kind of body for pants.

> You never do anything right.

> You wouldn't understand.

> This hurts me more than it hurts you.

Oh, that looks like the same ring he gave his first wife.

Your brother never had these problems.

Do you know what's wrong with you? You can't take criticism.

My mom says she'll quit smoking when I get my life together. Meanwhile, if she dies of cancer, I'm to blame.

Don't you ever consider anyone else's feelings?

Why do you make me hit you?

How did you ever manage to keep your breasts so small?

I really like that dress—if you hang on to it, it will probably come back in style.

I hope she's smart because her sister is much cuter.

We can't imagine that he'll ever amount to anything.

You are always a problem.

I wish I'd never had you.

People will deny they are critical when you stop them. They claim they are trying to help. But criticism is the opposite of helping. Criticism is used to compete, to compare, and to denigrate the victim—all of this disguised as being "for your own good." Criticism tears people down; encouragement builds people up.

Criticism:
"Mom, I got three A's on my report card!"
"Well, what about the other grades, why didn't you get all A's!"

"Dad, I mowed the lawn and I even put the lawn mower away!"
"Well, did you wipe off the blades first? I'll bet you forgot that again; you're so careless."

"Look Dad, I just put together my first model airplane all by myself."
"I can see you did it without help; it's a mess. There's glue all over everything. I could do better than this when I was half your age."

Encouragement:
"Mom, I got three A's on my report card!"
"That's wonderful, I know you worked hard." Later that week: "I'm very proud of you and your grades, you'll do better each time because you know how to study. Would you like some help to get four A's next time?"

"Dad, I mowed the lawn, and I even put the lawn mower away."

"Thank you, Son, you really are an asset to this family. We all appreciate your help. The lawn looks great! I forgot to mention the importance of cleaning the blades off when you finish; let's go and do that together now."

"Look, Dad, I just put together my first model airplane all by myself."

"You put this together all by yourself? Congratulations. This is a really good start on building models. I see you had some trouble with the glue. That was hard for me too when I first started building models. It gets easier each time. I'll show you some of the tricks I learned."

Parents are like mirrors for children; their faces and comments tell us what we are worth. Encouragement instills a feeling of confidence— we're okay. Children who are encouraged and supported try harder and succeed more often. They are not afraid to make mistakes, so they do more.

Think back over your own experience as a child and as an adult. Think about the criticisms that still sting even years later. You will understand on a personal level the power of criticism.

Our sense of self has a lot to do with whether we are successful or not. If you feel you are not valuable you may not allow yourself to be successful. You will always assume any success you have is luck instead of your own hard work. Children who are constantly criticized and whose accomplishments are discounted by their parents often spend their lifetime discounting their adult achievements. Check yourself; check those inner voices. See where the negative thoughts come from.

My aunt, when she was seventy-five, attended a lecture I gave on criticism and self-esteem. She had tears in her eyes as we drove home. I asked her what had upset her. It was unusual to see her cry. She was remembering when she was ten years old a remark made by her Aunt Bess. "Dorothy has such a sallow complexion" was the comment. My aunt had never forgotten, and the hurt was still there sixty-five years later.

We criticize out of habit as well as a desire to hurt, humiliate, or control. We accept criticisms out of habit too. You may not even notice the small ones until enough of them pile up and you find yourself feeling blue and not knowing why.

Criticism undermines your sense of personal value. It's like sandpaper of fine to coarse grade. It wears you down and away. Your confidence, however much you started with in the situation or relationship, erodes.

What You Can Do

Recognize it. It's not yours. Either drop it, or hand it back. If the slugs that you're handed all look as though they belong to you, then someone has reduced your sense of self and it's time to reevaluate.

When you put the slug down or hand it back, you'll still feel the slime on your fingers, but that's better than holding on to the whole thing. Dig a pretend hole with your foot, drop the slug in, and cover it up.

If you ask people why they gave you that hurt, they might get angry, because people who have a lot of slugs to unload are afraid. Fear usually hides itself in anger and irritation. Sometimes they'll switch to tiny slugs, hoping you won't notice.

They'll also use slug sandwiches, two nice comments with a slug in between. My mother used to put ground liver in my orange juice so I'd be healthy. I always thought something was in the glass, but didn't know until I got to the bottom. Little slugs are like that. Give them back.

Register it. Let them know you noticed the slug. When at a party, if your spouse or a friend criticizes you, just go "Ohh!" as if you were hurt. Then go on with the conversation. Don't refer to the comment. If someone asks what's wrong, say you just felt a pinprick.

Set up signals. One family stopped slugs around the dinner table by using a bell. Whenever grandfather criticized someone, they rang the bell. He realized he couldn't get away with it anymore.

Drape it over you. A great strategy (if you have a sense of humor) is to agree with the criticizer. It eliminates the power of the slug by disintegrating it, just as though you had sprinkled it with salt. Here are some examples of how to agree with slugs:

Slug: You've gained weight, Dear. Aren't you about twenty pounds over-weight?
You: Yes. Actually, it's closer to twenty-five. Terrible, isn't it?
Slug: Aren't you going to do anything about it?
You: Probably not . . . I'm just going to be fat for a while.

Agree with whatever is said until the other person gets bored. Take the power out of the remark. It only has power if you grant it.

Criticizer: This house is a mess! [translation: It's not perfect.]
You: Yes, it is.

Criticizer: Well aren't you going to do something about it?

You: Probably not. I mean I didn't, so I probably can't.

Criticizer: You could learn to be a better housekeeper.

You: No, I've tried, and I think I'm just not good at it.

Criticizer: It's very hard for me to live this way.

You: Yes, I know, I worry about you. Maybe we could hire some help, or you could help, or your mother could come over.

Criticizer: It just does no good to talk to you.

Resist. Write a letter to each criticizer politely saying that you are not going to absorb any more of their slugs. Talk to criticizers you live with and inform them of your new resolution. When they criticize you anyway:

Ask them why they want to hurt you. They'll probably say it's for your own good.

Walk away, close your eyes, deflect the criticism.

Hang up the telephone. If it's someone you love, say "I love you" just before you hang up.

A woman told me her husband only criticized her in public. She began to carry a small towel. She put it on her head, covering her face, whenever he made a hurtful remark. He was so embarrassed by the towel that he stopped.

Record it. Begin a list today, and keep track of where your slugs are coming from. Start a notebook to write slugs in and give them a 1–10 rating. Which hurt the most? Just writing them down will give you perspective. You could have a "slug of the week" contest among your friends or family.

Catch them if it takes awhile. Sometimes you won't identify the slug you've been given until a few hours later. As soon as you do, throw it away. Keep track of who hands you slugs, and stop them, find a way to deflect them, or stay away from that person. If you cannot avoid them, start working on handing slugs back.

We repeat old patterns. Feelings and actions that are familiar feel safe, even when they're negative. If you were given a lot of slugs as a child and dutifully swallowed them, you will look for close companions who will make you feel at home.

Evaluations at work are different. Your family and friends do not have a license to criticize you—even if they think they do. An employer makes a contract with you that may include criticism. You have to decide whether it's worth it.

Remember

Don't criticize back or attack others.
Marriage or parenting doesn't give you a license to criticize.
Stop believing that criticism is constructive.

Encourage, don't criticize. A kiss or a hug, but never a slug.

25. I'm Jealous

Few emotions hurt like full-blown, 24-hour-a-day jealousy. It turns you green because it makes you sick. You cannot sleep; the images move through your mind. You compare yourself specifically, intensely, and with burning pain to someone you think he wants more than you. Your stomach hurts, and your body aches. You become a detective and a whiner for reassurance.

Jealousy is simply and clearly the fear that you do not have value, and therefore nothing is safe. Jealousy scans like a beacon searching for evidence to prove the point—that others will be preferred and rewarded more than you. Jealousy can be a burning pain as a particular lover chooses another or it can be a dull lifetime ache of comparison to everything and everyone.

Jealous people usually are unhappy in many areas of their lives. They may be dissatisfied with their mates yet still jealous. They are not sure what they want, but they know they don't want to lose anything they have.

Jealousy hurts because it is a devaluing of yourself and your security. We fear the loss and, even worse, begin to think we deserve to lose. She is probably better than I am. "It's not fair." "We're married." "He promised." "She was my friend."

Jealousy is so acute because it has its roots in our childhood. This is when we learned to define ourselves and our worth based on the attention we received from others. Most children feel that the only proof they are loved is direct attention. We think of our value as coming from the attention and love we can get from someone else. We are, therefore, in constant danger of losing it.

Men tend to be just as jealous as women, but they often handle it differently. Women become introspective, questioning their own worth, wondering what they can do. Men are more likely to take action, either through violence or replacement. They may quickly find another woman to restore their value.

Jealousy and power are closely connected. The power goes to the person least emotionally and economically involved in the relationship.

When power is unequal, there is always anxiety over getting hurt or being out of control of your life. That is why some people try to make another jealous or pretend they are detached.

There are many myths that surround and contribute to jealous feelings. It helps to know what they are.

- It has happened to me before so it will happen again: "I lost my father to my mother or sister or brother or another love." You may have been hurt early, lost a crucial competition before you understood the rules. Now you expect it.

  Jealousy causes so much pain that some of us change so we won't ever feel that way again. Others set up an expectation of abandonment and allow their jealous feelings to contribute to repeat experiences.

- I always love more: "I love you more than you love me." Translate this to, "I love myself less, and I keep score."

- Jealousy and craziness show how much I love you: Wrong, they show how terrified and out of control you are. You are unable to tell the difference between passion and anxiety, love and hysteria.

- No relationship will work: You are willing to prove it with tests and investigations instead of trust. You lack faith in relationships. Check your family and past experiences for reasons.

- I don't deserve it: This is always the bottom line in jealousy. I must, in order to feel valued, find someone to love me. But I never will be able to hold onto this, because I don't deserve it. When you feel you have no value you assume others will sooner or later treat you that way.

When Judith met him she thought her dreams had come true. He was, at six feet tall, big enough to take care of her. At night there would be sexual images of her father as she slept with someone who could dominate her with a hand or a look. He was the past, but she had no idea, then, of the pain he doubled for.

He was well known and people stared. She liked the feeling of being with somebody. She sure wasn't anybody herself. It was fun for a while, confusing, new. She decided it was a chance to be a real woman and love with everything she had. She could hear Frank Sinatra singing, "When somebody loves you, it's no good unless they love you—all the way."

This one would work! To believe that, to fullfill the hunger, she ignored immense anounts of information. It was the classic situation: everyone but she knew that true love was the last thing that would be happening to this couple. She ignored the cruelty he displayed toward his children and his constant depression. He seemed wonderful to her. She ignored the information from her own body. She lost weight, pierced her ears, and bleached her hair to be a "natural woman" for him. They listened to music together that she thought had deep meaning, not knowing two duplicate tapes had been sent to other women. She stopped having orgasms and found herself waking at 4:00 A.M. next to him, desolate.

"Shucks," she thought. "I just need to give more, be more open, vulnerable, loving, a real woman." So she cooked meals, ran errands, neglected her children and work, and answered telephone calls in the middle of the night when he was on the road.

Then, in love up to her newly pierced ear lobes, she began to trip over other women: groupies with pornographic cakes, housekeepers in his bed naked, ex-lovers who still had hopes (he was a collector of women), secretaries who had similiar hopes, his friends' wives and daughters, and women on the street. They were everywhere, lined up, offering body, soul, and cookies.

As Judith fell deeper into this love swamp, she became shakier and lost her ability to make sense of what was going on. She just tried to love more.

Here are some of the conversations she thought were reasonable.
Sitting in the bathtub together:

He: "You're number one, so why does it matter that there are others?"
She: "Number one" (pleased) "of how many?" (dismayed).
He: "There's no reason to talk about it." He then remains silent, refusing to talk, for the rest of the evening, unless one of the other women calls. She had upset him. Being number one had special rules.

Over dinner in a restaurant when the waitress has just tucked her telephone number in his pocket.

He: "I thought you believed in love."
She: "I do."
He: "Then, why would you want to stop me from loving as many women as I can? Why shouldn't other women have me too? You are really selfish."
She: "Yes, I see, why not? We can all be loved; there's enough for all of us. I shouldn't need to be the only one" (intense pain).

At a theater sitting next to a woman he had told her was just a friend:

His friend: "I wanted to meet you. Fred says you're a friend."

She: "Oh!"

His friend: "I want to start meeting his friends. We've already talked about having children together. He's helping me move out of my husband's place. We're divorcing."

She: "Oh!"

His friend: "He says you're very smart."

She: "Oh."

His friend: "You know, if you fixed your hair and put on some makeup, you could be really attractive."

Her children hated him; her friends were either intimidated or impressed; a relative was thrilled to have somebody she could show off. Judith didn't notice the slide into all-consuming jealousy until she had

—called him in the middle of the night to see if he was really home, forgetting that others did that when she was with him.

—had a drink with his housekeeper and two of his lovers.

—sobbed on his secretary's shoulder, even though she knew many others had before.

—dressed in dark clothes to sneak up to the outside of his house and peek in.

—gone through his drawers and tried to listen in on his telephone calls.

—confronted, in public, one of his ex-lovers and made her cry.

—gone to a plastic surgeon to see if she could be made prettier.

—gone ten thousand dollars in debt doing things for him.

—tried dressing like the model he liked.

—given up important professional opportunities.

—hurt her children and friends repeatedly.

She did all that—and more—until she ended up in my office for counseling. When he sensed she was beginning in therapy the first steps away from jealousy and toward self-value, he gave her a diamond ring but said it was really a friendship ring. Then he took it back. Judith held on to her love and made more self-destructive moves. She was consumed by the other women.

She slept with him Christmas Eve—after all, she was number one. He told her late that night that he would be getting up early to go to breakfast with an actress and her family. After he left she found, in his briefcase, a photograph of the woman, surrounded by yellow roses. On the back was a thank you to him for the flowers. He had sent Judith yellow roses too. He had told her they meant "eternal love."

She wandered around his house that morning and found three vases of yellow roses. She tried to find the little cards to see who they were from, and then she called me, ready to give up.

When I called her to ask permission to tell this story she laughed all the way through the torturous list of what she had done when jealous. He had called her, a few months after that Christmas, on his wedding night, and she had been able to hang up. Then she started to get well.

Jealousy, and the humiliation that always goes with it, come from deep personal insecurity. Tackle that problem first, and then the rest of these suggestions may help.

What You Can Do

Relax. Muscle tension holds anxiety. You can make yourself feel better just by using some stretching and relaxation techniques. Restore a little balance. Sometimes the body has to release jealousy before the mind can. Wait twenty four hours before taking any action.

Restrain yourself and analyze the situation. Being upset won't force anyone into giving you more attention, and it may do harm. Why are you feeling so devalued and threatened? What is your history?

Examine your worries. Jealousy occurs when we fear loss. Jealous people are very anxious people. Find out what you are anxious about. If you lost this man, would you survive? Try to do a reality check.

Break the pattern. Jealousy feeds on bad experience. You might have been okay until you ran into a man or two or a friend who abandoned you for someone else. Is this a lifetime pattern or just a bad year? Who are you choosing to love and trust? Do you need to take better care of yourself?

Work on your own life. Develop independence, the knowledge that you can survive alone. Don't stay home in a black mood because he is out with someone else. Put some energy into your life even if right now you have to work at it. Take a class, start a project, take a trip, exercise, call someone else; do something for you.

Negotiate. Ask your partner or friend for some changes in behavior. Ask for more open communication so you can build trust. Identify specific situations that make you uncomfortable, and work out a compromise.

Get to know your rival. What qualities does a rival have that you might envy? Are you in competition for the same or different things in the relationship? Is she or he really a rival? What improvements could you make to be your best self? Is it worth it to you?

Plan ahead. If certain situations make you jealous, plan how to handle them before they happen. Either avoid the circumstance, ask your partner to cooperate, or distract yourself. Avoid reading papers and mail that is private; don't listen to telephone calls not meant for you; ask friends not to report information to you.

End the relationship. If you usually are a reasonable person and a particular relationship is causing you constant jealous grief, think about ending it. Is the person you love really that wonderful? Is the hurt you feel worth what you are getting from the relationship? If the other person is doing things to trigger your jealousy (deceit, flirting, infidelity) why put up with it?

Forgive yourself. Jealousy and love are closely connected. You have given yourself to love; you have let yourself be vulnerable. You are willing to be emotionally intense, and jealousy is part of it.

There is only one way to reduce jealousy forever—that is to increase your sense of self-value. If *you* cannot love you, you will not believe you are loved. You will always think it's a mistake or luck. Take your eyes off others, and turn the scanner within. Find the seeds of your jealousy; clear the old voices and experience. Put all your energy into building your personal and emotional security.

Then you will be the one others are jealous of, and you can remember the pain and reach out to them.

Remember

Don't become a detective. Don't spy and end up violating your own ethics.

Try not to do anything to humiliate yourself just because it feels good at the moment.

Don't deny your jealous feelings. Sometimes they are reasonable and a signal to make a change in the relationship. They are also a signal that you need to work on your own self-worth.

You don't have to suffer to be loved.

26. I Know He's Unfaithful

Many otherwise reasonable people want to have it all. They want the feeling of being married and the feeling of being single. They want to have the security of a lifetime commitment and the sexual freedom of the single life.

Yet, commitment requires trust and respect. In most relationships that means fidelity. But in many marriages and long-term arrangements you will have to face the possibility of his being intimate with another woman. You may also feel desire for another man.

Infidelity is one of the most painful things that can happen in a woman's lifetime. Few things hurt as much as betraying or feeling betrayed by someone we love. Women are, by culture, less secure, more afraid of rejection, and more likely to be monogamous.

His Infidelity

The beginning steps are small, but finally your intuition starts signaling that your partner is intimately involved with someone else. The temptation is to look the other way. Painful knowledge is to be avoided. Instead, listen to the signals. The pain will be more intense if you don't validate your intuition.

Rejection in any form hurts, but you will survive this and your relationship may survive it as well. Here is a list of the classic signals:

There is diminished personal communication between you.

You overhear him talking quietly on the telephone or jumping to get the calls.

He starts insisting on picking up the mail.

He stays at work later.

Business trips get longer.

He wants to go off on weekend trips alone.

Dinner meetings end later.

He gets up and leaves earlier.

There's a sudden change in grooming habits.

New sexual techniques show up in bed.

You feel unexplained physical or emotional pain.

You have no sexual contact.

You feel shut out or that he is guarding a secret.

You feel detached from the relationship.

It all starts to add up, and you think he's seeing another woman. Your trust is breaking down. You start to play detective. You go through his pockets and his wallet. You try to check up on him and listen in on his telephone calls. It is demeaning and humiliating to your spirit. Try not to play detective. Instead, try to find out what is really happening and what it means for you.

First, could you be wrong? Do you have a fear of being abandoned that may color your perception? Has this happened to you before? Give your spouse/friend the benefit of the doubt. Try to think the situation through. Do not make accusations. Don't talk to friends or the children. Is there any real evidence?

Without confronting him with your suspicions, discuss your feelings about the changes you perceive and the loss of feelings of love and trust. Try to find answers to your questions and emotions.

If this fails to relieve your doubts, it is time to confront him with your suspicions. Choose a location where you will not be interrupted and a time when you can complete your discussion. Share your feelings, and gently confront him with the evidence.

Is there an explanation? Try to believe it.

If he admits to an infidelity and it is the first time, can you forgive? Can you take your share of responsibility for what has happened? Could you see a counselor and work out a way to rebuild trust?

If he denies the infidelity even in the face of an obvious fact, if he admits it but wants to continue the triangle, if he has been unfaithful before, or you are unable to forgive, the rest of this section may help.

What You Can Do

Face the emotions. Sort out all the feelings that are raging within you. Infidelity is rejection at its most powerful. When you fell in love you gave him the power to judge you and hurt you. There is no way to love and not be vulnerable.

Infidelity hurts the most when we think someone else has been chosen to replace us. Jealousy hits us in our softest spot, our sexual self-esteem. We think we are not desirable. There is great pain in the loss of status, the humiliation, the loss of reputation. Others will know we have failed in the most intimate sense.

Women are often hurt on another level too. We feel our security threatened because desirability seems to be the key to success as a female. The sudden sense of abandonment makes us lose self-confidence and imagine ourselves alone forever in a secondhand dress. We feel dependent.

It is time to slow down your emotions before you decide what to do with the information you have. It is easier now to face infidelity than it once was. It has happened to many, and your friends will be supportive. You know you have worth beyond that defined by men, and you know that you are still valuable as a person.

Hold onto your perspective and self-worth. Sit down and try to remember what your life was like before you met this man. If you have been married a long time, remember the times that you have been happy alone. Rebalance your perspective by taking care of yourself.

Do one thing to take care of you: have a cup of tea, take a hot bath, buy a small present for yourself, call a friend, exercise. Do one thing to make yourself more attractive: change clothes, put on some makeup, wash your hair. You may resist caring about your appearance, but it is important for your sense of self and his view of you.

When you are rested or at least calmer, lay out a plan of action. Find out what's really going on.

Get accurate information. You need to know what is going on. Confront your lover or husband, and ask him if he'll tell the truth. Find out what his intentions and plans are. Do your best to be loving and not over-concerned with your loss of value. He is in pain too.

Decide what kind of infidelity this is. Call, or go and see the "other woman." Your husband may deny the accusation and shift the burden of proof to you. He may blame the affair on the needs of the other woman. It is easy to set her up as the problem. Don't do it. Find out what she thinks is going on. Evaluate her intentions, and let her know you are a living, breathing human being.

Watch out for invalidation. Your mind will want to play tricks on you. You will be tempted to invalidate your common sense and your intuition. You will want to believe things that you know to be untrue. It will be difficult to save this relationship if you don't know what is going on.

Get practical information. You may not be interested in divorce, but you do need to know where you stand. Call a divorce lifeline or other information source. You will get legal information, access to a support group, and some ideas about marriage counseling.

Build your independence. It may take awhile to sort this hurt out. You need to feel strong. Evaluate your financial situation, and decide what you could do if your relationship broke up. If you are unemployed get a job or enroll in school or a training program. Don't sit home and worry about what will happen to you.

Organize social support. Turn to your friends, but not couples who will have to take sides. Try not to drag your family into this. There will be plenty of time once you know what the choices are.

Take good care of yourself. Start taking vitamins and eating carefully. Cut down on caffeine, sugar, and alcohol. You need to hold onto your balance, not sink into depression. Get into an exercise or relaxation program, and do something to make yourself feel more attractive.

Evaluate his behavior. How does he treat you? Is he expressing regret or just saying it's your problem? Does he listen to your feelings or invalidate and challenge them? What does he want? What are his plans? Do they match his behavior?

Decide what you want. If it is the first time, you may be willing to forgive. This confrontation may deepen your commitment to each other. You will learn from the pain to treat each other with more kindness and attention. If it is not the first time, you may be ready to leave.

If you stay, counseling will help you to discover what happened and how you really feel. Without help you may bury your feelings and exact revenge in other ways. You need to forgive yourself, the other woman, and your husband or lover.

Forgiving yourself may be the hardest. You will wonder if you should have worn lingerie to bed. You will wonder what is wrong with you and attack your image and personality. You will grind your teeth, comparing yourself to the other woman, wanting to know every detail, and hurting yourself with each comparison. To let it go, to stop the fantasies, you will have to forgive yourself for not being all things to all people.

Forgiving the other woman may seem unimportant, but it is. You will be tempted to blame her instead of recognizing that your husband or lover is an adult who made a free choice. She may have been lonely or devalued herself. She may have been taught to believe that men are entitled to more than one woman at a time. She may have believed a line about your relationship or his intentions. Whatever the circumstances, she is, in a sense, a sister. She also feels pain; she is part of a hurtful situation. Let her and yourself off the hook. She did the best she could given who she is and what she knew at the time.

Forgiving him is essential if you two are sincere about rebuilding your relationship. Without forgiveness you are just marking time until you can find justice in some other way. You will know by your personal fantasies if you have been able to give yourselves a new start.

A client of mine was unable to let go. She seethed, she attacked herself, she hated the other woman to the point of wanting to kill. She kept smiling at her husband, but he knew he was walking on eggshells. He asked her again and again to forgive him, and finally we realized that she needed proof of his love, a visible penance.

They agreed that every Saturday, for a year, he would wash her car. She would watch him from the inside if it was raining or outside if it was not. His actions would demonstrate that he loved her, was sorry, and would do anything he could to prove his love. For three months she watched him wash her car; it was so much more powerful than words. Then one day she walked out of the house and began to help him. She had forgiven herself; she had forgiven him. He knew it; his dues were paid, and they could let their love grow.

If you decide not to stay in the relationship, sometimes forgiveness is not the issue, preservation of your value is. If he continues the affair, has been unfaithful before, or you just know it is time to let go, then take action. Consider counseling to get you over the rough spots, read the section on breaking up, and take good care of yourself.

There is no question that a breakup connected to infidelity is about as horrible as anything a woman can face, but it is better than years of mistrust and humiliation. Men who have multiple affairs will do so until their death. Staying with a man like that, hoping that this one will be the last, will break your heart.

Remember

Try not to compare yourself to the other woman, saying "if only" I had done this or that.

Try not to do anything humiliating to yourself or in front of him. There is a long list of these in the breaking-up section. If you do these things anyway because the pain is so intense, forgive yourself; passionate people do passionate things.

If it still hurts, it's time to turn within and read the section on self-esteem.

It is harder to leave a bad relationship because fear may have kept us in it. A loving one is usually an independent choice.

"What is not love is fear."

—A Course in Miracles

27. I Want to Have an Affair

I frequently get letters from women wanting more passion in their lives. Their marriage is good, the children are okay, they like their work, but something is missing. They want the anxiety that used to accompany sex back when they kissed in school or in the beginning of a relationship. They cannot tell the difference between passion and anxiety. An affair or a one-night stand will give them anxiety masked as passion.

Some marriages can sustain sexual freedom, but most cannot. You know what kind of relationship you are in and what you want. Before you get caught in an infidelity decide whether you want to build intimacy with all its costs and rewards or whether you want the chemistry, the thrill of new relationships. You need to know why you want a sexual fling.

- Curiosity: Know yourself and your alternatives. In our highly sexual society you may feel that you are missing out on something if you have not had many lovers. The most experienced women will tell you this isn't true. Most of the pleasures of sex are in your mind and your sense of the relationship. Male bodies and technique will not make that much difference unless your husband has serious sexual limits.

  If you still want to see for yourself, consider renting a pornographic video, or ask your husband if he will go to an adult motel or film. Check out all the possibilities at home before you settle for less elsewhere.

- Missing parts: People often have affairs to find the parts of themselves they don't feel there is room for in their marriage. It may be a certain level of understanding or acceptance, the chance to start over and look new in someone's eyes. Try to figure out what your real desires are.

- Role models: If you were raised with infidelity or multiple marriages you may repeat the behavior. It can be both an unconscious pattern or a loyalty to the life your parents chose, whether they ended up happy or not.

- Anger: A common block to sexual desire is anger. You may want to hurt him or seek revenge for what you think he has done. Underneath anger is almost always fear. Clear both your anger and fear before you hurt yourself.

- Age and desirability: Sex is the classic way to prove one's masculinity or femininity. We all want the rush of someone with lust in his eyes. We are still desired; we have proof. We dream of one last fling before cellulite takes us out of the market.

- Self-destructiveness: Some women want to avoid intimacy, so they destroy good relationships. Some thrive on anxiety or trouble, so they create crisis. Do you have a pattern of hurting yourself or getting into situations where you are hurt?

Consider a worst case scenario. Assume you will be discovered, your husband will insist on a divorce, and your lover will abandon you. Could you handle it? Is it still worth it? I know this sounds like a scare tactic, but you need to know what you are willing to face.

My next-door neighbor was a lovely, fun, energetic woman with four almost-grown children. She had a wonderful husband, and they had been married since she was seventeen. At forty she felt she was missing out on something. It was at the height of the 1970s "sex as exercise" attitude, and she had only been with one man. She announced her intention to check out the scene. Her husband tried to go with her but dropped out.

He accepted her infidelities for a year, then asked for a divorce. By the time she realized what she had lost, he had fallen in love with another woman. She now lives alone, hurt and angry, with a violent lover and is unable to handle her bills even with a generous divorce settlement. Her life has totally fallen apart, and she is not sure why.

It's impossible to have an affair by yourself, so consider the feelings of the other man and whether or not he is involved with another woman. If the affair becomes public you will also have to decide what to tell children and relatives. Accept the difference between flirting and infidelity. You may have been brought up in a sheltered environment with very little experience of flirting. Under these circumstances you might think the first sexual step commits you to action. It doesn't.

Some men will act as if it does. You may get grabbed at a party, and you need to know that you can say no. If you want to flirt, enjoy it, but be thoughtful of your husband and the women who might be hurt by your actions. If you want to have an affair, decide on it in cooler, more rational moments.

What You Can Do

How to Avoid an Affair

Have fantasies instead. It is fine to dream, set up imaginary sexual encounters, read novels, giggle with women friends, directly ogle men, and anything else that pleases you. Just remember to separate your imagination from action.

Keep busy with other passions. Boredom can lead to sexual boredom. Check out the rest of your life before you decide on sex as entertainment.

Think before you act. Redecide what you want and what your values are and whether it is worth it to you.

Don't meet men you are attracted to in dangerous places. Meet them for lunch, not dinner. Meet at public restaurants that are not particularly romantic. Don't meet in hotels. Avoid out of town trips with such men, and if you find yourself on one, don't accept a dinner invitation unless other people join you and you return to your room before they leave.

Be clear about your intentions. When you feel the sexual tension in the air, admit to attraction but state your preference for friendship and your assumption that he feels the same way. Sometimes it may be better left unsaid, but usually you can break the sexuality just by bringing it out in the open.

Stay away from alcohol or drugs. This is not the time for anything that impairs your judgment or gives you an excuse to forget who you are and what you decided in more rational moments.

Arrange your own transportation. The two of you don't need to drive home together alone. If you share a car, make sure you are dropped off before you would end up alone with him.

Watch out for vulnerability. Don't seek out a man you are sexually attracted to when stress and problems make you vulnerable. You may seek solace sexually and later realize it has only made things worse.

If You Decide to Do It Anyway

Try to get permission from your spouse. There are many indirect ways of testing how your spouse feels about either a more open marriage or your attraction to others.

Be discreet and thoughtful in whatever you do. Don't humiliate or embarrass or force a confrontation. Don't assuage your guilty conscience by telling your spouse what will only hurt him.

Protect yourself. Avoid pregnancy or sexually transmitted disease. This is not the time to let romance supersede using a condom.

Avoid married men. Have respect for your sisters who could be terribly hurt by your infidelity. Respect your friends and the men they are involved with.

Remember

Try not to have an affair. If your marriage or relationship isn't working, finish it honorably. Then you can go back out into the world looking for magic.

Anxiety is not the same as passion.

28. I'd Like to Know More About Men and Sex

Men and women are rarely honest about sex. We are afraid to fail, to offend, to be insensitive. The sexual trigger is so fragile that there is fear of damaging it. The end result can be misconnection, pretense, and resentment. Couples who love each other and want to stay together find themselves longing for a new lover just for the chance to start over and set up different patterns.

We have such high, romantic expectations for sexual intimacy. It is the magic we long for that will transform us. Many women feel at their ultimate when they see naked desire in a man's eyes. (That was thrilling just to write.)

Men say we want too much. We want it to be too perfect, instead of just enjoying ourselves and them. That's why they like us to have a few drinks first so we will relax and not notice little imperfections.

Stop for a minute, and think of all the barriers you put in the way of making love even when you are in a good relationship. You are at home, and he is due home soon. It's been a good day for you, you're not tired, so you think, "Maybe tonight's the night." Then the "ifs" start:

"Well, *if* he comes home on time."
"*If* he is nice to the kids."
"*If* he helps with dinner."

Well, he's on a roll—in a great mood, helps with dinner, chats with the children, and even cleans up the dishes afterward. Then the "ifs" start again:

"Well, *if* he doesn't bring up any negative topics."
"*If* he doesn't watch a football game on TV."
"*If* he comes upstairs early."
"*If* he brushes his teeth and doesn't wear his shorts to bed."

It must be catching. He senses something is in the air. He does it all, and soon you two are snuggled in bed together.

"Well, *if* the kids go to sleep."
"*If* the telephone doesn't ring and the dog doesn't bark."

All is quiet. He begins to nuzzle your neck.

"Well, *if* he remembers not to blow in my ear" (his first wife liked that).
"*If* he doesn't lean on my arm so it goes to sleep."
"*If* he slows down, even though it's been three weeks."

There are so many "ifs" that most of us just give up unless we're on vacation where a different atmosphere changes the expectations.

Many people give up desire rather than risk compromise.

The following complaints men make about women and sex were listed by Ken Druck, author of *Secrets Men Keep*, and by men I have interviewed:

Men want women to initiate sex more often. When you are in the mood, go ahead and let him know. Let him lie back, be soft, and let it happen.

Men want greater sexual honesty from women. Men know women fake sexual responses and orgasms. They dislike it, because it implies they can't learn to love in different ways. It also leaves some men never trusting their partners, because they cannot tell what's real and what's not. With that feeling they give up and turn to using sex for themselves instead of to build intimacy and the pleasure bond. Be honest about what works for you and what doesn't. Have an agreement that you don't need an orgasm every time. Some men find that hard to accept, but you can explain it. Women love closeness and pleasuring, and that doesn't always mean an orgasm. You both need to be free to do what you want to do instead of what you think the other person expects.

Many men know very little about female sexuality. They've learned most of what they know from other men, movies, and innuendo. They aren't sure how to tell when a woman has had an orgasm. They are confused about how to stimulate a clitoris or where female erogenous zones are or when to rub hard or soft. They complain women never tell them or wait years to say anything. It makes them uncomfortable to ask. Tell him, show him. Make jokes to take the tension out of making love. Make it safe for both of you.

When there are sexual problems, men often blame themselves. There are lots of things women can do to help with impotence or premature ejaculation. Just sharing the problem, taking off the pressure, can make a difference. Women can fake it when they are anxious; men cannot.

Men need to have their penis approved of just as women like to be told their bodies are attractive. There is tremendous anxiety over penis size despite physicians' claiming they are all the same. Men don't believe that, and neither do women. Let him know you accept and appreciate his body. Cooperate with him to adjust sexual position so you are satisfied.

Male orgasms vary in intensity and pleasure, just as women's do. The older a man is, the more likely he is to choose carefully his partner and circumstance to maximize the possibility of a "good" orgasm. Ejaculation is not necessarily pleasurable for men without the extra feelings that go beyond the release of tension. Men sometimes play act the intensity of their sexual responses, just as women do. You need to be able to know your man's responses and be able to talk about your own.

Some men don't feel free to say no to sex. A gentleman is never supposed to turn a lady down. A man may be tired, bored, angry, or depressed, but his need to prove his manhood overrides everything. The result of sex as obligation can be impotence, which is terrifying. Make it easy for him to say no, and don't take it personally. Think of all the times you've wanted to say no to someone you love.

Some men don't know what they feel and want. Many men are not in close contact with their emotions. The "sex on call" issue is an example of denial of feelings. They learn to tell women what they want to hear because it's safer than telling women how they feel. One man put it well, "A lot of times I can't separate horny feelings from those of wanting to be taken care of. I'm not sure exactly what it is I'm asking of my wife."

Some men feel that good sex and nice girls don't go together. When they get to know and like you or you two get married, passion dies. Unless you can help him understand this madonna-whore stereotype, you may have to play "bad girl" enough to remind him you're a woman. If you don't want to pretend to be what you're not, then couseling may help.

Men sometimes prefer "quickies" to romantic sex. Sometimes just-for-fun sex is not romantic, even though the man is feeling lots of affection for his partner. They want to play "grab-ass" at least once in a while. Why not? You can do it too.

Most men have a secret fantasy life that their partners know nothing about. Men have been hiding sex magazines for centuries. They masturbate in the shower or other places that are safe. Inside men's imaginations, just like women's, sex can be safe, simple, exciting, and without limits. They feel that their fantasy world doesn't reflect negatively on their relationship or their wives' sexuality, and they resent women's attempts to stop these activities. Leave his magazines alone. *What this all adds up to is friendly passion.*

These are the things men say make sex wonderful:

- Closeness: Men feel especially close after sharing painful or difficult emotions. They like to make love after a fight with their partner.

- Self-esteem: Men say their internal feelings at the moment are very important to good sex. They want to feel desired, successful, anything that creates personal safety in the encounter. They also want to feel good physically, and they see a connection between self-esteem and sexual energy.

- Attractiveness of partner: They want physical attraction, a chemistry between them and their lover. They feel that an openness in the relationship makes a person attractive and so do good sexual techniques.

- Time: They do not want to feel they have to hurry. They want to feel they have all the time in the world. They love vacation sex.

- Playfulness: They want to feel relaxed, to experiment, to joke, and to have fun. Men like women who giggle when making love better than those who create serious drama.

- Variety: Creativity is a bit like playfulness, the willingness to be innovative, to try new positions, to create surprises. They like women who will dress a part or set up a sexy scene.

- Cosmic feelings: Men experience a special connection to the universe when they make love. They want to create spiritual feelings, intimacy with the environment. They like to make love outside or in some way connected to the earth. They also want to feel the connections with God.

- Firsts: The first time is always exciting. The first love, first time in a car, in the office, on an airplane, skiing, anything that is a special event. They love women who create firsts.

How to Hold on to Desire

The number one sexual complaint now is loss of desire. We may be trying to do too much (stress) and are too exhausted for sex. You may have problems with your own sexuality or your relationship.

Many couples marry for other compatabilities, not because of strong sexual desire. They then wonder after a few years why they don't have a passionate sex life. You may have made a good marriage and compromised to get the qualities necessary to a lifetime of commitment. Accept it, and use your creativity and love to put as much magic in the relationship as you can. Even if you never feel "crazy passion" you have probably made a good choice. Intimacy has its own rewards.

How you feel about yourself, as in so many things, is a key to sexual pleasure. If you do not accept the beauty of your own body, you will not want someone to see it, touch it, or view you out of control. You will be worrying if a certain sexual position is unflattering to you instead of feeling the pleasure.

Cosmopolitan magazine once advised on flattering sexual positions: ways to avoid him seeing the backs of your thighs (lie on your back), to keep your breasts from sliding into your armpits (by holding your arms at your side), or anything else (turn out the lights). With this attitude, why bother to make love at all?

Sex is an expression of affection, not just a physical release. Men want to feel loved. Show your love, be affectionate, tell him you love him. Let him know you want to be next to him for a long time.

Talk to each other about what you want. If it's too embarrassing to talk, then write him a letter. Give him a book or magazine article underlined. Put notes in his fortune cookies, but tell him what pleases you. Find out what truly feels like romance to you (not store-bought), and let him know. Find out what feels like romance to him.

Even someone who loves you cannot read your mind. Wait until a neutral time (not just after making love) and tell your lover what you want and ask him what he wants. Silence will only make things worse, because it will become more and more difficult to talk. He may think you jerk your head because you love him blowing in your ear instead of because you hate it. Be light, use humor, and ask him his preferences too.

If you think there is a problem, find out what it is. Talk about your feelings in a gentle, nonjudgmental way. Sometimes you are unsatisfied with sex but don't know why. Talking can help you find what is really going on.

If you are preorgasmic, join a women's group or see a counselor who specializes in this area. You will not want to make love very often if there is no real satisfaction. Take full responsibility for your own sexual response instead of waiting for your partner to do it to you.

There has to be room for pleasure to enter your mind. You may need to learn to accept pleasure. Use relaxation techniques to let go of the day and all the things you worry about. Suspend reality for the time you are making love. Let go of your need to keep yourself in control. Let it be safe to roll over the cliff knowing that you will not be hurt.

Do everything you can to eliminate distractions. Women have keener hearing for problems because they feel physically less safe unclothed than men do. They also tune in to children very intensely. Set up an environment for desire by thinking ahead (unplug telephones, put locks on doors, bring the dog in).

Use your mind to start the sexual encounter already aroused. Dress with romance in mind, create sexual images or use literature, touch yourself to create sensitivity, and then communicate your desires to your partner with whatever signals you two use. Getting a head start, putting your mind in a sexual frame, makes a significant difference in sexual pleasure. Men still warm up a little faster than most women.

Each of us has a unique set of sexual triggers. Stimulation, regardless of how skillful a lover is, cannot lead to orgasm without a corresponding fantasy. The fantasy may be tuned in to your current reality (partner, events, place) or Victorian England. It doesn't matter. Whatever enables you to be open to a complete sexual experience will please your partner and, of course, you. Develop a repertoire of fantasies, and tune into them when you want to.

You can also ask your partner to cooperate in a fantasy. Tell him the words that turn you on, the touches, the gestures. Men want to please and need information to do so. If it seems uncomfortable to talk at the time, show him by moving his hand or your body. Give him signals on pressure.

Women can be martyrs around romance and sex just like everything else. "Oh, it's all right that you didn't notice the special things I did," or "You go ahead, I'll have an orgasm next year." When you don't please yourself in a sexual encounter, you rarely please your partner. Quickies or "This one's for you" are fine now and then, but as a steady diet they breed resentment and frustration.

Make sure that you are comfortable in a position. Slow him down if you need to. Touch yourself if it helps you become aroused. Zero in on your own sensations instead of watching his reactions. Concentrate on where you are being touched and how it feels. Move so deeply into the sensation that you cannot be easily distracted. Allow pleasure to happen to you.

Sensate focus is a skill taught by sexual therapists to patients who have a problem with "spectatoring." They watch themselves making love instead of making love. Sensate focus starts with nonsexual massage between partners. One directs the other to touch certain areas in just the right way (have you ever guided someone in scratching your back?). Each person, in turn, learns to concentrate on the intensity of a single focus, gradually building up to sexual contact. Massage in any form is a wonderful way to warm up to making love.

What Damages Sexual Desire?

All marriages and long-term relationships have times when the passion level is zero. That's when we ask, "Is this all there is?" The loss of romance and passion is probably one of the most important and least talked about sources of "the blues."

We think it should happen like magic and last forever. We forget that a lot of the "chemistry" in the early stages is anxiety. We don't know this person. We are taking chances. It is an adventure. Then it isn't anymore. It is impossible to marry someone, live with him for years, and still create the perfect mixture of security and danger essential to full-blown passion.

Unrealistic expectations and ideas about marriage and sex create disappointment, resentment, and a feeling that something is wrong. All couples report that their initial romantic euphoria wanes after six months to a year. Marriage shifts sex to an obligation instead of a sudden inspiration. It can become work, a conscious decision to be considered every night or weekend. Sexual desire doesn't work if it is on a "to-do" list like taking out the garbage.

Resentment can build up over years, interfere with sexual desire, and never surface until the divorce. We are so good at hiding our hurts, assuming it is the right thing to do. It's like making love wearing a suit of armor. Clear the air; voice your grievances. Fighting a little is better than loving only a little.

When you are angry, especially if it is hidden anger, it isn't safe to be intimate. Your emotions are not geared to being gentle, to trusting. Your real desire may be to hurt or frustrate the other person. It's such a relief when anger is resolved and desire floods back in that some couples like to make love most after a fight.

We often destroy love and desire with criticism. Telling your husband he is gaining weight just before you make love limits his desire to respond to you. When he criticizes you it can take days to feel desire again. Let him know that.

Waiting until the end of the evening to make love is fine when your energy level is high. But if you collapse into bed exhausted the last thing you want to feel is someone's hand on your thigh. Save some energy for sex, plan ahead.

Ambitious, hard-working men sometimes marry a woman and then forget about her. They steel themselves against emotional distractions in order to succeed. They may prefer affairs, where they can maintain control, and avoid a wife who has too great a sense of equality.

One of the main reasons for loss of attraction is that you stop sharing good times together. Desire builds on other pleasures. You cannot build a bond just being roommates who worry about bills together.

There is an obvious image element in sexual desire. The unhealthy or overweight man or woman is a turnoff to most people in our culture. Take good care of yourself.

The security of a long relationship sometimes turns us into slobs. At home we wear old clothes, forget to comb our hair, or brush our teeth and bathe less. Some men and women unconsciously let themselves get dirty as either a test, "You should love the real me," or a way to keep intimacy at bay. Cleanliness is crucial for desire in most people.

Drugs and alcohol, medications, or substance abuse can also seriously impair sexual functioning. Even if the drug is prescribed for an illness, find out if has any side effects. Major problem drugs are tranquilizers, antihypertensives, and antihistamines.

Celibacy

There is nothing wrong with celibacy for a year or forever if it suits your relationships and your temperament. Many people like to channel their sexual energy into other passions. They don't feel deprived; they actually feel freer. Celibacy may give you a breathing period to catch up with yourself, your life, and your values. Just because everyone else seems to be sexual doesn't mean it's mandatory. In fact, in a 1985 survey single men were likely to be celibate for longer periods than single women. Women worry more if they are not sexually active.

Sexual interest may not be an important element in many very loving and satisfying marriages. Some couples feel they grow beyond sexual levels of relating at times. They want to experience intimacy and union on many other levels as well. The crucial issue is that you both agree to celibacy rather than just let it happen.

The renunciation of sex for a time is not a renunciation of love. It is a time for you to rest sexually and, perhaps, if it is your preference, to renew your sexual being. Others choose to remain celibate for life. Love is available in many forms.

What You Can Do

Let your feelings flow. Passion requires sustained attention and intensity. Let go of being calm and gentle long enough to be wild and spontaneous.

Be honest. Show your genuine emotions and set your own rules about what's okay. Do it your way, don't do what you think you should do.

Care about him every day. Don't take each other for granted. Stay clean, healthy, and attractive. Brush your teeth. You cannot get sexual unless you get physical.

Communicate. Talk about feelings. It is a real turn-on.

Give sexual passion priority. Leave energy in your life for sex.

Sex is not just for the young and beautiful or for new lovers. It is a lifetime gift for the open, innovative, and loving.

Remember

Try not to put off sex in favor of housecleaning or other projects. If you wait until you're sixty-five, it may be hard to find your spouse. Other lovers will be in short supply too.

Do it now.

29. I Want Romance and Intimacy

We will put tremendous creativity into the decorating our home, choosing the clothes we wear, or designing a garden; then we approach romance wearing flannel pajamas. Romance takes creativity, playing off each other's personal fantasies. Romance thrives on communication and creativity.

Beauty and romance cover a vast spectrum of stimulation. Sounds, music, smell, texture, colors, foods all contribute to romantic feelings, so do feelings of peace and your own sensuality. You need to be present. You need to care.

Routine ends romance. Wearing the same clothing around the house or to bed creates a faded image. Some of us dress up only to go out. You don't have to give up your overalls every day, but plan surprises. Men love affection, touch, stroke. Send mushy or funny cards; tuck notes in their socks or briefcase. A friend of mine writes notes on the hard-boiled eggs her husband eats for lunch.

Set up activities in which you two can build the pleasure bond you had while courting:

- a special dinner out once a week
- a weekend away instead of painting the house
- dancing lessons
- after-dinner walks

Have lunch together. Ask him to keep his afternoon clear and then slip a hotel key under his plate.

A friend of mind hired a chauffeur to pick her male friend up at his office and deliver him to a hotel room. The chauffeur just smiled and handed him the key. She was waiting with food, wine, and herself. Create an environment for romance that fits you, not just the stereotype (candlelight dinners and black lace teddies).

Get to know your partner's sexual triggers. Once a client as a joke put the backseat of a car in her bedroom. Her husband loved it. Romance is an attitude; when you feel it and put energy into it the other person catches the chemistry. The magic is always in your mind and how much care you are willing to put into this kind of loving.

If your thought at these suggestions are, "Why do I have to make such an effort, why can't it just happen?" you have bought the myth of everlasting passion—"If only I marry the right person." It is a myth, a painful one, that fills adolescent hearts with hope. You are a woman now with a woman's mind. You know that you have to work at creating the life you want. The magic is in your effort, not the moon.

Intimacy

Men fear intimacy, closeness. They are afraid that deep connections mean deep responsibilities, loss of independence, loss of freedom. They may want to leave you just because touching you brings tears and ambivalence. Leave them personal space and independence. Let them know you can take care of yourself.

Women need a measure of safety to be orgasmic and to truly trust and build intimacy. They may enjoy risky sexual situations but are less likely to achieve orgasms. I have always assumed that this need is connected to the desire of women for emotional intimacy and the age-old need to bear children in stable families. Men could take greater risks because they did not get pregnant. Evaluate whether you truly feel safe. If your partner is not someone you can trust with your love, it will affect your sexual pleasure. Women, unless they are working through serious self-esteem problems, quickly lose interest in men who are insensitive, critical, or unfaithful lovers. If you are hurting you may stay with such a lover for self-destructive reasons and then wonder why you desire him so much but are still not orgasmic.

What we both most want is to be truly loved by at least one person in our lifetime, to get so close to someone over time that we are known deeply—and then we are no longer alone. Lawrence Ferlinghetti once wrote in a poem about a woman who was "made more virginal by having lain long with her lover". Her constancy gave the love innocence—the pure light of acceptance and shared history. We want intimacy desperately, yet fear the exposure of self, the possible rejection, the vulnerability.

Men and women often define it differently. Men are more likely to want to maintain their boundaries. They feel when women try to reach inside them they are taking from them. They prefer to build intimacy by just being in a relationship. Men complain that women cannot recognize when a man is being intimate because they want soul-revealing information.

Fear of intimacy is a major source of loss of sexual desire. We get closer and closer to someone, feel entirely too vulnerable, and draw away. Each of us has a closely held comfort zone. It is a set amount of space we need between us and others to feel at ease. We learn it through the patterns of intimacy in the families we are raised in.

The act of commitment is an unveiling. Intimacy requires us to strip layer after layer of defenses from our hard-won personalities. It is a relinquishment of images, of ego, a laying bare of the child within. George Leonard describes it powerfully:

> Still, it is not merely the exercise of the common virtues that marks the High Monogamist but rather a sort of towering, vertiginous daring. For this state requires that we look directly and unflinchingly at our every weakness and flaw, straight down through layer after layer of cowardice and self-deception to the very heart of our intentionality.
>
> And in High Monogamy we are forced, as well, to confront something even more terrifying; our beauty and magnificence, our potential to love and create and feel deeply . . . human beings are ingenious at discovering ways to sabotage their own joy. Still, for those adventurers who can make the leap into commitment, the rewards are great; a rare tenderness, an exaltation, a highly charged erotic ambience, surprise on a daily basis, transformation.

What You Can Do

Set a model for intimacy. Intimacy is based on mutual and unconditional acceptance. You must give this to yourself before you can give it to another. Share yourself and your fears.

Create a safe environment for vulnerability. Don't question, don't correct.

Be absolutely trustworthy.

Be patient, it will grow over time. It may take a lifetime.

Try not to blame yourself when there seem to be many limits and barriers.

Try not to blame him. Building intimacy is the hardest journey we ever make.

Do your own homework; try to understand your fears of intimacy so you won't pass them on.

We hunger to be truly known by another and to know that other in turn. Yet, we all know that by our own uniqueness as a human being we are essentially alone within and to some degree always will be. There is strength in accepting this aloneness and courage in trying still to transcend it.

Remember

Try to be open, transparent, vulnerable even though you will be hurt.

Make it safe for others to take the same risks with you.

Love means giving even when nothing comes back.

30. Breaking Up Is Hard to Do

The only thing that devastates women more than the loss of a lover is the loss of a child. Losing a lover, you are facing a major grief that will shake your belief in yourself and life. All that we are as women has centered for centuries on being loved by a man. To lose that love, no matter why, feels tragic. To be unloved is to be in danger. To lose that love to another woman is a declaration that we will be unloved and perhaps alone forever. The pain is the evidence, overwhelming at times, that you love deeply, that you have given all of yourself.

What you may feel right now is a mixture, depending on your circumstances, of failure, grief for the loss, humiliation, fear, and rejection.

The failure of a love that we had hoped would last forever is still hard in our culture. Deep down is the feeling that a good woman falls deeply in love only once and then lives happily ever after. Don't underestimate the power of this myth. The loss of a love carries with it most of the feeling associated with divorce. If I have failed in this relationship will I ever find someone to love? This failure means that there is something terribly wrong with me.

The grief you feel is a measure of the depth of your emotions and character. If you could walk away from love without a backward glance, then you would not be able to love. You hurt because you care. You care because you are a person who can love deeply. You love deeply because of the quality of your character. The pain is a measure of your passion. You are a passionate person. There is always a price to pay.

The gift that is hidden in this pain is increased understanding of who you are and the patterns within you that set up your relationships. You are learning to love better and to take better care of yourself. You are learning the hard way. Most of us do.

Try to protect yourself by controlling your behavior, not your emotion. Long after you have survived the love you now feel you've lost, you will remember the humiliation of your actions. When you devalue yourself, let another person judge your worth, or violate your own code of behavior, the pain is intense. These are the words of one of my friends.

I don't know why I called him. We had been apart six weeks. I had survived the holidays (we broke up just before Thanksgiving). I hadn't been able to sleep all night, so I started calling people at six in the morning. The pain was so intense I didn't think I would survive. I called three friends and my counselor, and all of them had on answering machines. It was Sunday morning.

When I dialed his number I knew it was a dangerous thing to do—even though two weeks earlier he had sent a card saying he would always love me. He answered the telephone, sleepy; he told me that he was moving on with his life, trying to grow, learning to love again. He used all the psychological "hits," and each one found its mark. Then he said he really couldn't talk anymore because he wasn't alone.

Men are much less likely to humiliate themselves than women are after a break up. Most men find another woman as quickly as possible. Men are less willing to go through the grief and introspection. They are unwilling to be put down by the power of their love or pain. It is a sex-role difference that some men transcend, but most do not. If you call or ask questions about him, you will feel replaced before you are ready. You will always imagine that she will be the love of his life because she is better than you.

Underlying all the possible sources of pain is the greatest fear: the fear that you will be alone forever. If you were in any way abandoned as a child, this fear can tear you apart. Surrounded by evidence to the contrary (friends, work, past relationships) you still will feel that the failure of this relationship means permanent, overwhelming loneliness.

You will think that every arrangement from now on will be a sort of compromise. You may find a man to live with or marry, but it will not be a "great love." You will keep moving through life, but the luster will be gone. Some inner part of yourself is lost forever.

It's not true (as many people will tell you), but you will think you are different. The pain is too great to be able to think, let alone feel, life six months down the road.

Hope will get in your way too. Your ambivalence can be the worst torture of all. It strings you out endlessly. Others will think you have given up, but you still will be holding onto fantasies and secret hopes. You can hear Ray Charles singing, "I can't stop loving you." You hear Linda Ronstadt singing, "I can't help it if I'm still in love with you." You dream.

If you can just give him up, let go, your pain will begin to lift. But it is hard to let go. Holding on is much worse.

One of the sources of the resistance and pain that is the hardest to deflect is the feeling of rejection and failure. Even if you precipitated the breakup, you will feel rejected. Somehow there is something wrong with you. You were not pretty enough. You dressed wrong or weren't smart—or something. One woman with tears in her eyes said to me, "If only I'd kept my nails polished."

The feeling is so overwhelming that you reject yourself. Whatever self-esteem you may have had is gone, and you become worthless. He or they become the judge of your value. You may be tempted to call or write in hopes you can reverse the judgement or soften it, even momentarily.

If you discover he is with another woman, the rejection is complete. Someone else will reap the benefits of your pain. All the talking you and he did, all the growing he did with you, all the possibilities, the dreams, someone else will have. It's not fair unless she is more deserving than you.

The litany of pain I'm listing is long. You will be able to add other arguments as to why you are unlovable, deserve to be hurt, or will end up alone. It's time to turn to healing.

What You Can Do

Some of the suggestions in the grief section may help, but the loss of a lover has other elements that require strategies to limit the dues you have to pay for having risked loving so deeply.

Recognize the loss.
Accept the pain.
Give yourself time to heal.

If just getting through the night is a problem, if your "blues" are overwhelming, please turn to the depression section for help on making it through the night.

Nurture yourself. See friends, exercise, watch nutrition, get a massage, get a facial. Start nurturing yourself as if you had been hired for the job. You often will feel more like hurting yourself, but try to take care. Look good even though you don't feel it. It's time to play the role a little until you can do it and mean it.

Stress from a breakup can make you ill, which just makes things worse. Do some preventive work. Take vitamins; try to get enough sleep; stay away from alcohol.

Take care of business. There will be a temptation to do self-destructive things. You feel you don't deserve anything. Be careful about spending money and making important decisions. Go to work every day, even though you're thinking of asking for time off. Even if you do C+ work, it is better than absence. Build into each day some self-care. Lunch with friends, get a massage, or exercise after work. Set up a treat for having survived the day. You cannot afford to stack up failures. Don't make work or your business life more of a casualty than it has to be. One day still sticks in my memory. I was lecturing at a local college. I cried all the way to the lecture in my car. I parked on campus, found a bathroom, washed my face, and covered the redness with makeup. Then I gave a good speech on something, the women in the audience told me what a good role model I was. I thanked them, ran back to my car, got in, and cried all the way home.

I did give the speech. I was on time. I took care of business.

Get help. Go to a counselor, or join a support group. Read books and talk to friends about your circumstances. Hire someone to come in once a week and clean your home. If you are an independent professional, get someone else to carry a little of your load for a while. Do what you can to keep going while lightening the load.

Don't ask about him. When friends start to tell you what he is doing, stop them. You'll feel better while they are talking, as if you've reconnected, and then crash as soon as you are alone. Don't call him, write to him, or make contact even if you're feeling you can do it unnoticed.

Skip the following:

Parking near his house or business for a glimpse.

Going places you used to go together.

Sending presents to him just because you saw something he'd like.

Calling late at night and hanging up when he answers. He will know it's you.

Don't try to be friends. If this was an intense love affair, friendship will have to wait awhile. Try to end the relationship early rather than late. If you reconcile when you know it's over you only stretch out the pain. You may go back a few times, most of us do, but try not to put yourself in the down position. You'll know it, and so will he. *Remember that you are vulnerable.*

Cry. Indulge yourself once a day if you need to. Listen to sad music, watch sad movies, read sad books when you need to let the tears flow. It's okay. You will not cry forever. Then take a shower.

It's okay to hurt. Be patient with yourself. It's normal. Hurting deeply usually lasts from two or three months to a little over a year. Most women feel free and able to love again fully within two years. Give yourself time to heal.

Clear your mind. Thinking of your loss constantly will sap what little energy you have, so use tricks to clear your mind. It's like changing a habit. Any of these techniques will interrupt the pattern: yell no, stamp your foot, or clap your hand, snap a rubber band you keep on your wrist, take a deep breath, count to ten.

Set up a dream. Think of a place you want to go or a project you want to do when you recover. You will. I had always wanted to go to a Caribbean island and lie in a hammock for weeks. When I started feeling a little better I began to plan a trip for a year away. It was a gift to myself for the heartache. I took the trip eleven months later. It was wonderful. Dreams will be hard to believe in now, but it's worth a try.

Don't date. You have years to meet men. Try to avoid looking for a replacement for a few months; otherwise you may increase your grief. You will enter a room, and none of the men will be even slightly interesting. Nothing compares to him. He is the only one, the last perfect man. You will go on a date with someone new and have to force yourself to get through the evening. Just accept that you'll need to take some time off to recover and that no man will look good to you until you have.

This is the time to have a love affair with yourself. Learn more about you. Take some pleasure in solitude. This is a time to catch up with yourself. You may find you prefer being alone.

Avoid rebound. You may feel desperate to fall in love again, but chances are you will pick another destructive situation. Try not to. Try finding friends instead of lovers. Don't open yourself up to more hurt. At least be celibate until you are stronger. This is not a time for more vulnerability. You will make too many mistakes.

Keep in touch. There will be a tendency to isolate yourself in your grief. That's okay for a while but you need to be social at least once in a while. Set a goal of once a week doing something that puts you in contact with other people.

Forgive yourself. It's easy to be consumed by "if only." The idea that if we had just said different things, or looked better, or something, the relationship would have worked out. This is especially true if he is with someone else. She has what you didn't. Forgive yourself. You did the best you could with who you were and what you knew at the time. There isn't any more you could have done or been.

Being in Pain Is No Proof of Love—Don't Hold On

Let yourself off the hook. Stop any put-downs in your mind; try to reduce reminiscing that brings back hurts. Avoid measuring your worth against his. If this seems impossible, try the "altar ceremony":

Cover a TV table or small chest with a lace cloth, towel, or scarf. Put a photograph of him on it. Then add some fresh flowers (it's the least you can do), candles, and incense. Every day for fifteen minutes, kneel in front of the altar and say you're sorry.

"I know it's my fault."

"If only I could have been different."

"I couldn't help it if I wasn't pretty."

"I'll love you forever."

"She deserves you, I don't."

Do this every day until you start laughing ("Can you believe I'm doing this?") or become disgusted ("He doesn't deserve this much attention"). When we do our penance directly it takes on a different meaning than when we keep it inside. A little exorcism ceremony can sometimes kick us back into moving on with our own life.

Forgive her. One of the things that will keep you connected to the past is your feeling of rejection and replacement. If you think she was dishonest, hurt you intentionally, is a slut, and so on it ties you to her. View her for a moment as a sister: another woman who will be hurt by a man who cannot love, or a woman who has paid her dues before and deserves a chance. She is not your rival. She is a woman, like you, trying to survive. Save your hatred for him if you need to feel it. But understand that anger is always an expression of fear: if she is loved then the fact that you are not means there is something wrong with you.

She may be loved now, but what about her past and her future? She is more like you than different. In another time and circumstances you might have been friends.

Forgive him. It may be too soon, but letting him off the hook will let you off too. Like all the rest of us (with varying ethics), he did the best he could with who he was and what he knew. Let him go. You may not be able to see his pain, but it is there. He has taught you something no matter how unintentional or painful the lesson. Learn it and move on.

Stop fantasies. It's okay to practice a little escapism, we all do. Watch out for fantasies that keep you in the relationship. Here are some samples:

He will become ill and you will rush to help him out. He realizes your true worth, and you are reconciled. You live happily ever after. One day the two of you are walking and holding hands. You notice a shabby woman drinking in an alley. It is the woman who once replaced you.

You find out you are pregnant but don't tell him. Four years later you and your little boy (who looks exactly like him) are playing in a park. He walks by, notices you, says hello, and realizes the boy is his. He is immediately struck by passionate love for you because of your great sacrifice.

You get the idea. We each create our own. It is natural to want to work out a less painful future where everything works out, shades of Cinderella. It's a problem if the fantasies slow down your reclaiming your own life. There are women who have lived their whole lives on a fantasy of the one great "lost love." It is easier sometimes than living your life and taking other risks, but the cost is enormous.

Stay away from him. If he calls, don't talk. Provide neutral information, and say good-bye as soon as possible. If you run into him, do the same. Don't be tempted to talk it out again. It will prolong your grief. If you are still hoping for a reconciliation, then you haven't yet lost the love. That's okay, but down the line if things don't work out you will have to go through the grief over again.

You can make a list of all his bad qualities and habits to keep for emergencies. Grief makes us concentrate only on the good parts of the lost love. A little reality helps. It might make you giggle too, if you're willing to make a truly gross list.

Write down your feelings. This seems to be the time when we can write poetry even though we were never interested in it before. Write out your feelings and thoughts. It can help you clear your mind. Other days when you look back through your journal you'll see how much progress you've made.

When you are tempted to call him write a letter instead, but don't mail it. The words are really for you and your sense of justice. He wouldn't understand, or you would still be together.

Heal at Your Own Pace

Don't try to do everything. Some women go into a high-activity stage to avoid grief or to feel successful at something. They go everywhere and do everything and then crash. Anything is better than being alone. Stop; don't overload yourself. You need time alone so you can stretch and move forward.

Unload the memories. If you haven't already done this, now is the time. Gather up all the photographs, letters, gifts that have special meaning, pressed flowers, or anything else that triggers memories. Put them in a box in storage. You can get them out years later if you want to, but don't keep them around now.

Try to remember what it was really like. You may be remembering wonderful moments when they were very rare. You may want to think the relationship had wonderful potential, but what about the reality? Was it really fun? How often did you feel safe and loved? Were you orgasmic or did you just pretend? Did the truly wonderful moments really outnumber the bad ones? Was a lot of the pleasure just relief from anxiety when he called or showed up?

Check your perspective. The wonderful walks holding hands that you think (when it's a beautiful day) happened frequently—were there really only three in a year and a half?

When your head and heart are clear, you may realize that a lot of what you lost was never there. We often fall in love with what we think someone can be, not what they actually are. We grieve for illusions.

There will come a day when you wake up and feel good. You look forward to the day and only belatedly remember you are recovering from grief. A feeling swells up in you that you're going to be all right. You will be able to live well alone. You are free. In your mind you will say, "This is who I am and it's just fine." Whatever happens or doesn't happen, life has value for me.

Remember

Celebrate your strength, your ability to love and your recovery.

There will be someone for you to love who will love you.

31. I'm the One Leaving My Lover

Many women find it hard to leave a relationship, even if it's obviously over. Some loyalty or commitment "gene" keeps some of us with anyone with whom we have shared sexual intimacy. The emotions are confusing. The good woman "stands by her man" and learns to do with less. When we finally make a decision to leave, we are afraid of the man's responses. There is always more danger inherent in a woman leaving a man. This is a time to call upon your assertiveness.

When you are the one who has decided to break up, don't string your lover along. This prolongs the grief and sends mixed messages. If you are going to reject someone, be strong, direct, and firm. Seeing a little less of someone, each week is pure torture. Holding out hope that maybe things will change is just as bad.

Remember, one of the rules of love is that when one person knows the other wants out, he or she falls much more in love. Rejection is so painful that we will do anything to avoid becoming the victim. If you act confused and try to take care of another's hurt, you will often drive that person to humiliation. Long after he is over his love for you, he will hate you for the humiliation you were a part of.

Make sure you are ready to break up. The emotions you create when you reject someone cannot be taken back. This is not something to play with, so he will prove his love by his grief and passion. Setting up love tests will backfire.

Have you evaluated the problems in the relationship? Are you aware of your mistakes, your part in the conflict? Are you willing to work things out or ready to quit? Have you talked to a counselor so you know what is going on? No love is easy, so make sure you've given your best.

What You Can Do

Consider the timing. What is happening in his life—holidays, illness, new job? Try to pick a weekend so there is some time to recover. Do it in person, not by mail. Be honest but avoid criticism or a litany of what's wrong with him. Instead, concentrate on your own problems and feelings.

Let him vent his anger. Listen to his frustration, or grief, and try to avoid defending yourself or arguing about who is right. You have the control, and you can afford to absorb some of his hurt. Take the blame if anyone has to. Make sure your message is clear, and hold onto it, repeat it, even in the face of strong emotions.

Don't let him feel easily replaced. There is no need to talk about who you plan to date or if you have found someone else you are interested in. Don't let yourself get caught with someone else, be discreet and protective of your former lover. It's inexcusable to cause him the pain of discovering you with another man. If you've arranged it, you are asking for a lifetime of hurt.

Let him go. Don't count on friendship, or even bring it up. When time has passed you might end up friends but not in the midst of the break-up. What you think is magnanimous will be interpreted as arrogant by the person you are rejecting. Don't sleep with him again; don't date; don't do anything that rekindles possibility. Don't be a collector, a woman who keeps men on a string as an insurance policy.

Settle practical details. Get any goods exchanged of financial obligations settled quickly, before the desire for revenge sets in. Prepare to be replaced, and don't be surprised when he gets over you quickly.

Check your patterns. Stop now and look over the number of break-ups you've participated in. Are they alike? What can you learn from this so it doesn't happen again.

Men are much more likely to get out of the house and take action. If all this seems intimidating, it is. There is a temptation to vanish, to stop answering the telephone, to leave town to facilitate a breakup. None of us want to face these emotions. Hang in there; be honorable; don't leave someone who loves you without answers to his questions. If you treat him with kindness and respect, then maybe you'll reap the rewards the next time someone leaves you. At least you'll feel good about yourself.

Remember

Try not to stay in a relationship you know has no future while you wait for the right man. You will convey mixed messages to other possible men and be exploiting someone who cares for you.

The failure of a relationship does not determine your worth.

III. MY FAMILY

32. Relatives I Wish Weren't Mine

It's harder for women to be independent of "family", because our survival depended so long on being "approved." Men might be encouraged
to go their own way but not women. Rebellious women paid a high
price. If they were thrown out of the family they had few alternatives.
Traditionally, many prostitutes were women who had no place to go.
Women could lose custody of their children if they upset their family.
More than a few times independent women found themselves declared
"insane" by their parents.

Our patterns with relatives usually are of long duration, thus difficult to change. They may prefer we not change so will fight against it.
They may not want you to be more comfortable if it affects them. Your
independence may violate their rules for life, so they will try and stop
you. Within your natal family, they had control over you for so long it
is very difficult for them to view you as an adult. Since relatives are
"forever," they may feel they have a license to abuse you because you
are family. You may agree.

You carry within you a historical fear of the emotional and economic
power of relatives. It was once a reliable survival strategy. Now there
are more options and freedom for independent women. Remember
that, when you feel afraid in family conflicts and are not sure why.

Blues that last a lifetime can arrive with new relatives, not just your
own. You are caught when you find you cannot get along with or at
least are irritated by your mother-in-law, son-in-law, mother's or father's
new spouse, sister-in-law.

There often is a cultural issue at the base of in-law problems. Some
cultures welcome new relatives with open arms. They think "the more
the merrier." They are prepared to welcome you, love you, put up with
your idiosyncrasies, and have a good time. This attitude makes marriage easier.

Other cultures view everyone outside the "blood" family as an outsider. They view new relatives with suspicion and plan for an immedi-

ate power struggle. While you are thinking, "Oh goodie, now I have a sister," they are thinking, "How can I keep this bitch under my thumb and restrict her power and popularity?" Harsh, but true.

If you marry into this competitive-style family you will need to understand that they will not change much. They might mellow over time, but you will continue to be an outsider. Your spouse will always be pulled in two directions at once.

If you find yourself in a basically friendly family or a mixed group and still run into problems, you may need to check your motivations. Most of us need at least one person in our life we cannot stand or who cannot stand us. Maybe it keeps the juices of survival flowing. That person is almost always a relative so we cannot escape the problem.

Mothers-in-law may not want to give up their sons so may get them into a triangle of "Who do you love?" The son loses either way. Many men just pull out of the triangle, and let the women chew on each other forever.

The last element to add to the various psychological power plays is that being related, even having shared the same house for years, does not guarantee love or even affection. Some of us would have chosen very different relatives, given the chance. Some of us are still hoping to switch in-laws or move far away.

Decide whether it's worth it to change your family relationships. Am I worth it? Do I care enough about myself? Do my relatives want to live my life and theirs too? Do I care enough about them to change the relationship? Am I making assumptions about how they feel that could be wrong?

The best and most difficult survival strategy is not to take the actions of your relatives as a personal judgment of your value. Their attitudes toward you have more to do with old family patterns and loyalties than with who you are. You can question your motives and actions until you are blue in the face and never find out why you have been rejected.

A friend of mine married into a family and was delighted at the prospect of getting to know her husband's brother's wife. She was a dynamic, intelligent woman, and my friend Sylvia saw great possibilities for gaining a sister. Her new relative felt just the opposite. She saw Sylvia as competition. Karen had always been the dominant woman in the family, and she took one look at Sylvia's attractiveness and her doctorate and felt threatened. Even though Karen was only a few years older, she began to act like a mother-in-law. She told Sylvia what was wrong with her and her husband, set up family feuds when she felt her family wasn't given preference, refused to attend holiday celebrations if they were held in Sylvia's house, and generally made everyone miserable.

The key to survival for Sylvia in this situation was to assume that Karen couldn't change and not to take what was happening as having anything to do with Sylvia herself. The next step was to organize holidays anyway and let Karen stay home or go elsewhere if she wanted to. It took five years of Karen's husband showing up for holidays at Sylvia's house for Karen to decide grudgingly to come too. The two women have missed out on what might have been a great friendship, but they have learned to be civil.

The biggest problem was that my friend was so hurt. What had she done? What could she do? Why did Karen treat her so badly and complain about her and her husband to others? These laments drove her husband to distraction and led Sylvia to bouts of the blues. Karen's husband was putting up with the same irrational comments, and the two brothers could only roll their eyes heavenward and sigh deeply.

Families have good and bad aspects and members. The important thing is to find a comfortable place for yourself given the family you have. Once you're free, they'll look like a better group to you.

What You Can Do

Start on them one at a time. Tell the involved relatives what your feelings are, listen to theirs, and then refuse to debate or argue. Use the "broken record" approach; just keep repeating, "This is what I've decided." Remember, they have no real power over you, they rely upon your willingness to stay trapped.

If you continue to show respect and affection while living your own life, the decision will be up to them. If they choose to fight your independence, it is they who precipitate the break, not you.

Take time off. Sometimes it does take a break of contact with relatives if the dependence has been of long duration. To convince them and yourself, you may have to limit contact. It need not be permanent.

Clarify the conflict. Don't let someone else's problems define your value, behavior, or state of mind. If you are just starting out with a new set of relatives or willing to try and mellow out a conflict you are already in, the following ideas may help:

Be civil. Do this because there is a danger of lifetime animosity, and you don't want that grief in your life.

If it is too late for a new start, reclaim what you can. No apologies are necessary, just pleasant behavior when in contact, appropriate cards on special occasions, and no negative comments that those involved might hear.

Do some introspection. If you are still stuck, look inside yourself. Try to find out why this person gets under your skin. What are you afraid of? Could it be (it often is) something that is really between you and someone else? Try figuring out what motivates the person who upsets you! What is the source of the bad feelings on either side? Is it something you could let go of or forgive?

Sylvia realized how unhappy her sister-in-law was. She had not been able to pursue the academic career she wanted or to have children. A lot of the bitterness was just pain, and Karen found anger one of her best defenses against that pain. She didn't like being reminded of her hurt by Sylvia's presence. Understanding may not change a situation, but it makes it easier to live with.

If your mother-in-law picks at you, is it because she has little love in her life and is afraid of losing her son? Are you pushing him to choose you over her when it would be okay to encourage him to see more of her? Isn't there enough love and time for both of you? How secure are you? Do you need a sacrifice to be made in order to feel safe?

Try the reverse of resisting. Start being loving and complimentary around and about his mother, if she is the problem. Encourage him to see her, alone if you prefer. Drop out of the tug-of-war, and it will go away. It takes two people to pull the rope. When he complains about her suggest they talk it out, since you don't have that problem. Don't let him give you his mother problems. Don't complain about her yourself.

Relatives are for a lifetime, even if we create our own friendship family. We share many memories with them, and you can do your best to make them positive. There is another generation to think of as well. It is not worth it to be cut off from grandchildren, nieces, and nephews. They need you too. Do the best you can to keep the lines of communication open. Don't expect justice, and always be ready to start over again if someone opens the emotional door to let you in.

Whatever the consequences of your living your own life instead of your relatives' version, it can't be worse than giving up your life to try to pay an unending debt. Remember this as your children grow up.

Remember

There will always be the temptation to scream, "Why do I have to be nice to that ———?" Don't give in to the thought even once. Run into the bathroom, and stuff a towel in your mouth.

Try not to set up long-term feuds and demand that people take sides.

There is no ideal, happy set of relatives. Blood ties aren't the same as those between carefully selected friends.

Very few things are truly important.

33. How Can I Make Peace With My Brothers and Sisters?

You compare your successes and failures to those of your brothers and sisters. Visits with your parents leave you feeling they prefer another child to you and always have. They seem to play favorites among the grandchildren. Sometimes you think about your inheritance from them, and you wonder if it will be fair. You can't stand a sister-in-law or brother-in-law and think he or she is hurting you.

We are told that our sisters and brothers are special friends for life, so we wonder what is wrong with us when it doesn't turn out that way.

Some brothers and sisters work out great friendships as adults; some barely see each other; and many cannot stand each other. It is a myth that most siblings end up best friends. Your relationship with brother or sister reflects your parents' treatment of you and the unfinished business of childhood.

Two women I know who are in their seventies are still trying to pretend they are loving sisters when they cannot stand each other. It is difficult to be around them, even though their visits together are rare.

The older sister, Agnes, sees herself as the serious one who should have been preferred by their perfectionist father. Agnes behaved herself, but her little sister, Pearl, did not. "How can Father prefer Pearl?" When Pearl was born their mother developed anemia, so Agnes still tells everyone that, "Pearl took all the blood out of mother!" Their mother remained an invalid from that point on, and Pearl was therefore a bad baby.

Agnes had to take care of Pearl and suffer all the indignities of competing with a rambunctious, cute, risk-taking little sister. She thought being serious would make up for being plain. She thought being religious would bring her close to her father, a religious man. He never was close to anyone, and he always found Pearl more interesting.

Pearl married and had children; Agnes did not. Pearl was a mixed blessing as a parent, given her models. Agnes, by then a P.E. instructor, was sure she would have been a wonderful parent. The competition became so constant, the bickering so petty, that the two sisters could not drive somewhere in the same car and decide which way to turn.

Pearl decided to escape the parenting of her older sister and removed her family from the country. She emigrated and put great distance between them. She essentially said to Agnes, "You can have both our parents; I'm getting out." Agnes became the doting, caretaking daughter, and when they died took control of the heirlooms. She had to pass them on eventually to Pearl's children, and this gave her one last bit of leverage to continue the battle.

When I last saw them the bickering was as strong as ever, even though Pearl has weathered many difficulties in life and Agnes has become a lay sister at a convent. Agnes told stories about what a terror Pearl was and how their father preferred Agnes. She also pointed out that she had always had bigger breasts than Pearl and was more sincerely religious. Pearl fought back halfheartedly and planned how to cut the visit short.

They will both die having never understood or resolved the fight that began with Pearl's birth. When I raise issues that might resolve one of the conflicts it always brings tears or anger to whichever sister I am trying to talk to. The pain is still close to the surface. It is as if they are ten and seven again and not feeling loved or preferred. It is easier for them to continue the battles of more than sixty years. "You know, Pearl, Nanny told me before she died that you were the most difficult child she ever took care of."

Parents and teachers often use comparison and competition to motivate children. Since all of us want to be unique and uniquely loved we hate losing such intimate competition. If an older brother or sister is the good kid or the smart one or the pretty one you may decide not to take second place. Instead you'll opt to be bad, athletic, unconcerned about your appearance—anything that is an alternative route to attention. If it works, great. If it doesn't, you may end up feeling in second place your whole life.

Some parents up the level of competition as a power play. As long as the adult children are vying for their attention they remain in control. The competition continues through the grandchildren. Check and see if your parents are still pulling any strings that lead to your feeling anger toward your siblings or their spouses.

What You Can Do

Decide to drop out of the competition. If you want to build a friendship set up a meeting with your brother or sister on neutral turf so you won't be tempted to play out old patterns. The issue is who you are now, not the rivalries and complexities of when you were growing up.

Tell your siblings what you want. Refuse to discuss or defend yourself on any issues from the past. Make your conversation stick to the future. Be prepared for trust to build slowly. Say only positive things about them to the family or to friends.

Give up any idea of justice. Stop trying to or win your parents' affection. Aim for friendship and love. Sometimes we wait for illness and even death to make the power of our connection to siblings known. You can do it now, before it's too late.

Remember their history. Understand that your siblings were only trying to survive in the same family. It's often true that winning (if you think they did win) had negative side effects. Agnes's devotion to being number one with her parents took away her chance to build a family of her own. Work on forgiving your siblings for the struggling children they once were.

Try to forgive. Sometimes spouses or children are used as buffers between sisters and brothers who are afraid of each other. Siblings who have shared hard times as children often fear reminders of pain. By putting a spouse between them and letting the spouse absorb the anger and fear, both siblings can stay away from more dangerous emotional territory.

You are the one who must understand and change. You may not be able to get back to loving closeness; it may have never been there. But you can become comfortable together, thoughtful and not victims of family manipulations. Be the brother or sister you want to be and that you want for your children, regardless of the response you get.

Remember

Try not to involve your children. Let the cousins enjoy each other without competition or having to take part in parental feuds.

Don't fight over inheritances. It's not worth it. It is a cold hand from the grave still manipulating you with parental approval or disapproval.

Family is forever.

34. I'd Like to Feel Grown Up

It's possible to go through a lifetime dominated, directly or subtly, by parents. What comes with this tie is a low-grade depression linked to the feeling that your life is compromised, that it isn't really yours. No matter what you do, it won't quite please the ultimate judge of your worth. There are not enough rituals in our culture to signal that we are adults, on our own, able to listen to our own counsel.

Making the final psychological separation from parents usually occurs when we are around thirty and beginning to feel in control of our lives. We begin to question what we owe to our parents. We consider what kind of parents we are. Do you evaluate how much you are controlled by your parents economically, physically, or psychologically?

Do you borrow money from your parents (not just a down payment on a house, once, but living expenses)?

Do either one of your parents tell you what to do and make threats if you don't comply?

Do your parents criticize you?

Do they handle you physically as if you were a child?

Do they violate your privacy?

Do they generate guilt in you with their health problems?

Do you think of their reaction before you make decisions?

Do you act more like a child when you are with them?

Do you hide things from them?

Do you see them or talk to them on the telephone more than you want to?

Do they talk about you to others, in front of you?

If you answered yes to any of these questions, it's worth looking further. Some parents try to tie their children to them tightly with economic or psychological control. It leaves you stuck, feeling like a little girl whenever you are around them. You may have your father fix your car or balance your checkbook because it's easier. It seems as though you are getting a service, but you end up never feeling like an adult.

Just because you, as a child, always did what your parents wanted is no reason to continue to do so. They may find it very difficult to let you shift to adult status, but you need to break the pattern of catering to them. You can take care of yourself, even if it displeases them and goes against what they want.

Watch out for guilt traps, heavy sighs, complaints, and martyr statements. "We've given you so much and look what you do to us," needs to be ignored with a smile and a "Well, I know being a parent can be disappointing."

Be prepared to fight for your independence. Some parents will not let go without a direct assault (major battle, marrying without their blessing). You may face threats of their never speaking to you again, disinheritance, or other punishments—just as when you were a child. Be diplomatic, but hold your ground until it becomes clear that you can no longer be dominated.

I finally resolved my feelings of anger toward my mother by writing her a very long letter telling her everything that was wrong with her. It's possible to write such a letter and not send it, but I mailed mine. Normally my mother would have fired off an even longer defense and a new set of accusations, but this time she took the letter to the priest at her church.

He was a young man, with new ideas. He suggested that they burn the letter on the altar and that mother write me telling me she accepted my comments and opinions and asking if we could start over. I was thrilled, since I had offered at the end of my letter a chance to start over. I went to see her and took her out to dinner, and we have built a better friendship since then.

She stopped criticizing me, became much more loving in her behavior, and began treating my brother and son with more sensitivity as well. Three years later when we were enjoying our new closeness she let me know that the letter had been burned on the altar. "God knows what you said." I was able to laugh.

The ability to find your balance is keyed to the type of parenting you had. If it was very abusive, you may be able to resolve the control and pain only by ending contact.

Many things make it hard to let go, be on our own, and feel grown up. Certain kinds of parents and certain life situations can make it more difficult, but you make the choices.

- Very successful parents: Even loving, supportive parents can be hard to separate from if they are wealthy or otherwise successful. You may feel less of a person away from them. You may have enjoyed the shadow of their protection or notoriety. You may feel compelled to follow in their footsteps. Stake out your own territory, and stop trying to compare your life to theirs. Don't let them or others make comparisons either.

- Dependent parents: You may have started taking care of them as a child. They never grew up, so you had to. Alcoholics, parents with health, economic, or relationship problems will count on you to take care of them forever. They use your guilt, the blood relationship, and anything else available to keep from being responsible for themselves. Take back your life.

- Dominating parents: You may be afraid of them. They have controlled you for so long that you have no self-esteem or confidence. The thought of standing up to them and staking out your own life is terrifying. Try doing it in small steps, such as making purchases without their input or leaving the room when they criticize. Consider counseling to build up your self-confidence.

- Personal failures: If your life has not been successful you may want to go back to feeling like a dependent child. When things are too much for us, we don't want to be adults. Try to resist the temptation to go home when you are sick or unemployed. The momentary feeling of safety will soon be replaced by recognition that you have lost ground and may not regain it. It will be harder to take control of your life once you have given it up.

- Divorce: You are at a low ebb during divorce, and sometimes parents make it worse. They may side with your spouse, reject any new relationship, or demand that you stay married regardless of the cost. Let them know you need their support. Try to understand their pain while you work to reduce yours. Take care of your needs, and let them have time to adjust before you participate in a confrontation. If they call you names or commit disloyal acts, warn them, but try to hold off judgment until the trauma has subsided.

- Expected inheritance: Parents can manipulate you and your siblings your entire lives if you count on them for money or material things. You will end up suspicious of your brothers or sisters, worried about your mother's remarriage, or waiting for your parents to die. You will not make a full investment in your own life, because you will be waiting to inherit theirs. If they bring up inheritance as a bargaining chip, tell them you prefer not to discuss it.

- Siblings: Parents can manipulate your relationship with your brothers and sisters just as they did when you were children. If they compare you, ask them not to. Don't provide information to your parents or join with them against a sibling. Keep out of triangles where they try to manipulate one child by going through another.

What You Can Do

Learn through your own children. Children want to leave home. They want to put together an independent life. When they have trouble doing that, it scares them and their parents.

It isn't a process that begins at eighteen. It begins when children are toddlers. You may not notice it until your child starts to push, around the age of twelve. Children express it in different ways. Some will "talk back"; some will skip school. Others will run away overnight. The child begins to struggle with opposites: the need to have a home and roots and the need to be independent; the sad feelings of leaving the safety of childhood and the exhilaration of newfound power and control.

Younger children express it whenever they want to make decisions for themselves, whether it is about ice cream or clothes. Independence should be encouraged as early as a child seems ready. Let children make decisions when possible, take care of their property, handle finances, earn money, cook, do their own laundry.

Listen to yourself as the children grow. Are you comfortable with their growing up? Can you let them make mistakes? You are the key to their feelings of confidence. If you believe they can handle things, if you think mistakes are part of learning, they will too. If you express fear or lack confidence in their abilities, they won't want to leave home. It won't seem safe.

At what age is your child an adult? If you cannot answer this question you may be relying on your feelings, not your child's needs. It's hard to let go as parents, because of old patterns, but also because we don't want to admit it's over. You have the same problems with your own parents.

When my son got ready to move out at nineteen I tried to stop him for a few hours. We had agreed months before that it was time. He was fulfilling a contract we'd drawn up his senior year. It wasn't until he was actually loading things into his car that I was hit with fear. I suggested that I read him one more book and laughed; I'd always wished I'd read to him more. When your children grow up you feel you're received a parenting grade. It's final, an A or B or C. There is a temptation to hold on longer to try to up your grade. Our parents feel the same way.

When you let go of your parents and take over, you own life. You are not only accepting them as no longer parents but yourself as no longer a child. The child within you may be trying to get a higher grade too.

Forgive yourself. Until you have accepted yourself and the way you were parented as a child, you will not be able to grow up. Repeat over and over to yourself, "They did the best they could with what they knew and who they were at the time." If you feel you must make amends in some way, do it. Then let go.

Issue your parents a blanket apology certificate. Give one to your grown children too. Remember that they need to feel right about their perception of your/their childhood even if you don't think their view has any connection to what really happened. Stop fighting their memories, and they will no longer need to fight with you. Use an impressive gold seal and your version of the following words:

This is a complete and all-encompassing apology to you for the incredible number of mistakes I made as a parent/child. I wasn't perfect, or even close, and it's time to admit it.

You will only receive this one certificate, and it represents an apology for all errors up to this point in time.

None of us were or will be perfect parents. We are so vulnerable; we want so much to do the right thing that we often refuse to admit to any chinks in the armor for fear the whole defense will collapse. Give up, give in, admit to being a marginal parent, accept the limits of your own parents, and keep your sense of humor.

Forgive them. They may or may not be exactly what you wanted. Accept them as having value and being worth your love as they are right now. Don't wait for them to become what you want them to be. Forgive them for being themselves.

Grieve for what never was and now cannot be. Letting go will bring grief for the childhood you never had or the parent you were unable to be. Let go of the illusions; feel the pain and disappointment, and decide what to do with the present. Put energy into your own life. If your life is interesting and successful you won't be tempted to put your hands on someone else's. Check your empty spots and fill them yourself so you don't call on your parents or adult children to do it for you.

Be generous with affection. They want more than anything to feel your love and approval. Always remember birthdays and special events. Say "I love you" whenever you can, even if it makes you both cry. Find positive things to say about their current life and your memories. Don't remind them of how awful they once were and how you suffered. Touch them when appropriate, and hug them whenever you can.

Accept their life-style. You are not responsible for another life. Try not to judge their choices harshly because they are different from your own or scare you. Don't blame yourself for their desire to live differently. Learn from them. Be creative. Try to stay open to the idea that they are probably right about their needs. They are not you, and they don't have to live the way you do.

Be available. There is some wonderful balance between hanging around too much and not seeing them at all. Ask them what is a comfortable balance. My mother calls me every other Saturday. I wouldn't want her to call every day.

Fight dependence. Sometimes the most loving thing you can do is help people be independent. Sometimes we have to kick our children into their own future. That may mean forcing them to leave your house. Try to keep your parents independent too.

Restrain criticism. Treat them as you would good friends. Restrain yourself from correcting them, and don't be tempted to say, "Well, if I can't tell you, who can?"

After years of battles with my mother over criticism, she sent this card. I felt loved right down to my toes.

> DAUGHTER,
> Here's a card
> You're sure to like—
> It doesn't
> lecture,
> advise,
> debate,
> discuss,
> argue,
> persuade,
> dispute,
> or disapprove—
> It just sits in your hand and says
> HAPPY BIRTHDAY

Be prepared for death. Make your peace with your parents as soon as you possibly can, even if it means walking away from the relationship. You need to feel clear inside, so they cannot haunt you from the grave. Write the loving letter that forgives. Have the fight that lets you clear the air. Be the daughter you want to be regardless of the parents they are. The important judgment is the one you make of yourself.

Try to think down the line a few years to the relationship you want to have with your own children. They will be your children forever, and the sooner you allow them to feel like complete persons, the easier it will be for them to love you.

Remember

Don't assume that they can't survive without you. They probably will do quite well. The real issue is whether you can survive without them.

Be the daughter and mother you want to be regardless of their responses. You need to feel at peace.

Try not to count on your spouse to fight your parental battles for you. You need to resolve it directly instead of complaining to him and expanding the battlefield.

Don't leave your feelings in limbo until it is too late. Make your own choice.

I can take good care of myself.

35. I Need Help Choosing to and Surviving a Divorce

Divorce has become an event most of us will have to cope with. We may end up divorced ourselves, or our parents, children, friends, or relatives will ask us to understand and help with theirs. Next to the death of a loved one, divorce may be the most painful experience anyone can go through. It can last for years or forever. It affects our self-esteem, our security, our life-style, and our children.

I Want a Divorce

The hardest part of divorce is deciding it's what you want. It takes an average of three years from the first thought of divorce to actually announcing it to one's spouse. There is so much fear and confusion around loving and not loving someone that it is difficult to sort out. If you think you want a divorce, try the following exercise.

Relax, take some deep breaths, and imagine your life in five years if you leave your spouse. How do you feel? Can you support yourself? How do the children feel? Can you handle the potential loneliness? Did your family take the news well? Do you still feel attractive and lovable? Does your life look better, or worse?

Then imagine your life five years into the future if everything stays just the way it is now. How do you feel? How well are your children doing? How is your spouse and the rest of your family?

Your visions of the future, coupled with the other information you have, should make the decision clear. It is not easy, there are negatives and positives to either choice. Your emotions rather than your logic will ultimately make the decision.

Once you have a sense of certainty start learning from the process you are in. Try to figure out what happened to your marriage. Do you understand the part that you played? Do you know why you married in the first place? Are your current feelings long-term, or are they connected to a crisis (unemployment, illness, infidelity)? Is there any other solution?

Sometimes just living apart can change your mind and change behavior. It can also be a way of easing into a divorce if there is opposition. Don't suggest it just as a way of pretending that you believe reconciliation is possible. Do consider it as a way of being sure about what you want.

Some people claim to have had "good" divorces. It may be possible with counseling. Crisis is always a time when we learn an enormous amount about ourselves. A marriage counselor can help you uncover what has really happened to you. He or she may be able to show you the difference between a problem in your marriage and a personal issue that is too painful for you to face directly. There may still be a lot of love between you and your spouse, but buried under resentment. A counselor can also help you put the children first and end up feeling reasonably decent about what you are doing.

Announcing of your thoughts about or intention to divorce can never be taken back. The insecurity it introduces into your marriage may provide an opening for counseling, but it is more likely to start the divorce process. Make sure it is what you want. There are suggestions for announcing your decision to your spouse in the section on leaving your lover. Don't be surprised if he has been thinking of divorce too. We rarely develop our emotions about a marriage alone unless we are very disconnected from our spouse.

He Wants a Divorce

If the divorce wasn't your idea or it isn't a mutual desire, the process will be much more painful. Some of the hardest changes to deal with are those announced by someone else. We immediately dig in our heels, feel threatened, lose our self-esteem, and become irrational. Divorce intensifies all this because it adds the feeling of rejection. Someone who knows you intimately doesn't want you. For some of us, that is as painful as being rejected or abandoned by a parent. We think no one will ever want us again.

A certain innocence is shattered by divorce; it changes forever the way we view love and relationships. We rarely assume divorce will be positive. In fact, we are growing up and letting go of the last stage of the Cinderella complex. Letting go of these illusions gives you an opportunity to truly love and be loved. This is a time when it is hard to see the future, but your new awareness will eventually bring you more pleasure, and you will realize how much in your marriage you just learned to live with because you didn't know there were options.

All our fears come to the surface. We question our attractiveness, doubt our personality, think about financial disasters, and forget that we know how to take care of ourselves. You may offer to change your whole self, to be what he wants if he will just change his mind. You will go through all the stages of grief: denial (he will come back), anger (I'll make him pay), bargaining (couldn't we stay together and live separate lives, or I'll change, I promise), acceptance (my marriage is over), and rebuilding (I will survive).

What You Can Do

Take care of yourself. Use every technique in this book for feeling better. Read about grief, stress, jealousy, and happiness. Do things to make yourself look and feel better. Gather your friends around you for support but be careful not to wear them out. Do the things that you are good at to remind yourself of your own competence. Tell yourself over and over again, "These feelings will not last forever."

Wait until you have survived the initial grief before you make any major decisions or negotiate a divorce settlement. You need to be able to shift out of the emotional and into the practical. There will be a temptation to continue the communication difficulties that led to the divorce. Do you know what you need to rebuild your life? Make a list. Talk it over with a counselor.

Be realistic. Divorce is a time when our own interests seem crucial, but we also have an obligation to carry it out in as decent a fashion as possible. Long after the divorce is final you will still be angry if humiliation is added to all the other grief.

Read the section on breaking up, and make a plan that offers the most in terms of protection for you and sensitivity to your spouse. Don't be surprised if he has already made his own plans. More than once in my experience a client has been about to tell her spouse she wants to separate and he has announced his desire for a divorce first.

Talk about your feelings without blame, but avoid laying out a practical plan for dissolution. There are a number of emotional stages for your spouse to go through before he will be willing to accept that you have already made plans. He or you need a place to stay; you two need to tell the children and make the public announcements. Then, you can negotiate the first stages of the separation.

Tell the children. As soon as possible after you two have talked the children need to be told. Otherwise they will feel the tension and be upset longer than is necessary. Agree on what you are going to say, and tell them together. Let them ask any questions they want. The key issues for children are, Is it my fault? and Am I going to lose a parent? Reassure them over and over that they are in no way to blame for this adult decision. Make it clear that even though one parent is moving out, they still will see that parent regularly and be able to call anytime.

This isn't the time to jockey for loyalty, either. Trying to get the children on your side, however subtly, is unfair and will backfire. You may feel scared; you will want to draw them around you as family; but it will hurt you in the long run. They will make up their minds based on what they see and feel, not what they are told. Sooner or later they will balance out what they were told at four with the insight they gain by fourteen. If they have been misled or used, they may find it hard to ever forgive you for what you have taken away.

Tell everyone else. Each of you needs to tell friends and relatives what has happened. Except for your closest friends, try to stay away from details or justifications. Do your best to get your family's support without turning them against your spouse. When there are children they must still work out some relationship after the divorce.

Some of the bitterest divorces involve grandparents working out their anger. Make it clear when you tell them your plans that you want their support but you will conduct your own divorce. Ask them not to share hurtful information with the children and not to berate your spouse. You may enjoy their outraged support for a few weeks, if that is their response, but it will quickly become a major problem.

Consider getting help. There are alternatives to counseling per se: mediators, divorce services, and attorneys who are also certified counselors or mediators. You may be able to ease your grief, understand your divorce, and ease the process with a neutral advisor. When appropriate, include the children in these sessions or at least let them know what is happening.

Dating again. Give yourself time to adjust, grieve, and let your tension level drop before you decide to date. Give your children and your friends a chance to adjust before introducing the possibility of new men and more changes. Avoid the "rebound" by waiting until your self-esteem is stronger before you go out and test your attractiveness. Dating is rarely what we imagine it to be when we are married. One of my favorite statements was made by a wife: "The best reason to stay married is so you don't have to date!"

You will fare better in the divorce process if your spouse thinks you are not dating. Even if you both want the divorce there will be jealousy over who found a new person first. If you do, he may feel less sympathy, more concern for his children, and a desire not to share as much of the community property as he originally would have. Putting off dating can be both an emotional gain and a financial one.

When you do begin to meet men, try to go slowly. Just because you have been married doesn't mean you cannot put the brakes on sexually. Watch your thinking. If you are worrying that you'll end up alone you will start making painful compromises. It usually takes two years to get from the announcement of a divorce to the possibility of a new marriage. Give yourself time.

Stay in control of the legal process of divorce. Early on in the separation draw up a paper of intent with your spouse. State your views (both of you) on custody, finances, property, personal items, life insurance, medical insurance, living arrangements, children's expenses and education, visitation, pets, and wills. Do this together before either one of your sees an attorney. Get some idea of how you feel and what your bottom line is before you enter the adversarial process.

Try to get experienced divorce attorneys, one for each of you, but stay away from "tough" or "shark" lawyers. The blood and money that gets spilled is too likely to be your own or your children's. A divorce can take a few months with reasonable fees or years with half of what you have paying for the attorneys to fight over the rest. You can also do a dissolution yourselves if the trust and agreement level is high enough. Get one of the manuals on setting up your own divorce.

Expect grief. Whether the divorce was a relief to you or not, don't underestimate the grief. You will feel alone and depressed and wonder if you've made the worst mistake of your life; you'll feel guilty anxiety about the future, ill, and stressed out; you'll have accidents and be tempted to behave in ways that will hurt you. There is always a voice inside saying, "You must pay for this sin of divorce." Some family members may tell you things that will hurt you and reinforce the voice.

Even if you feel wonderful and free, try to prepare yourself for a crash. When my ex-husband moved out, I celebrated. I felt minimal guilt; I didn't care what my family thought; I felt my son would be better off. I walked out on a dock near my house and cried into the wind, "I'm free! I'm free!" Three weeks later I met what I thought was going to be the love of my life and within six months was in the deepest depression of my life. Take care of yourself. Don't run out into the world trying to catch up on everything you think you have missed.

Draw around you all the support you'll need. Make sure you have a job, economic stability, a comfortable place to live, friends, family, and professionals (counselor, attorney, physician). Take steps to protect yourself even if you think that you'll never need it.

Some Other Issues

A Message to Grandparents

The grandchildren are going to need you. Be loyal to your adult child without alienating the ex-spouse. If you participate in a bitter battle you will damage everyone, and you may never see your grandchildren again. Custody battles can escalate into "sides of the family" battles, and you are the easiest to dispense with. It may be difficult for your ex-daughter-in-law to deny the father visits, but she may be able to exclude you. Try to be supportive without interfering. Put the children's needs first and offer to help out with them. Don't get into a custody battle yourself.

Harassment

Divorce brings out the worst in some people, and you need to fight efforts they might make at harassment or exacting revenge. If this becomes a problem for you, keep a record of incidents, talk to a women's abuse crisis counselor, talk to the police, and consult an attorney.

Approach harassment as a business problem, and try to avoid letting whoever's doing it hook you emotionally. If all they get out of their acts are nonemotional, civil responses and documentation, most abusers will stop. Don't let harassment raise your stress level, and do everything you can to protect yourself.

His new spouse. Whether she is the "other woman" or not, it is a waste of time for her to be the target of your anger. He is the decision maker, and forgetting that is just a way of blaming it on someone else. He can think; he makes decisions.

She may be a woman whose values you question, or she may have been someone he met after you separated and who under other circumstances might have been your friend. Whatever she is or seems to be, you need to direct your energy to the dialogue between you and your ex-husband, not a triangle. Any attacks on her place him in the position of her protector and create the opposite of what you may desire. Tell yourself over and over, "She is not the problem." Any number of women could have ended up with him.

Children Again

Divorce for children is not a brief crisis, the possibility of a new marriage, and a chance to start over. Children feel divorce as a lifetime issue. They cannot replace their parents or their natal family. Even when the new situation is better in most ways, they will feel grief.

The problems they have may result in anger, acting out, or depression. They may feel overburdened by adult problems. They often find themselves pulled one way or the other by both parents. The new man or woman in a parent's life adds more stress for children who often take second place to lovers.

Sex with your ex-spouse. Couples who have had a good sex life often want to continue it after the divorce. Obviously it sends a confusing message to children. They will think you are getting back together. It also makes it very difficult for you to be truly available for a new relationship. You will convey this sense to men that you meet. The sexual tie is an intimate one, and a divorce means a separation on all levels.

If your spouse left you for another woman it may seem like a wonderful way to get even with her, but you are the one being used. He still has two women.

Bringing Lovers Home

Unless you are planning to be married soon, having a lover stay overnight hurts everyone. Your son will feel compromised as a male and will see you as a questionable kind of woman. Our culture may seem more liberal, but these emotions run deep. Your daughter sees her mother being openly sexual, and it sets a model for her own behavior. It also puts her in an uncomfortable sexual position when her mother's lover is her friend, not her father. You'll feel the tension and some guilt, and it will impair your ability to make good decisions around the relationship.

Family Gatherings

If you've been able to forgive each other for the failure of the marriage you may not need to ask everyone to take sides. It ruins family meetings when everyone is keeping score. You can try for loyalty in very difficult divorces (violence, alcoholism, child abuse), but you may not get it. Do the best you can to avoid loyalty tests.

Let him come to the wedding, the graduation, the special event. Let him bring her. Encourage your new man and your old one to be civil. See if you can at least make an acquaintance of his new wife even if you suspect she's only twenty-one. It will be easier if you have all acted honorably in the separation, divorce, meeting of new partners, and remarriage. Don't create a lifetime feud.

A couple I worked with recently joined with his ex-wife in seeing their seventeen-year-old daughter off to France for the summer. They waved good-bye and had a lovely dinner together. The ex-wife, besides being an interesting woman, seems like family to them. The husband loved it. He didn't have to feel guilty; he can still enjoy the personality that first attracted him to her; and his wife gets extra love because she's not fighting for it.

Remember

If your marriage has not been destroyed by abuse, if it's just sick, it's a better investment to fight to save it than to start over.

You are the only one who can take care of your inner child.

36. It's Hard to Be a Parent

All of our relationships are forever touched by memories: familiar rituals, moments of understanding, songs, silly ways of talking, family traditions, just being together.

There are so many memories created every day. It's wonderful and terrible: parenting is one of the most important things we ever do and yet the one that can change our lives in ways we cannot cope with.

Some of us grow up in successful families and learn how to be a parent from good models. I never learned how to be a parent and was terrified when I first brought my son home. I was of the generation of mothers rescued by counselors and Dr. Spock's baby book.

There is not room here to discuss more than a few of the basics of helping yourself through parenting. There are some excellent books on parenting in the bibliography. What I can offer are some bits of information that may help your perspective. Parenting can be the source of the worst blues any of us face.

Most of our parenting style comes from the way we were brought up. We either imitate our parents because it's familiar or try to do the opposite because of the bad experiences we had. Neither is a good option. Parenting needs to be thought out in terms of the particular child, your spouse, your values, and what works.

You may think spanking works because you turned out okay, but it may be very harmful in the more sensitive culture we now live in and to your particular child. You also might not be in touch with the amount of pain you feel inside from physical discipline. Do your homework. Analyze how you were parented and what you accept or reject about that parenting style. Read books, consider classes or counseling, and make sure you know what you are doing to your child and why.

This advice comes from thousands of parents who have realized many years later that they did to their children what they most wanted to avoid. It is a lifetime source of guilt to not be aware of the kind of parent you are.

It takes deep soul-searching to understand what you want from your children and what you want from yourself as a mother. What are your expectations? Are they valid? Where did they come from? How much do you care what others think of your family? How powerful is your parents' approval or disapproval? How much of your parenting style is habit, and how much is carefully chosen? Tape-record yourself talking to your children. Plan out your role as mother, don't just let it happen.

Loving and nurturing children is the core of a woman's being. It has been our central role from the beginning of time. It is the most important thing we do. Take the time and energy you would put into anything else that is vital to your well-being, and figure out who and what you are as a mother.

Women were so long the caretakers of children that many men don't feel welcome helping or don't feel competent to help. You may find you shut out your husband because you "know best" or you spend more time with the children. If you don't encourage your husband to be a father, you may end up a martyr, and believe me, no one will thank you for it.

At a lecture I gave a decade ago to a group of Air Force colonels, I was surprised by some of the beliefs men might have. One man said that men had different hands than women. Another said that men could not hold infants as well as women because women had a curved bone in their forearm that made a better cradle. No one laughed. At first I was stunned and then I remembered the times I had been in a room with a newborn. Many of the women present would coo and ask to hold the baby. The men would usually stand back. Once a man did reach to pick up the baby and the mother yelled, "Don't drop the baby!" This man was a neurosurgeon during the day but could not be trusted to hold a baby after hours.

If you feel your husband doesn't share the load, try to figure out why. What is he comfortable doing? What would he be willing to learn? Can you take classes or read some books together? Are you willing to not interfere?

Set up a contract with him so that he won't lump you with the kids as a source of stress. You need a "we and them" view of you and the children not a "he and them" perspective. Some men say they've got to get away from the wife and kids for a while when they really mean the kids. You get lumped in because you identify yourself—or he identifies you—with kids. That hurts!

If the father is absent or unavailable, carry the burden yourself. Don't convey to the child that anything is wrong with the other parent. They will think it is a reflection on them. It is an unsafe situation for a child to be half bound up in someone who is either unknown or disliked by you. Forget about creating loyalty to you; that will be automatic. Try to create a balanced feeling in your children about their other parent. When they are older they can sort out the facts.

When you are down and feeling alone, look at your own relationships and take care of yourself before you decide that someone else is the main problem. When you feel stronger and less stressed, evaluate your family situation.

What You Can Do

Try to understand why your children misbehave.

Low self-esteem. They have been convinced they have no value so their behavior doesn't make much difference. They will either try to hurt themselves further because they think they deserve it or give up entirely and refuse to cooperate. Rebellious teenagers and obstinate little children are sometimes protecting themselves. They refuse to invest in your demands because of the insecurities of your treatment of them.

The only way to change this is to find out why you are so critical and to work on your own self-esteem while you try and build the child's. Make a clear shift to the positive. Find successes. Learn more about less destructive styles of discipline, and get help if you need it.

Abuse or abusive environment. If you use physical punishment on your child or let anyone else do it, you are an abusive parent. Physical or sexual abuse can lead to a lifetime of problems. Constant criticism, humiliation, or teasing can be equally destructive. Children raised in abusive environments will try to survive in any way they can.

No marriage or relationship is worth abusing your children for. Get counseling and change the situation or get out of it. Tell your children you are sorry, and try to build a safe, structured environment for them. They may seem able to adjust, but consider counseling for the hurts that are hidden.

Attention. Most of us want attention, and children think their life depends on it. Survival depends on attention for infants. It doesn't matter if the attention is negative or positive as long as they are noticed.

Notice what you respond to. How often do you respond to negative behavior? Do you respond at all to positive? What are you reinforcing; what do your children get attention for?

Expectations. Children know when we are trying to steal their identity by deciding what we want them to be. You may want a disciplined doctor and your daughter may be a creative adventurer. Sooner or later she must fight your expectations or lose herself. Try to know your children as unique personalities, not as raw material with which to live out your dreams.

Watch your family's expectations too. You may be tempted to please your mother or compete with your sister, using your child as the ammunition. Try not to ask your children to be or do things that you don't think are important just because somebody else might criticize you.

Competition or comparison. Children want to feel unique and uniquely loved. They hate being compared to another child. When you say, "Your brother was never like this," you are asking for trouble. The instant response is either low self-esteem (Mom thinks the other child is better than I am) or resentment at your setting up a rivalry. We rarely compare children favorably. We always find a child who is doing better. It is just another form of destructive criticism, and children know it. Try not to make comparisons of any kind.

Revenge. Children have a strong sense of justice because they have to rely on it for protection. They know that when you hit them it is only because you are bigger. Psychologically it is behavior no different than that of the bully on the playground. When you make unfair demands, humiliate them, punish them inappropriately, or destroy anything that is theirs on purpose, they want revenge. They will wait for a chance to get even.

Try not to act in anger or retaliate when your children misbehave. You can retaliate with much greater power, and it only reinforces their sense of inadequacy and desire for a sneaky revenge. It's a cycle that you need to stop.

Power. Most of us want to be our own boss. Many children feel significant only when they are in charge. They may feel the need to control an unsafe environment or just want to run the show.

You have the power as the adult; you don't need to engage in power struggles in which you end up screaming like your ten-year-old. Develop discipline strategies that don't require you to prove your power. Remind yourself over and over, "I am the adult; this is a child." If you forget that, you've lost too much power.

Some of us did not learn how to negotiate with our parents, so we find it difficult to negotiate with our children. If you were raised in the "Don't talk back" school your negotiation skills were short-circuited by threats. You will find the same desire to shut your children up by force that you encountered when you were a child.

Imagine yourself as an all-loving, all-wise adult. Pretend you are Solomon making a decision for the good of the people. Put on your robes. You do not need to question your power or be afraid someone doesn't respect you. Solomon wouldn't get upset if someone he was speaking seriously to laughed at him. Solomon would thoughtfully make his decision knowing it was based on his wisdom and love.

Listen to their arguments, make your decision, and then stick to it. You don't have to be talked to death or harassed into a power struggle. Have faith in your ability to parent. Trust yourself to use your power in good ways, and your children won't need to fight you for it.

Discipline works only if there is a positive personal relationship between parent and child. Both need self-esteem, quality time together, a sense of trust, realistic expectations, and attention for what is right and what is wrong. When these ingredients exist there is far less conflict.

Discipline requires that you know what you want and trust yourself. It must be consistent, predictable, and reasonable. Children understand logical consequences (If you are antisocial, you must leave the room). Always separate the deed from the doer. The child is okay; the behavior is not. Avoid violence, avoid pity (it makes children feel there is something wrong with them that they need to be comforted for), and avoid being out of control. Take good care of yourself so you can take good care of them.

Remember

Don't try to go it alone because you've been hurt by your natal family or a divorce. It can be heartbreaking and exhausting to take care of any child without a friend to lean on and share with. If you are new to a city or don't know where to start, get involved with a parenting group. Call your community information line and choose a group you're comfortable with.

Try not to think of yourself as a bad parent because things get out of control once in a while. Don't just wait for them to "grow out of" problems. Get help to learn new strategies.

Never put your children aside to pursue a relationship or a career. It will eventually break your heart.

You are not alone when times are hard, and you're worn out. There are many loving parents feeling just as you do.

Don't become a martyr, giving up everything for your children. If you do, you will hurt them with guilt, future expectations, and the destruction of your own life value.

I did the best I could with who I was and what I knew at the time.

37. It's So Hard to Forgive

You feel a constant tug from unresolved relationships. Your teeth clench when you think of certain people or situations. You complain to friends about things that happened to you years ago. There are more than a few people that you avoid. You set up loyalty tests and participate in feuds. When you forgive, your ego feels that you are losing.

"I won't forgive them, no matter what it does to me."

"It's hard to think about my future when I have not received justice in the past."

The hurt part of our mind keeps score; the healthy mind enjoys life. Some philosophers call it little mind versus big mind. We do not forgive to benefit others but to benefit ourselves. Forgiveness releases us from the pain and conflict. The other person may not even care. Forgiveness is the letting go of past abuse or past misunderstanding, pain that interferes with your present sense of self and peace.

You may be afraid to let go, to change, to feel better, to grieve. When you can forgive others, you can forgive yourself, and you may not be ready to do that. It's hardest for martyrs and perfectionists to forgive, because they keep score over a lifetime.

Forgiveness is acceptance of humanness. Inability to forgive is based on fear. Fear of what we think we are or what we are afraid others will do to us. When we feel we are being attacked, we attack.

What You Can Do

List your fears. Some will come to mind automatically when you just close your eyes. Others will turn up as you go through your week. Try to jot them down to get a handle on the barriers you have to forgiveness. Try to examine each fear and find out why you are upset.

List people and situations that you cannot forgive. Include the ones that you cannot forgive yourself for. Then try the following strategies on each of them until you find one that fits.

- Grief: Often we have to grieve for what never was or never will be: the parents we didn't have, the love that disappeared, people who don't live their lives the way we want them to. Find the source of your grief so you can let it flow and begin to recover.

- Penance: Paying for the crime sometimes helps. Assign yourself (or the other person) a penance so you do not have to feel guilty for a lifetime. Make it fit the crime.

   Penance has a long history in our culture and our religions. Endless guilt takes the energy out of you. It's important to us to have justice, so appropriate punishment or penance creates a balance and a second chance.

   I forgot my lines in a high school play. At thirty it still bothered me at odd moments. Instead of saying, "How silly," I decided my punishment would be to attend three high school plays. It worked; I was off the hook.

   An aunt I loved very much, who had been very kind to me, died when I was too worried about other things to visit her. I felt terrible for years. Then I realized I had another aunt I could show love to. I turned the guilt into energy to extend myself to someone who needed attention.

   You can set up a penance even without the cooperation of the other person.

   Send an anonymous gift to someone you want to apologize to if you cannot do it directly. Give money to a charity in someone's name. Send your ex-husband his favorite books, which you hid during the breakup.

   Use your creativity; make the penance fit.

   A young woman I worked with was deeply depressed about an abortion she'd had as a teenager. She could see no possibility of forgiveness for such an irrevocable act. None of the arguments that she may have made the right choice for her at the time carried any weight with her conscience. She had decided on a lifetime of guilt.

   We talked about penance, and she came up with the idea of volunteering her time to work with unwed mothers. That seemed appropriate. She could help care for infants and young mothers who were struggling with a different choice. The problem was her feeling that it must be for a lifetime. We compromised on two years of two afternoons a week. Five hundred hours was an arbitrary number, as penance prayers often are, but it brought her peace. She put her energy into something positive instead of a lifetime of looking backwards.

- Written justice: Write out your version of the situation, in detail. Be as angry as you want; make your accusations of injustice; try to put all your feelings on paper. Then add a way out. Write that you are willing to let go of the past now that you have had your say. You are willing to start over, never bringing up, or even hinting at, what has gone before. Tell the other person you care. Then either send the letter, burn it, or file it. Whatever works for you is the test.

- Dialogue: Set up two chairs in a private place. Put yourself in one of them, and imagine the person you cannot forgive in the other. Put some time into creating an image in your mind. What does the other person look like? How is he or she dressed? Try to connect with your own feelings.

  Even though it may bring grief, tell the one in the chair how you feel. Express your sadness or anger. Say it is time to let go of the past. Ask the other person to apologize, and make your own apology. Practice until it feels right.

  Sometimes you can convert this into a real dialogue. If you do, concern yourself only with what you need to say, regardless of the response. Remind yourself that you need to forgive whether the other person does or not.

- Hot coal: This one works best for me. Imagine that the anger or hurt you carry is a hot coal in your hand. Close your fingers tightly around it. Who is getting burned? You are! The person you don't want to forgive isn't. You are the one being hurt. How long do you want to hold onto that hot coal? Let go!

- Trading places: Put yourself in the other person's consciousness and try to understand the other position. You don't have to accept it, just understand it. Become the person you dislike as deeply as you can, and you will usually find a part of yourself. It hurts, but it's hard to change without pain.

- Rebellion: Look deeper into your refusal to forgive. Repeat to yourself and the other, "I won't forgive, even if it ruins my life!" Say this often enough, and you may decide that hurting yourself is not worth it.

- Grudge: Refuse to forget or forgive anything, even if justice turns up later. Remind yourself that it is better to ruin your life with frustration and meanness than to let go of any grudges for a minute.

Write each one down on a card, and put it in your grudge file. Grudge files should be glass bowls or jars so you can always see them clearly and riffle through them when the mood strikes. After a while the grudge bowl gives us a clear view of what our problems are.

You are never upset for the reasons you think. Do some personal homework, and find out what is really upsetting you. Chances are it's something within your own character that this conflict triggers.

When it seems impossible to forgive, there is always a very personal and painful hidden agenda. There are old feelings, sometimes going back to childhood, that make the hurt go too deep. It seems inappropriately deep until you understand why you are upset.

Sometimes letting go of the past means letting go of the hurts of all of the generations of parents and grandparents that preceded you. Get to know your grandparents and their parents through talking, memories, aunts and uncles. You will find more of yourself there than you ever thought possible.

Look into your own doubts and conflicts before you believe that your inability to forgive is someone else's problem.

It often is easier to forgive in imagination than in reality. When we next see the person all the old feelings come back. It's hard and embarrassing to make the shift. Aim for small steps, a smile, just a hello and no more. Maybe just being in the same room but not catching the other's eye. Say something nice about the person to someone else, and it will flow back to him or her and ease the connection.

Start where the emotional load is easiest for you to carry. If it is a relative maybe you begin by just sending a note or a book you liked. If the other person needs to tell you his or her side, try to listen without judgment and not defend yourself.

Some situations require a fight for justice before we feel able to take the forgiveness step. Women who fight unfair divorces, protect their children, sue for respite from discrimination or sexual harassment are working for fairness. It will be easier to fight if you can forgive. The energy behind your efforts becomes clearer.

Childhood victims of sexual abuse find terrible pain in the forgiveness process, because so often the abuser refuses to admit or repent. Understanding the terrible fear he feels may not temper your pain. Care enough to confront. Abusive behavior must be controlled (with legal steps, divorce, denial of custody) or changed.

Forgiveness does not mean being a victim. Don't deny your anger or your fear. Work for justice and resolution, but accept that it may not always be possible. Make a conscious choice to let go of the pain and anger, but hold onto your own value.

Remember

If you think constant suffering over a mistake will earn your release, it won't. Grieve, make amends to the best of your ability, and accept that you must release yourself.

Hold onto what you learn in each process of forgiveness so you can forgive sooner and deeper next time.

If you have been terribly hurt it will take time to heal. That's okay.

It's a short-term thrill, but ultimately being right will hurt if you cannot forgive.

"You're forgiven, now leave me alone": this is a way of faking it. Closing the door on your emotions doesn't get rid of the problem.

Try not to be a martyr. "I will never say anything. They will never know the pain they caused." You will carry it forever, resentful as hell beneath your halo.

"The holiest of all the spots on earth is where an ancient hatred has been replaced by a present love."

—*A Course in Miracles*

Part Two:

SOURCES OF UNDERSTANDING— STRATEGIES FOR LOVING

Learning new strategies and thought processes makes life easier but it isn't enough to create a foundation for action and joy. That takes self-value, an understanding of yourself as a woman, and knowledge of the cost if you want more than others seem to want. Part Two addresses those issues and helps supply what is needed for that foundation.

Self-esteem has been the new "buzz" word for this decade. It's finally okay to think about and like yourself, although that's easier said than done. The next section presents the setting for the development of your self-esteem and some steps you can take to understanding your own experience and feelings about yourself.

Directly linked to basic individual value is your value as a woman and in relationship to men. It is inescapable that women will rate themselves, in part, on how well they succeed as the companions of men. The second section of Sources of Understanding is simply a cultural framework for women and men. Check the traps you've been caught in, the perceptions that color your view of yourself and its effect on your self-esteem and your satisfaction with life.

The third section, about women of high potential, is deeply connected to both self-esteem and our relationships with men. You probably wouldn't have picked up this book unless you were already aware of feelings and wanting more. Women with high potential suffer very early losses as children and continued pain as adults in an ambivalent culture. Understanding how you may be caught intellectually and emotionally often sets you free

The truth hurts, then it sets you free.

38. Self-Esteem and Childhood Pain

The foundation of happiness is liking yourself. Few women do. All the strategies discussed in this book are dependent on your feeling you deserve to feel good.

Where do you get self-esteem if it doesn't develop in you as a child? First, by accepting that most of us share the problem of not valuing ourselves enough. We were raised to believe in a different set of survival skills. Sometimes it seems as if we are unique victims, but we're not. If your parents didn't seem to love you and your teachers criticized you, they were just doing their job the only way they knew how. You may have had intentionally abusive parents or disturbed parents (the section on childhood pain is for you), but most of us were just caught in history.

Caught in History

Americans still have a pioneer spirit, the idea that only the tough will survive and an underlying acceptance of cruelty toward women, children, and minorities. Concern about sensitivity and self-value is a relatively recent element in our culture. Before 1970, group feelings and group control were still considered more important than individual feelings of worth.

Back in the fort, the ideal was to keep women and children safe by protecting them: protection through control. It is hard to control people who think for themselves or who think well of themselves. Their low self-esteem made it much easier to control women.

If your father or mother screamed at you in anger and called you names, maybe they were saying, "How can I protect you if you don't do what I say to do?"

When you were berated, belittled, and otherwise embarrassed or humiliated by adults you were being taught basic survival skills. Cooperation was a bigger problem in pioneer days than self-esteem. Self-knowledge was confused with conceit. Conceited people couldn't be counted on to support the group or to sacrifice when necessary. They thought too much of themselves. Running a family then was like running an army. Safety depended on the leaders not being questioned.

It is hard for middle-class women now to remember when the security fear was, "Will I have enough to eat?" The current issue is, "Will I eat too much?" Surviving had a different meaning at the turn of the century. Your time in history affects your self-esteem. In an affluent, multiple-choice society self-value is essential. In a limited choice, subsistence culture it was less crucial.

The old survival skills were designed to make us fit the cultural norm. We were taught not to vote for ourselves. I lost two elections in high school by two votes, mine and that of the conceited person who did vote for herself. My face would turn red even today if I voted for myself and other people could see my choice. Fear of conceit was the value I was raised with. Can you vote for yourself openly? What would you teach your child to do? Why run for an office if you don't think you're good enough to vote for?

During the sixties I took a college course that required each of us to assign our own grade. Even though I had been an *A* student in all my college courses, I could not give myself an *A*. Guilt overwhelmed me, and it was a fight to assign myself a B. "Never put yourself forward," I had been taught. People who put themselves forward probably got scalped; anyway, they endangered the group.

What were you taught about compliments? Can you accept them, or are you tempted to say, "Oh, this old thing," or "I really didn't do anything." What if someone gives you lots of compliments? What do you think of that person? Hustler, wimp—obviously someone who says nice things about me either wants something or has bad taste. Some women learn to want only men who don't want them, because it eliminates the dilemma of thinking well of themselves or suspecting anyone who does.

Can you stand in front of a mirror and say "I love it all!"? Why not? Because you've been told from the moment of birth what is wrong with you by everyone who could possible tell you in order to avoid any chance that you might think well of yourself. Their version of the truth is constantly repeated. Given the competitive spirit, it starts early:

> "Tell me, does the baby turn over yet? No? Well, my little Susie turned over in the birth canal! I'm sure little Helen will catch up soon."

> "Look at those feet! She'll grow into them one day, I hope!"

> "It's a shame she ended up with your family's nose."

"I hope you're smart, since you're not as pretty as your sister, are you, dear?"

Remarks we heard when we were too young to fight back still sting. My aunt at seventy-five still remembers with tears in her eyes being told at ten she was unattractive. Her youngest sister, my mother, was the pretty one. My aunt, in a part of her being, has hated her little sister her whole life for that blow to her self-value.

Even the most loving parents were cautioned to civilize the little beasts within their children by guarding against the development of self-awareness and selfishness. We admonish them to put others first. See if you can remember the old messages that still move through your sense of self.

You are four years old, and it is summer. Your mother puts a bowl of fresh, washed cherries on the table in front of you. What is the normal, logical thing to do, assuming you love cherries (substitute plump, seedless green grapes if you prefer)? Eat every one of them as fast as you can with great joy. Your mother sees what you are doing. How does she respond?

Historical response: "You little pig! What are you doing? How can you be so selfish? There are others in the family who like cherries. I'm disappointed in you! Can't you share," and so on.

Rational response (that builds self-esteem): "Those cherries are good, aren't they? I'm tempted to eat them all too, but there are others here who will want some, so let's divide them up so they get their share."

Depending on your family and your time in history, you may have picked up a lot of irrational fears and labels that have nothing to do with who you are. Sometimes it's as if we're given a fishbowl to wear on our heads at birth and everyone around us puts labels on the bowl: selfish . . . slow . . . liar . . . plain . . . short . . . tall . . . hyper- . . .

We grow up and view the world and ourselves through the labels, never realizing that we can peel them off and see the world and ourselves clearly.

The main reason we can now work for a clearer view of self or consider self-esteem as the foundation of a good life is that we can afford to. Safety has been achieved for most Americans in food and shelter at least. They are free to ask questions and seek qualities beyond basic survival.

"Am I happy?" *not,* "Will I survive?"

"Am I living up to my full potential?" *not*, "Will I be able to find work?"

"Is there enough passion in my life?" *not*, "How can I get there first?"

Survival strategies have changed. To survive and be at peace in a complex world requires a commitment to self-knowledge. The fort, where a woman's obligation was to keep everything clean, tight ("Waste not, want not"), and in order, has opened its doors. We are now asked to look within ourselves, not just to the group, for value. We have shifted from fear of conceit to an absolute requirement for self-knowledge.

Sources of Self-esteem

It is possible to explain why our culture valued low self-esteem, especially in women, but it is not easy to explain the sources of self-esteem. These are the four major elements that affect personal value: fate, family, experience, and perception.

Fate

The time you were born in history is determined by fate. We give different messages to our children than those given to us. This is not because we are better, but because our survival needs have changed. My twenty-two-year-old son understands self-esteem. I didn't know the meaning of the term until I was thirty three.

Fate includes such factors as sex, race, geography, culture, and disability. If you were born a woman fifty years ago you were already one down. Now it's becoming tougher for men. If you were born of a racial or ethnic group that was perceived as less valuable you suffered blows to your self-esteem. In a racist and elitist culture members of in-groups have higher self-esteem than members of out-groups, unless the negatives are mitigated by understanding and family support.

Geography can put you in the middle of a revolution or isolate you, limiting your chances. Culture can be warm and passionate, filled with love and humor, or cold and hard, with tight stoicism. A disability in a perfectionist society can put you down again, whether it is physical, mental, or just being unattractive by the agreed-upon standards.

Fate is unchangeable. You are tall or short, Asian or Caucasian, blind or sighted. Perhaps time or changes in politics or preferences will modify your fate, but the original value message will always remain within you.

Family

Family is the most talked-about source of self-esteem. How did they treat you? Were you loved or not loved—openly or who knows? Did your family stay together or fall apart? Were you rich or poor, together or separated, violent or nonviolent, disturbed or balanced? Did anyone die or abandon you? Your first family will seem like the most important to you even though you later build others.

Your family was also caught in their history. Take time to understand your background and the behavior of your parents or whoever took care of you. You need to know what happened to you. I found out that some of my fear of abandonment came not from being left by my parents because they didn't care but because I was sent out of London, to foster care, for my own safety during World War II.

Within the framework of your family and culture is the most personal of all self-value sources—the pain or pleasure of your earliest years. The pain of an abusive childhood is a lifetime pain. It begins with the recognition that our very survival depends on the goodwill of others, that if we cannot appeal to them we will not live. Early on, the unique self within us compromises if survival requires it.

The truth will make
you free—but
first it will make
you miserable.

A talented, successful woman of forty shared with me her earliest memories:

For most of my life I have not been able to recall any of my childhood. The memories began at about ten with only shadows before. I knew there should be more, and as my life became safer in other ways I began to remember.

I am two days old, and I realize it isn't safe to nurse at my mother's breast. She does not like females, and I am one. She is angry at my presence, and her breast is cold. I am afraid to touch her.

My refusal to nurse, and to thrive, results in my being forcibly fed milk from a teaspoon. I will not suck. This memory brought back pain that washed over me in waves.

I decided to check the accuracy of my senses. The next time I talked with my mother, I asked her what she fed me with as an infant. She answered that I refused to suck. She had to feed me with a teaspoon and block my nose so I would open my mouth.

Many adults hurt in childhood cannot remember the child within at all. They cannot make contact. They have chosen the defense of denying the existence of a separate and once whole self. Their ideas about what they were like as a child are drawn only from the stories and descriptions of others who know them. They do not easily recognize themselves in childhood photographs. Alice Miller has written that "This self is like a prisoner in a cell; no one believes in his innocence, and as a result, rather than remain alone and isolated with the truth, he too finally loses all knowledge of it."

The child within us remains hidden and withdrawn. It is a protective device to avoid living out the pain that was misunderstood when we were so young. We sense that we are not authentic. There is an absence of a true self. We have only the compromise made long ago and a hint of memories.

There is a split in our personality: the good but false self that has learned to compromise but does not feel real, alive, safe, true or passionate; the bad, rejected self that hid early, sensing she was unacceptable, yet still shows up and reminds us of the fear within. The fear that some of us carry is only a small child asking to be cared for. Without recognition and support, this split self may slip into depression.

The consequences of childhood deprivation, in all its forms, are an interlinking of love and hate. The child is helpless, totally dependent, and is being hurt, taken advantage of by the person he or she must turn to for survival and solace.

It is not safe to express the hurt or anger, in most circumstances, for fear of losing what care there might be. Ambivalence about trust, love, and intimacy become the foundation on which all future relationships are built.

The childhood emotions, unexpressed, are lived out endlessly as an adult. Love must mean pain and sacrifice. Love is humiliating. Love hurts. Love is ambivalence. I must love or I will not survive, but who I am will not survive if I love. We learn to keep people at bay, yet we hold onto them as if our lives depended on it.

Most do not choose recognition of the child within, because of the memory of pain and the desire not to complete the grief experience. Instead we resort to defenses, perfectionism, control, self-destructive behavior, or a rigid, protective view of appropriate behavior. We tie ourselves tighter to avoid the threat inherent in loose thoughts and actions. Control prevents access to the true self. Self-destructive actions destroy it.

The god of my childhood wears black robes, has horns on his head and carries an ax in his hand. How in the world was I still able to slip past him?

All my life I have been creeping stealthily through my landscape, under my arm the little bit of life I keep thinking I have stolen."
—Mariella Mehr, *Steinzeit ("Stone Age")*

If you have read this far you already know you have no choice. You are too aware of your loss. Your body reminds you daily. Your heart feels a sharp stab of pain at unexpected moments—impossible not to go forward yet reluctant to keep having to work on "it." "When will I be healed?"

I once asked a therapist why he couldn't issue graduation cards like Red Cross Life Saving cards, so you knew when you were done with your childhood. I wanted a little card I could carry in my purse to show people I was complete. I had taken my classes and paid my dues. There is no card, no guarantees; it is a lifetime journey through layers of protection, a journey toward the heart.

I used to dream at night of a Chinese puzzle box. It had many moving panels that you could slide to eventually get at the prize hidden in a little spring drawer deep within. It was very difficult to open the panels in the right sequence and hold them open so you could get to the inside. When I left the box alone for a few months I would almost forget what to do to open it again.

When I entered therapy the dream shifted and the puzzle box became a Chinese chest with carved and inlaid doors. As I repeated the dream every few nights the outer doors of the chest opened. Inside there was another set of smaller doors. They were more beautiful than those I had opened. Over months I slipped through many sets of doors, each more beautiful in carving and inlay than the ones before. I finally reached what I sensed was that last set of doors, but I was afraid to open them.

I felt a premonition that inside this innermost chamber was a spider: a black widow spider, the kind we used to be scared of as children, the one that could kill you with a bite you hardly noticed.

I felt tremendous fear, and months went by with no attempt on my part to open the last doors. The dream was intermittent, but the image of darkness was the same. In my therapy I was trying to "lean into the pain," as I call it, so I could get through to the other side. I did not share the dream with my therapist or understand its obvious metaphor.

The dream returned; the inner doors were ajar, and I could see a beam of light slipping through the crack. I opened the chamber, and it was filled with light. No spider was within, only light. It has remained so ever since.

It takes a long time to open the doors. Often we don't even see the most obvious responses or think to evaluate our dreams. There is light inside every one of those complicated boxes. I gave a friend of mine, who was in great pain, a Chinese puzzle box with a pearl in the innermost drawer. I gave her an illustration, step-by-step, how to open it so she would never forget.

You must do your homework. Dig up the past so you can see your value clearly. You must find and create safety for the life you tucked away decades ago. She must be invited to join you now. She is your heart, your soul, and your passion.

This is not work you should do alone unless you have absolute confidence in your ability to handle the grief. The tears unshed for past losses will need to flow. They will not last forever, but there will be pain.

Find a picture of yourself as a child, perhaps an awkward one, and put it on your bathroom mirror. Talk with this little girl, and recognize her innocence and her fear. Reassure her that you are there and that she has your love and support. You can take care of her. You want to take care of her.

Leave the photograph there until you can look at her directly and neither wince nor cry. Leave her there until you can smile. Give her everything she needs until you feel her relaxing within and beginning to trust.

Write to her in your mind or on paper. Tell her you understand how confusing and frightening it must have been. Remind her that you are both safe now. You grew up, you're okay. You're able to take her hand and help her join you. She no longer has to hide.

Let her write back or talk to you until you feel you are one. Then let her forgive herself and finally those who hurt her because they too had been hurt before memory. Dig up the past together so you can plant your own future. There really is no choice.

Even when you have made your peace there will be times when you feel low and wish that your childhood had been different. You assume that then you would be and feel different. I'm not sure that is true, but regardless of the impact of your natal family, the key is now this:

Who is now taking care of you?
Who is now your parent?

For two years I had a call-in radio program. It was so intense, that two years was all I could handle. During that time a man called upset about a problem in his office. He was an architect, about thirty four, and tended to have "snits" in the office.

A snit was a sort of fit that resulted whenever too many things went wrong, he made a mistake, or someone criticized him. Sometimes he just scrunched up paper or broke pencils. Once in a while he was tempted to bend machinery to make it work. "I'll just kick it or hit it or smash it!" That day he had gotten so upset he had tipped over his drafting table.

His colleagues were getting a bit wary of him: "Walk on eggshells around Mark." He was afraid that he might lose his job.

"Snit" was a new word to me, so I asked him where it came from. He said his mother used it. Aha! a clue.

"What age child might have a snit?" I asked.

"About a ten-year-old," he replied.

"What kind of kid were you at ten?"

"I was a mess, uncoordinated, and not doing well in school. My mother said she couldn't remarry because no one wanted a package deal."

"Can you remember any time in your childhood when you were truly okay, lovable, and capable?" I asked.

"No."

"What about when you were four? You know how cute little kids are."

He said, "No, I wet the bed when I was four. My mother said she'd give me diapers for a wedding present."

"How about three months? Babies are just beginning to smile then."

"No, I had colic. I kept Mom awake at night. I nearly drove her crazy."

I was lost. The radio time was ticking away, and a commercial need-ed to be played. When had this man had any value?

"Wait, were you born in a hospital?" I asked.

"Yes."

"Were you a healthy baby?"

"Yes."

"Imagine yourself in one of those bassinets at just one day old. Your mother is in another room; the nurses are taking care of you. You are not a problem yet. Now reach into the bassinet and pick up the baby."

"What?"

"Pick up the baby!"

"Okay, I've got him."

"Now, tell the baby that you will take care of him."

"Wait a minute! I don't know how to take care of babies!"

"You can read books, can't you? Talk to friends who have children. Tell the baby you will take care of him."

"Okay, kid. I'll take care of you."

"Now send me a card every time the baby has a birthday."

"What?!" he exclaimed, then hung up.

As I listened to the buzz on the line, I wondered if he had understood.

About a year later I got the first card. "The kid is now four," he wrote. "I've been taking him to the zoo and out for ice cream. He's not a bad kid at all. I don't mind if he's a little uncoordinated."

A few months later I got the card I'd been waiting for. "The kid is ten. Now when he comes to the office with me and something upsets him, I just reach in and hold his hand and remind him that he's safe because I'm here and I'll take care of him. No more snits."

The last card I received came three years after our first contact. The card said, "I'm scared to death. The kid is twenty seven. I'm afraid he's going to leave me."

What happens when you begin to take care of your own inner child is that the child starts growing up until one day you become one. It is painful because we have not let go of the past, all the explanations as to why things are not the way we want them to be. When we parent ourselves, we take full responsibility for the way things are.

I wrote back to Mark and told him not to worry, the child within him would always visit. Whenever things are tense or you feel unsafe the child will come back and remind you of the ten-year-old you once were. You can say hello and then remind him you are an adult now and able to take care of yourself.

Experience

What happened to you the first time you toddled out into the world? Did you get hurt or abused? Were teachers supportive? How were the kids in the neighborhood? Did anything terrible happen? Were you hit by a car? Did your house burn down? No or yes to questions like these has an impact on what you think about the world.

Experience piles on experience and affects self-esteem our entire life. Marry a perfectionist, and watch your self-esteem tumble downhill. Stack up bad love affairs or rejections, and you will feel no one can love you. If your husband runs off with another woman, it will have an impact on your sense of self-worth.

Positive experiences do the same: friends who are loyal, neighbors who care, teachers who like children, spouses who treat you with kindness and respect—wonderful!

Do you feel you've had more negative, or more positive experiences? Try to add them up in the columns of your mind. What do you choose to remember? What kind of experience are you creating now?

Perspective

More important than fate, family, or experience is perspective. How do you choose to view your past? Perspective is learned from our family or culture (like optimism or pessimism), but there are many people who seem to create their own. They decide to interpret their life events in terms of challenges and possibilities not losses and injustices.

The examples of perspective on fate are ones we are all familiar with, Helen Keller and Martin Luther King, Jr. These people turned their fate into something spectacular. I like to remember Martin Luther King, Sr., who even after the assassination of both his son and his wife said he viewed the world with love. You have your own examples of people with similar fates who created very different perspectives on it.

Check your perspective on your fate: Negative? Positive? Somewhere in between? Has it changed over time? Are you more attractive or more intelligent than you once thought?

Perspectives on family experience change as we grow up. It takes longer to tell your life story at twenty than it does at forty because different things seem important. We may now find humor in a remark by a parent that brought fury when we were sixteen. My mother said that my first husband looked like a gopher. So, to spite her, I married him. Even with all the pain that followed, I can now laugh at her insult and my response.

Understanding ourselves makes it easier to understand others, especially members of our own family. The control and criticism that once made me hate my parents can be translated into their experiences as children and all the generations they represent. The competition I may have felt from my mother has a lot to do with her childhood pain as well as mine.

Gloria Steinem, in her autobiography, *Outrageous Acts and Everyday Rebellions*, tells the story of an older woman who touched her at a lecture.

I was sitting in an ethnic hall in Detroit, at a local celebration of *Ms.* magazine's tenth birthday, and being tapped on the shoulder by a small, gray-haired woman with gnarled, hardworking hands and a starched cotton housedress that is clearly her best. "I just want you to know," she says softly, "that you are the inside of me." All reward came together in one moment. Remembering now that woman's touch and words, I still feel tears behind my eyes.

We are the inside of our parents as well as the outside. My father's suicide, which once seemed like a betrayal on his part and a failure on mine, now has become a gift. A reminder to value my own life and to be aware of the pain in all lives.

When did you last update your family experience? When did you last talk to siblings, parents, relatives, or neighbors about the way it was. As Richard Bach puts it, "You are always free to choose a different past and a different future."

When we are rigid about our perspective on the past, especially our perspective on our family, we make it impossible to change our self-value, because then the old explanations would no longer fit.

A couple came to me for counseling a few years ago. He was forty; she was thirty-seven. She wanted a divorce. I asked her why, and she described her husband as depressed, unsuccessful, and having very low self-esteem. She didn't see any possibility of change, and she wanted out. I turned to him, and he agreed with her evaluation. He did not want a divorce, but he saw no alternative.

After a number of sessions with little progress, I pushed him for his explanation of why he had so little sense of value. He said, "My father never loved me." His father had left him when he was four. He had been abandoned. His father had been a construction worker, a bit of a drifter, a man with a drinking problem who had walked out and never returned. He hadn't loved his son, or even liked him, and now he was dead.

I asked him when he had last updated this story by talking to someone who knew his father. He answered that it had been thirty years since he had talked to anyone about his dad. Was there anyone now alive he could talk to? The only person he could think of was his mother, who lived sixty miles away. I called her, and she agreed to come in for three visits with her son and me.

The first meeting she agreed with her son's version of family history. She hadn't worried much about it, because she had always planned to remarry and get the boy a better father. She was surprised when she did not find a second husband.

At the next meeting I pushed a little harder for information about my client's father. I told her I was concerned because her son's depression was deepening, and with the divorce I felt there was a risk of suicide. There was silence in the room for ten minutes, and then she began to cry. She started to tell a different story of her separation.

She was an ambitious woman who liked order and control. Her husband was easygoing; he liked a beer after work, but it wasn't really a problem. He traveled from one construction job to another, and he loved his son. He did not want to divorce. He finally agreed to leave at her insistence, but he kept visiting the boy.

She, assuming she would marry a more successful man who would take over as father, discouraged the visits. She pointed out that it upset the boy. He was excited before his dad showed up and sad when he left. Sometimes visits were missed because he was working out of state; sometimes he showed up late.

When he was away he would call, but she wouldn't bring their son to the telephone. She reminded her ex-husband that he was hurting the boy by interfering with his life and routine.

This was a time in our culture when men were often treated as second-class parents. The father didn't have much confidence and wanted what was best for the boy. He became discouraged and visited and called less and less, but he kept sending cards and gifts.

Everywhere he went he sent the boy souvenirs, balloons, postcards that squeaked, dippy birds, rock collections, and photographs. He did this until his death when his son was sixteen. He had not seen or talked with him since he was ten, because the boy and his mother had moved to another part of the country.

The son, now a man, would believe none of this new information about his father, because he hadn't received any of the things his father had sent. His mother had never given them to him. "I didn't want to upset him," she said. For some reason she had not thrown them away, she had kept them all. She agreed to bring in the boxes of old stuff from his father for our last meeting.

She arrived with three old boxes of cards, letters, and odds and ends—smashed Kewpie dolls, yo-yos, funny pencils, and hats. Her son cried as he sifted through everything. Then he refused to believe that his father had cared.

It took three months of counseling this man alone before he could accept that his father had loved him. Updating his perception of family didn't save his marriage, but it gave him a new sense of value and love.

You can alter your perception of your life experience with more information or with just the passing of time. Can you remember something terrible that turned out wonderful? Moving to a new place, dread-ing it, and finding out it was better than where you had lived? Losing a job and ending up with a better one?

Perspective changes, memories change, because they have a continuously evolving meaning. It often helps to search out the meaning of painful memories by recreating the scene.

Visualize a painful scene from the past until you can make it come alive. Then evaluate what happens. What are the people like? What is the emotional climate? What is happening? Who has the power? What is your response? What have you always believed about this scene? How do these beliefs affect your life now? Do you want to keep or revise these beliefs in any way? You are making the choices.

We are often told that time is a great healer. It heals because of what life experience teaches us about the motives of others. We find bits and pieces of ourselves in them or them in us. We react in similar ways and begin to understand why. Age makes some people more rigid and judgmental, but most of us mellow, understand, and expand our perspective.

Stop trying to change your parents, your fate, or your past. Check how many times you say "if only" with a sigh. Take a step into *your* present. Make a commitment to yourself: "I am in control of my perspective." How you see yourself is everything!

Like yourself now; be ten years ahead of your friends.

39. Women and Men

Your self-esteem (and thus your blues) is deeply connected to your sense of value not only as a person but also as a woman. We link love, satisfaction, and passion with masculine and feminine. None of us think of ourselves as generic beings.

We are caught now in a time of powerful redefinition. Almost everything has changed: the way we dress, our decisions about having children, our degree of independence, our concepts of lifework, our relationships with men, our very definition of happiness.

There are many who still feel the changes are merely political and can be reversed. In fact, the changes in men and women have little to do with politics, psychology, or philosophy. The shifts are economic. Cultural change is almost always survival-oriented. You need to know the history of the economic choices your culture has made. That history underlies your place, your sense of belonging, your feeling of womanhood. There are many books and theories on women and American culture so I will present only a brief sketch to provide a framework for your understanding.

Where We Have Been

For 98 percent of our history we human beings were hunters and gatherers with very limited technology. Our survival was based on our physical strength, speed, vision, and reproductive abilities. Men were more successful as hunters because of their speed and strength. Women were pregnant, usually from the onset of menses, and were either carrying, giving birth to, or nursing children. It is hard to chase antelope when you're pregnant or have an infant feeding at your breast.

This was a time when it made more sense to be the third wife of a Charles Atlas than the only wife of a Woody Allen. Ability to provide food was more important than sensitivity in a spouse. The successful woman was good at reproducing (many tribes had trouble maintaining their population, given the high maternal and infant death rates), had good eye–hand coordination for digging roots, catching small animals, producing crafts—all of which often made the difference between life and death.

Important ethics grew out of this survival balance. The ideal man knew that his masculinity was more important than his life. If anyone's going out on Main Street or into mortal combat with a boar, let it be the male. The ideal woman stayed close to a man when she was afraid and did what she was told to do.

Men and women still typically have different response patterns to danger. Men, regardless of a variety of civilizing influences, will feel the urge, when pushed, to fight. Women, knowing that men are physically stronger, are more likely to submit in hopes of stimulating protection. Our patterns of fear and our strategies for self-defense are centuries old.

As we shifted away from constant nomadism and began to establish small communities based on horticulture and eventually agriculture, private property was accumulated. With private property came interest in inheritance and in passing whatever we have to those who are most like us, our own children, people whose destiny we felt we had some control over. Codes of virginity, bride price, rape laws (originally property laws), seclusion or separation of women, and other sexual controls began to become established.

Past relationship differences still dominate our consciousness. Women always knew who their children were; men only knew what women told them. How do you control paternity if you are male? By controlling access to women by other males and women's access to any male other than you.

Shifts from agriculture to industry brought profound economic changes and changes in our values. The first factories required strength, and the workers were men. Families moved into urban centers, and men worked fourteen-hour days. Their children were asleep when they left for work and asleep when they came home from work. Men gradually lost the closeness to child rearing that had been such a part of their lives in an agricultural society. A philosophy developed to justify the new economy. Men never *gave up* their ties to their children, they lost them to economic change, change based on new technology.

The ideal male for most of our history was the strong, silent type. You needed a man who was unafraid, a stoic who didn't waste time talking. He was a doer, a "man's man." "Still waters run deep." "Tall and silent."

The ideal woman was a mother but a sort of pseudo Virgin Mary, a woman who reproduced but with no dangerous sexuality. The homemaker was submissive, faithful, hardworking, and willing to sacrifice everything for her family. The dangerous woman was the loose woman. She may have a few years of fun, but life would catch up with her. An independent woman could face a lifetime of a having a "bad reputation."

Despite what now seem like inequities, the system worked, we survived. Other economic and social organizations did not. Male strength and risk, for the most part, provided females and children with food, shelter, and protection. Women provided environment, process skills (food, clothing, gardening, gathering), and children.

When the two main determiners of survival, reproductive needs and production technology, changed, we changed as well. The reproductive mandate was once to have as many children as possible. You could win a prize at the county fair for having the most natural children of any family in the county. Now what do people say about you if you have twelve children? The average number of children per woman of child-bearing age has shifted downward every recent decade until it is now 1.5 children and still moving lower.

The corresponding drop in the maternal death rate and better health has contributed to women having a much longer life span. It has expanded from the late thirties in early history to around seventy eight today. Women are living much longer and having fewer children. The economy could not tolerate that many women not actively participating. Women's energy was bound to be directed into the external work force. We couldn't all crochet.

At the same time production shifted into communications and services, creative fields and high-tech. Men found themselves struggling with a massive redefinition of their role as technology removed the strength differential between the sexes. The forklift truck made almost as much difference to sex roles as contraceptives did.

Women have superior eye–hand coordination. After centuries of talking their way through life (because they couldn't arm wrestle and win) they also have excellent communication skills. We are used to providing service. Women's skills now fit the economic marketplace.

The stoical stud now finds himself referred to as "macho" and being told to learn sensitivity and develop a full range of emotions. His previous success strategies are becoming obsolete. A different worker, a different manager and a different lover are needed.

All these changes have left most of us unsure of what the ideal male or female is. We try to be everything, madonna, sex kitten, and successful businesswoman or stud, sensitive man, and highly competitive go-getter. Some women want to be just like men of the past. The confusion leaves us empty and frustrated. As Gloria Steinem has said, "We've become the men we once wanted to marry."

We're confused about what we now want in a partner. Women joke about having the sensitive man to work for and be with until about eight at night and then making a quick shift to the stud. One woman asked if she couldn't date the wild guys until she was thirty and then settle down with the other kind. Other women worry about becoming "displaced homemakers."

It is a lot easier to raise consciousness around equal pay and work opportunities than it is to change centuries of sexual fantasies and physical dominance. Some women still want to be thrown over the saddle and taken off into the sunset. At parties we may still throb to the arrogant man who looks through us rather than the sensitive man who admires our work. The blues originate in this place of intimate cultural conflict.

Heterosexual women question a life without the "right" man. It isn't just a nice man we can get along with; we want someone who will "light our fire" for thirty years. Lesbian women find their quest easier in some ways because they seem to understand each other better than we understand men. There's a good chance they get more help with the housework. The rest of us have created fantasies out of our culture and our family experience, and new expectations seem hard to live with.

Test yourself! List all the qualities you would want to have in a man you could love and live with. Imagine the two of you together every day for years. Order your criteria in terms of most important to least important. Do you know any man like this? Remember your list the next time you are out at a party deciding who you are attracted to. Here's a sample:

- honest
- sense of humor
- employed
- willing to talk
- physically attractive
- successful
- available
- believer in equal rights
- fair

- good parent
- creative

Tonight, when you get into bed, create a wonderful sexual fantasy of you with the ideal lover. What does he look like? What are the circumstances of your being together? How does he treat you? What are your sexual triggers? What does he do or say? Who is in control? Make a list of his qualities. Here's another highly individual list-yours will be different:

- handsome
- gently dominant
- married to you
- clean
- strong
- hairy
- experienced
- willing to talk
- creative
- sense of humor
- older
- well-built
- good dancer

Check your first list against your fantasy list. Do they have anything in common? Is your lover employed, and does he have a good sense of humor? Is he honest and fair? Does he have good values? Is he a good parent?

I spent my first thirty-three years longing for men much like my father, emotionally unavailable. Men who were big, uncommunicative, unfaithful, and disrespectful seemed the height of passion to me. I was afraid of them and desired them. My father was a very sexual man and a violent man. My sensible half tried to marry nice guys I would end up bored with, and my passionate, anxious half wanted dangerous men as lovers.

This split in my personality reached its height with a relationship with a man who was an exaggeration of all my fantasies. He was so powerful he could pick me up with one hand, just like Dad. He was unfaithful constantly, just as my father (in a little girl's fantasies) kept sleeping with my mother. Sometimes he didn't come home, just like Dad.

He would offer total love and passion, give me a diamond ring, and then invite a flight attendant to sit next to me at a public event and chat about their affair. I hung around for the thrills of this "perfect love" until something within me broke open and the pain was more than I could bear. I slipped into a deep depression, and when I hit bottom I knew that it was time to let go of men just like Dad.

A few months later I was at a friend's wedding when a man who was very much like my lover came up to ask me out. I said, "No thank you, I've been out with men like you before." He said, "You don't even know me!" I answered, "Yes, I do." I walked away from him and reviewed the list in my pocket of the men I could love who might love me. It wasn't sensitive to reject one man on the basis of a stereotype, but I knew by the thumping of my heart that I was in danger.

It took months to train myself to walk away from my old pattern of heart thumps and to spend time with men who had the qualities on my rational list. I had been through enough pain to understand the difference between passion generated out of anxiety and passion based on the attraction of shared values.

You need to know yourself well to be able to choose men who offer some balance between who you can live with and who turns you on. Riding off into the sunset over someone's saddle is not what it used to be. Once, it might have promised survival but not anymore.

Until you find some measure of peace as a woman in our culture it is difficult to build self-esteem or to resolve the question, What do I want? The confusion is everywhere: executive women, efficient, capable, but with quarter-inch bright red nails and stiletto heels. When we doubt our femininity we just cross our legs. We forget that thirty years ago red nail polish identified a loose woman. We don't note the conflict between a business woman's efficiency and the time it takes to maintain the nails.

Men now buy cowboy boots to wear with their three-piece suits. After a day of being a sensitive man, when doubt about their manhood starts to creep in, they just look at their feet and find reassurance. Women do it with business suits and long lacquered nails. Men and women are both confused and hungry to understand the conflicts we feel.

We are left with powerful differences between us because of our reproductive roles, our use of technology, the strength differential, and thousands of years of conditioning to other survival patterns. It's easier to love each other when we understand these differences. Understanding our history provides fertile ground for developing tolerance and compassion for ourselves and the men we love.

Where We Are Now

Some women miss the dependence we have lost, but most of us suspect it was always a mixed blessing. Dependence and protection had an abusive side. We once compared pickles and children; now we compare careers and children. Using the feminine charms that once enabled us to gain power with men is now considered unfair. It is harder now to know when you qualify as a successful woman. Can you live alone? How much do you have to do? The difficulty of choose between old and new requirements of "woman" has increased our stress. We try to do everything.

It is hard to discuss male gains because so many of them are subtle, emotional possibilities that one cannot put a price tag on. Men are building better friendships with both men and women. Men are reclaiming their children by spending more time with them and pursuing joint custody in divorce. Many men now feel confident in caring for tiny babies that they once were afraid they would drop. Men are told they can laugh and cry, although there is still ambivalence: women mistake kindness for weakness, and men fear being called "wimps." The qualities men are moving toward have been devalued by their long association with women.

Men have been given permission not to be lifetime meal tickets. They are taking better care of themselves. Their stress level is dropping, and 1986 marked the first year male life span increased at the same rate as female.

They no longer have to pretend, to conceal emotions, to fight over everything. One man told me that equal rights to him meant, "If there is a burglar in the house, my wife and I can take turns checking it out."

The losses are much clearer. Men have lost the sense that they are in control of their home and family. Dominance is now questioned instead of rewarded. Women demand that men communicate, that they help to build intimacy, that they make love in more sensitive ways.

Misunderstanding between us is one of the most constant sources of frustration and "the blues." It's hard to relate to someone who seems to think and feel differently than you do. It's like dealing with a foreign language. I remember translating a father's words for a teenage girl once:

He said: "I can't trust you. You dress like a cheap hustler, and you're nothing but trouble!"

She thought: "He doesn't understand me. He thinks I'm bad. He doesn't love me."

Translation

He really said: "I'm afraid for you because I love you so much and I don't seem to be able to control your life anymore. I'm afraid you'll be hurt. I need to be in control."

When she could hear his feelings and not his words, there was a chance for some reassurance and change.

Check your ability to translate what men are saying and doing to you and what you are saying and doing to them.

The differences described next may be stereotypes, but we all encounter them daily. The behavior and perceptions become so much a part of us that we don't even notice until we are confused, in conflict with someone, or depressed. We drive down the road unable to read the cultural signs that would let us know where the potholes and detours are.

Feelings. Women have a full range of emotions, and we carry them close to the surface. Our sensitivity, our intuitive abilities, were essential to survival. Being able to read your mate's moods in the cave—given his superior strength—was crucial. Finding ways to get along with your mother-in-law when living in an extended family was key to any kind of comfort. Women survived by being in touch with their emotions and everyone else's.

Men were taught the opposite. Their power was in stoicism, the ability to deny feeling. You don't want him shedding tears for an antelope that is about to be killed. If a woman needed protection she didn't want her protector saying he couldn't go out on Main Street right now because he was feeling blue. War required personalities with an ability to control emotions, including fear. Men needed physical strength. Women needed emotional skills. He may be telling you he loves you with his work, but you cannot hear.

Communication. Women seem to be able to talk about everything. They can sense intuitively when they are with someone they can tell everything to, usually another woman. They can tell virtual strangers about intimate details of their lives and laugh and enjoy the process. It is one of our most basic survival skills.

Many men were raised when talking was still considered feminine. It was once possible to "grunt" your way through marriage. A man might walk his daughter down the aisle on her wedding day with tears in his eyes because he had no idea who she was; they had never really talked. Men talked sports and politics but rarely emotions. Imagine a man in the trenches in World War I telling his buddies that he has low self-esteem and doesn't get along with his mother.

Men feel women are too nice in conversations and that that is misleading. Women will nod supportively when they disagree with what's being said. He thinks she is agreeing with him, but she is just being supportive of *him*, not what he is saying. Conflict results when he thinks she has changed her mind after agreeing with him only moments before. The misreading of conversational signals between men and women leads to a lot of problems.

My favorite misunderstanding is the attitude that when women ask a man for something they are nagging but when men ask for something they are just making a request. Women are afraid that when they want something they will sound bitchy or end up whining. We still choose passivity to avoid being assertive.

Power. Women's power is primarily verbal, manipulative, emotional, and moral. We can talk most men to death. It's 2:00 A.M. and you are talking with your lover. He wants to go to bed. You say, "We're not finished talking yet." We learned our verbal skills because of the incredible difference in physical strength. When we want something resolved, we talk.

We manipulate by using emotional strategies based on our intuitive knowledge of men. We can cry and seem defenseless, use sexual gamesmanship, children, or the community against them. Read some of the books on how to manipulate a man (like Marabel Morgan's), and you'll get an idea of how sneaky we can be.

My mother used to buy something and not tell my father. She would have a new washing machine installed in the basement and then wait for him to discover it. When he finally noticed, she would claim they had had it for months. Since she paid the bills, he would assume he had forgotten. Once she bought a fur coat and convinced him she had won it in a contest.

Moral power is exercised by women through guilt, gossip, ostracism, and control over children and sexual favors, whether its who gets into pep club in high school or games played within the family. Women's power is usually based in the home; women define personal morality.

Some women also have power through physical beauty or charm, the ability to "turn heads." Beauty is a property that others want, and it can lead to wealth, respect, privilege, and other sources of power.

Men are assumed to have power by the mere fact of being men. Women often must prove their power if it is in a traditionally male skill. Men exercise power through control, physical control over women or just the threat of it as their body tenses up. A smart woman recognizes every increment of tension shift in a conversation.

Most women are afraid of men, whether they will admit it or not. Many have been the victims of male physical power. Men can also intimidate by the language they use, by their willingness to swear or call names that traditional women freeze at, or by just refusing to talk at all.

Male power is primarily outside the home. Many see power as something you hold on to. If you have twenty power points and give five away, you only have fifteen left. Men find it hard to give power up to colleagues, spouses, girlfriends, or teenage sons.

Women think in terms of empowering other people. They assume if they share power there will be more for everyone, including them. Women give to get. It's a parenting model. You have to empower children so that they'll be able to take care of themselves. If you give to them when they are little, they will give back to you when they grow up.

Men are becoming willing to give up some power. What we underestimate is how difficult it is to give it up with no path to follow. When women demanded more power they gave speeches, wrote books, marched and protested. Women are generally nonviolent. Men have told me they are afraid of their violence if they get in touch with what using their power has cost them.

Some men have told me that when they confront their anger over the emotional limits of men's roles they want to use their old power styles. They feel overwhelming grief. They don't want to march, protest, or give speeches; they want to break things and physically change the balance. Their anger is much more dangerous than women's, and they have fewer patterns for channeling it into nonviolent resolutions.

Perspective. Men think in shorter time spans that women and see parts of systems better than they see the whole. They can invent something or set a policy and not feel responsible for its wider effects. They can operate their section of a project disconnected from other sections.

Women want to know everything that is going on. They think in twenty-year spans. Our perspective is geared to the length of childhood. We need to connect to the whole system, perhaps because of our experience living in caves with an extended family. We understand that a problem can spread and feuds last a lifetime unless everyone's feelings are considered.

Leadership. Based on our differing views of power and perspective, we lead in different ways. Men think in terms of control, women in terms of facilitation. Women are still afraid power and money will make them unattractive. We worry about being feminine so choose a sister or mother model. Men choose Dad. Dad ordered, Mom talked; Dad punished, Mom comforted.

Change. Women handle change more easily, perhaps because for so long they didn't have control over it. They were forced to be adaptable. If he said, "We're moving to Poughkeepsie," she said, "Fine, you go ahead and I'll stay here and sell the house, pack up, arrange the children's schooling, find a new house, move us in, and call you when dinner's on the table." This is an exaggeration, of course, but we prided ourselves on being able to make a home anywhere.

Men often see change in more threatening terms, because they have always had to bear the responsibility for the economic success of the move. If it didn't work or everyone ended up unhappy, Dad was at fault, because everyone else had just done what they were told. There is a lot of stress to being in control.

Risk. Men are better risk takers than women are. Perhaps they've had more experience (the hunger again)—or just less chance to avoid it. Sports, war, competition, business have provided circumstances in which being able to take risks is important.

Women have a background of seeking security. You don't attempt to jump the Grand Canyon on a motorcycle if you have small children to take care of. The security of children is a primary instinct for women. Our lack of physical strength and the traditional dominance of men has traditionally curtailed our risk-taking ability.

Conflict. Women are afraid of conflict because of our long history of being physically dominated. We will usually take a reactive posture, waiting for trouble rather than confronting it. Men will walk away from a bad relationship; we will hold on. When we disagree with someone and cannot resolve it, we decide that person is awful and we never want to see them again. We either worry a conflict to death or turn it into a personal lifelong dislike.

Men, perhaps because they have spent more time learning to work on teams, handle conflict better. They know when to stop hassling. They rarely personalize conflict, and they continue working with or seeing someone they have had a fight with. Their confidence comes from a sense that they can protect themselves.

Women's fear of conflict goes very deep. We know that men are stronger than we are even when they are the same size. If a man is threatened his body will tense up and he has the idea if no weapon is involved that he could land a punch or outrun the attacker.

Women, unless we are trained in self-defense, automatically submit to protect ourselves and our children. When we are threatened we cry. We do a "belly up" response in hopes that it will trigger the protector role in the male. If we are nice, we shouldn't get hurt.

A friend of mine was in her apartment alone, except for her little boy. An armed robber broke in. He was wearing a mask. He pointed the gun at her and asked for money. She told him she didn't have any and when he threatened to shoot she dropped to her knees. It was an uncontrollable response. She said to him, "I'm a mother." It popped out of her head with no thought. Three thousand years of history overcame any other assertive statement. He took what he could find of value, and she was not physically hurt.

Love. Men see love the way they see money. There is only so much to go around. If they give it away they will have less. If they have to share it with someone, they will have less. Before some of the changes in parenting many men viewed children as competition for their wife's affection. A new baby meant the man got less love, time, and attention.

Love also leads to increased responsibility for men. Men want to be free to wander and love whom they will (maybe we all do) and still have the familial love that sustains the responsible man. Men sometimes see love as limiting their lives.

Women usually see love as expanding. Nurturance is our skill. We want to take care of everyone. We overflow with love for the whole family when a new baby arrives. We literally cannot feel the loss of love the male fears. Love means we will be taken care of, secure.

Self-esteem. Both men and women hurt inside from blows to their self-worth as children. I'm sure we are equally vulnerable, but men seem to need less approval than women. They find it easier to ignore criticism, and they often overestimate their accomplishments.

Women devalue their achievements. They always think they should be doing more. We have a much greater need for approval. We care too much about the opinion of others—an old survival tool, a woman will give in to be liked. We worry much more about appearance, cleanliness, and criticism. We are more likely to read slights into the behavior of others and to keep score of our social position.

God. All these differences seem to be summarized in the different ways men and women see religion. Many men see the church as a hierarchy with rules and ritual. Once something has been agreed on, that is truth. The way to get to heaven is to obey the rules and make sure everyone else does. That is one of the reasons the pope gets so upset when one of his archbishops develops a personal relationship with God. One is supposed to go through channels.

Women think they *are* God. They think they will go to heaven if their hearts are full of good feelings. When they have opened up to God and become good people, the Spirit will enter them. They cannot imagine any reason why they shouldn't serve at the altar or should sit behind a curtain when the connection is love. They feel free to talk to God whenever they want.

Where We Are Going

We are trying to pull all of this together. Old and new, all the old traditions and feelings are melded into all the new options and possibilities. It is hard.

We hurt ourselves in so many ways. One of the deepest is our old sexual fantasies. We dream of men who hurt us or seduce us. Our sexual triggers are often not tied to equalitarian fantasies. Along with consciousness raising about comparable worth and equal rights we need groups to help us clear up destructive sexual images in our own minds. Practice within your own mind sexual excitement connected to respect, commitment, and intimacy. Perhaps women can learn to create their own sexual dreams instead of being drawn to the images of Victorian pornography.

Women are just as ambivalent about independence. We often don't plan our lifework. Many high school seniors still just say they'll get married and let their husbands work. They don't see a need to have an independent source of income. They wait to be chosen (like Cinderella) rather than taking responsibility for their own personal development.

Some women don't connect the idea of a job with a career; they separate personal goals from career goals. They usually believe in the justice of the economic system: "If I am a good person, I will be treated fairly." They are less likely to look ahead and plan for personal gain. They are more likely to wait for a problem to develop and then work on solving it.

Women sometimes wonder if they will have to work to earn a living. Men assume that they will have to work their entire lives. Women who prefer to work within the home build their security on the relationship with and the health of their spouse. The name "displaced homemaker" labels those women who through divorce or a spouse's death ended up unable to support themselves or their children.

Balancing independence, personal security, and the care of children may be the biggest unresolved issue. The most important thing we do in life is take care of the next generation. Women cannot compromise on the care of children while waiting for men to share more equally.

How we care for children will ultimately determine the quality of our own life. Two parents sharing the support of a child, each of us willing to help those who bear children, is crucial to our future. Yet, in our society we are still ambivalent. Perhaps our greatest hypocrisy as a culture is the gap between the way we talk about children and the way we actually care for them. The conflict is very hard on women. Children are at the heart of what a woman is. We cannot feel fully alive and at peace when children are hurting anywhere.

The differences between men and women are culturally difficult to understand for us as individuals. They operate deep in our history and emotions. Our sense of "woman" is based on all the women who have gone before and set the model: the women who have loved us, taught us, the women men have loved and lived with.

"Woman," in this part of the twentieth century, is a mixture of mind and heart. We're working with logic (equal pay) and struggling with emotional acceptance. We are beginning to know where we've been and where we are. It is still a struggle to understand and to look ahead.

The old messages may run through your head as you set your life's direction:

"I don't deserve it" (I have no value).
"It will upset someone" (who might hurt me).
"I don't have a choice" (I have no power or skill).
"It's too late" (after twenty-one, it's all downhill).
"I'll just wait for someone" (Cinderella).
"I'll sacrifice" ("Stand By Your Man").
"I'm not able to do it" (women are incompetent).
"I'll make things better" (I can smooth things over).

We feel these things inside, along with many positive aspects of our history. Sometimes we feel untrue to our sense of what a woman is when we let go of the old ways. Your mother may challenge you as she sees you doing what she always wanted to do.

Some men and some religions will try to get you to go backward—until you become a caricature like Tammy Faye Bakker. With a longer life span, better health, technical support in homemaking, and unlimited opportunities, none of us should give our lives to makeup and shopping. There is a reason Tammy Faye seems to be crying all the time.

Men are hurting too. There are still many men who feel under siege. They don't like the changes, and they refuse to give up their dominance and control. Men who score high on tests measuring hostility toward women tend to have traditional sex-role beliefs. They believe the husband should dominate in public and in private.

Men are afraid that they won't be able to get jobs, and their identity is much more closely tied to what work they do and how much they earn than is a woman's. They also fear a loss of male bonding as women enter where men once dominated (in mines, press rooms in printing plants, police precincts, fire stations, telephone line shacks). If a woman can do it, then the men who do it are no longer special.

The gains for men through the changes in sex roles seem far more subtle and hard to evaluate than the losses. The old male survival roles (Rambo, for example) have cost men tremendously in terms of their psychological development. They know it and they feel it. Many men envy women their ability to love, to foster intimacy, to communicate, to build friendships. Some men do not know how to show love to women when they don't any longer seem to need their earning power, their money, their companionship, or their ability to take the lids off jars. They sense our ambivalence.

Perhaps the greatest loss is their view of themselves, a lost ideal. The hero, the defender and provider, now is called a batterer, a molester, an abuser, a warmonger. The rules and perceptions have changed, and many men are carrying the sins of their fathers. Once-acceptable behavior has become criminal.

I participated in the trial of an engineer who had molested little girls. The evidence was overwhelming, but many of his colleagues appeared in court as character witnesses. I asked one why he would testify when he knew the man was guilty. He told me, with tears in his eyes, that if this man could hurt children, a man who was so much like him, then what did that say about him? It is very painful to be an aware man and find your sex blamed for everything from the destruction of the environment to the rape and murder of women and children.

We are working on the possibility of each individual developing the best qualities of both sexes. We each want to become a full person not just fill a role. We want to be more direct and honest with each other instead of indirect and manipulative. It is difficult for men and women to redefine something as close to the core as masculinity and femininity. It will take many more decades.

Meanwhile one way we can avoid the blues is by showing tolerance for our shared history and sense of maleness or femaleness. There is no insidious plot to keep the war between the sexes going. Adapting to new technology, new environments, a new reproductive perspective, and all other new possibilities will take time. We need to be patient and compassionate with our own confusion and frustration and offer the same love to men. There must be more praise and reward for sensitive men and more willingness to support other women.

"Confused" is probably the best word for where we are, and confusion brings the blues. We are trying to be all things to all people. We want to be traditional women (baking bread, nurturing, being soft) *and* all the new things that seem available. It is possible to find a balance between the best of the woman from the past and the best of the future.

We have a unique perspective and a unique potential. Our emotional values provide sources of strength and a basis for a more aware form of living.

Being a satisfied woman requires remaining connected to your heritage and transforming it into a better life. But we are still afraid. Many women don't really believe they can take care of themselves. Underlying all our feelings about being a woman, and the depression we sometimes feel, is fear for our safety. It runs very deep because of the physical (rape, battering, molestation, other abuse) and cultural (discrimination, humiliation) patterns we are connected to. We may never fully realize how afraid we are.

It takes a lot of courage to decide, now, to step outside your culture and redefine "woman." The alternative is to repress your unique value and face depression. Alene Moris has expressed it well:

The real task for woman today is to close her ears to all the outside clamoring and simply take responsibility for the lonely pilgrimage called "growing up." Coming to terms with the fact that each of us is profoundly alone and individually responsible to the Creator is a scary but totally exhilarating experience that should be wooed, not avoided. Realizing that nobody else can make us happy, we can then set about the business of doing those things which can lead to the satisfactions of maturity.

Much of the joy of life for us now is reaching our full potential. That means being fully aware of the world we live in. After centuries of limits women in America can chart their own destiny and shake off the "security blues." It's hard, but wonderful, to own your life and your own possibilities.

Move beyond your history.

40. Women of High Potential*

Though it would not seem so, being a woman of high potential can be a source of the blues. If you are such a woman, you must go one more step for self-value. Your awareness and sensitivity will lead you to face more than your share of pain, but you will perhaps feel more joy as well. You are a woman who knows. Whether through intelligence, energy, or sensitivity you see and feel more than many others. It is hard to pretend you are less than you are.

Being a woman complicates your heightened awareness. You can feel, see, and think of many possibilities, yet you live in a culture that will attempt to screen your vision and limit you. The ambivalence, rejection, and confusion you feel growing up as a talented woman are difficult and may deeply affect your sense of self-esteem.

Ask yourself these questions:

"Are you a woman with an extremely active mind who can retain, comprehend, and process large amounts of information?"

"Do you have high expectations of yourself and others?"

"Have you always felt a little different or special?"

"Have you felt frustrated at limits imposed on you by others, or by your society?"

"Do you sense men are sometimes intimidated by you?"

"Are your thoughts and philosophies original?"

"Do you synthesize events and thoughts into simpler forms that you can share with others?"

"Do you sometimes wonder if your feelings run deeper than those of others?"

If you answer yes to any of these questions, then you are a woman of high potential. You may worry that you are just egotistical or even pretentious. You are not.

*This title is taken from a conference title "Women of High Potential: Enhancing the Joys and Meeting the Challenges," held at the University of Washington in September of 1986. Some of the thoughts in this section were generated by the Board of Directors of the conference, especially the first three of the list of questions on this page.

Others might use the word *gifted*, and maybe you were a gifted child. "Gifted," however, is not broad enough to contain the level of emotion, creativity, and awareness that are included in this definition of high potential.

The word "potential" is itself ambivalent. When is potential reality? If you had unique potential as a child, what are the limits? When have you reached it? If you are now forty, have you lived up to your high potential? Is it possible at some point in your life to say, "I am no longer a woman of high potential, I am living up to the promise within me"?

As Kathleen Noble has written, women like this need to feel challenged, to have opportunities to develop their vision. They are very curious, have many interests, and are persistent and goal-oriented. They can do many things and consequently have a hard time deciding what to do with their lives.

When they do not feel that they have lived up to their awareness, when they are not satisfied, they feel failure. They have not used the gift; somehow the promise has not been kept. There is the deep, inner sadness of a path not taken. The pain is in the awareness of potential, the gift, the possibilities that are then blocked because the ability to value self is blocked.

Such women must cope in a culture that is uncomfortable with their power. People can sense it within you. They may respond with competitiveness. Men who love you may leave because of the power they sense in you.

There are many more barriers set up in our culture for bright women than for bright men. Barriers are present at birth, in childhood, in adulthood, and within yourself. You need to know what makes you hesitate to feel and be all that you are.

Culture

Our culture defines much of our potential at birth. Even with all the consciousness raising around male and female options we are still limited today. There is the possibility of more losses (children, home-making, femininity, marriage, friends, sexuality, role) if you are an aware woman. Marriage may be difficult or not possible because you may not be willing to compromise enough. It will be difficult to find a man who will love you and stay with you if you are all you feel you can be. Some women can step outside the expectations of their culture and find a place. But it is very difficult.

Women throughout history have redefined "woman" (Indira Ghandi, Eleanor Roosevelt, Madame Curie, Sojourner Truth, Margaret Thatcher, Elizabeth Barrett Browning, Harriet Tubman, Barbara Jordan,

Joan Benoit, Amelia Earhart, Emily Dickinson, Althea Gibson, Yoko Ono, Golda Meir, Katherine Hepburn), but it is not easy and always painful. There is always ambivalence.

My father told me when I was little that there was a machine that you could put little girls in and they would come out the other end as boys. I knew that it was better to be a boy, but I held on to my femaleness. It was very hard; I had intense emotions. Finally, after months of soul-searching I went to him and said I was ready to be put in the machine. I remember steeling myself and clenching my teeth before I went in to make my announcement. He then told me that there was no machine. I cried for days, betrayed.

The ability to understand what has happened to you if you are a woman of high potential, what is now happening, and its cultural base makes life easier. You can observe and not feel victimized. You can understand why you are alone.

Childhood

Awareness and sensitivity when you are too young to protect yourself can be painful. If you use your earliest intuition and intelligence to adapt to difficult family circumstances or to being a girl, you may lose your true self in the process. You remain aware of the potential within you but unable to motivate the core of your being to act.

You learn the art of not feeling, because feelings are so intense for you.

You create a false self that accommodates to your environment.

You find it difficult to stand alone.

You develop intellectually but lack an authentic emotional life.

Adulthood

You carry through the adaptions learned in childhood, but the awareness tugs at you. Many women find themselves involved in deviant and destructive behavior in an effort to shake loose the barriers. They feel everything intensely but cannot sort out their motivations. They cannot see value in themselves, so they try desperately to connect to those who seem to have answers or a strong sense of self. They make grave errors in judgement when choosing lovers and friends.

In order to survive some bury themselves in work or relationships or drop out of life. They show up as workaholics, perfectionists, or married martyrs, or they live on the fringe. They suffer high levels of burnout, compromise their emotions and their sexuality, and sink into depression.

Many women of high potential work through their depression and reclaim the loss of self in childhood. Others do not; the risks seem too great. The barriers remain.

What You Can Do

Accept yourself. Give yourself credit for who and what you are. Smile because you have survived. You still know. You can still feel. Your awareness and intelligence are within you. You can do your homework and reconnect. You may need help. It will hurt. But, for you, anything is possible.

Face reality. The world is not a just place. You will rarely, if ever, find unconditional love or approval. If you do, it may make you uncomfortable. You must dig into your own past, understand female history, and accept the difficulties and rewards of being who you are. Read books on women in American culture, and gather around you like-minded women. As you get older you will grow stronger, more authentic, and able to fulfill your possibilities.

Understand competition. It will be a continuing part of your life. Others will compare themselves to you and sometimes attempt to sabotage you. The temptation is to back down and be less than you are. Try instead to let others succeed with you; get them attention; learn the way systems operate; and compete only with your own standards, not someone else.

Accept your ambivalence. You will have days and nights when you want to be less than you are. You would like to try and "pass" as someone who fits in. You will think about being more dependent, more submissive. You do not have a choice. You are what you are, everyone will sense it so you might as well go with it. There is no passion in being someone else.

Expect envy. It is a lot like competition, but it will scare you more. Whether it is competition among women for cheerleader, marriage, or a promotion, you will feel the hatred of women who do not value themselves. There is nothing you can do except lower your profile when around them and provide opportunities for them to shine. It is also rational to stay away from people who give you feelings of emotional danger. Trust your intuition.

Expect to lose friends. You will find yourself a loner. You have a rich inner life and can survive alone. There will be close friends, but you will not fit in easily with an ongoing social group. They won't interest you, and they will sense it.

Let go of a little control. You will want control over everything to make up for the lack of control you felt as a child. The need will overwhelm you. It will show up as perfectionism, workaholism, or giving up and being totally out of control. You are an adult now. You are safe. You can take care of yourself. It's okay to be aware.

Understand the pain. You feel things very deeply, and there will be times of despair and depression. You must remember the price of awareness and carry around a big mental stick to beat the shadows off you. It is hard to know and feel what you do as early as you felt and knew it. Remember the gift, the increased joy.

Refuse the loss of femininity. Though there have always been women like you, they have not been celebrated for their beauty (even when they were beautiful) or their womanliness. The abilities you possess will always cause others to view your sexuality with ambivalence. They will sense more danger than submission.

You will often wonder about your own femininity and consider touches of lace and perfume to restore your balance. Surround yourself with pink if you want, whatever helps you knit the traditional definitions of woman with what you are.

The description of women of high potential and the problems they face may leave you more than ambivalent. Remember, it is not just frustration and pain, it is also the potential for incredible depth and beauty in life. The catch is that you have to decide; no one else can do it for you. You have to take all your power of mind and heart and beam it into your own future.

Women move forward by going deeper.

Part Three:

SOURCES OF PASSION—
STRATEGIES FOR THE FUTURE

Good survival strategies make life less unpredictable. Understanding of self gives us a strong foundation and deepens our experience. What we then want, as soon as our strength and self-esteem returns, is passion. We want to feel alive, electric, satisfied. We want to have it all. That's what Part Three is about.

Humor is the first step, the daily ability to see and feel the comedy inherent in our lives and desires. When you understand and participate in life with humor, your mind and body are safe enough to consider bliss. The section on bliss gives you ways to tap into the feeling of joy, the idea that you can decide, most of the time, to have it all.

You knew we couldn't leap directly into passion, it's too intense. It follows the safety derived from a perspective on life's ups and downs and an awareness that we can choose bliss. We create the high. Lifetime, twenty-four hours a day, passion is available. The key is the intensity of life you are willing to allow yourself and your ability to tap into your own life force. Take a deep breath, open your heart and mind. Roll over in the current you feel within you. Once you have been willing to move downward through your experience you will then find yourself drawn upward by the passion that is within you, always waiting.

41. Keeping Your Sense of Humor

If you could choose only two qualities to get you through life, the first would be self-esteem and the second a great sense of humor. If you cannot laugh at the absurdities that surround us, you'll never make it. You won't be open to passion.

Women are sometimes ambivalent about humor. There was a time when full-bodied laughter wasn't feminine. We were reduced to titters and giggles. Often women were the butt of jokes, so it became hard to laugh at what were really verbal assaults. Now we have our humor back, even if sometimes it's gallows humor.

The Soviet human rights activist Anatoly Shcharansky, when he was finally released from prison, said his sense of humor was a powerful weapon in dealing with the horrible conditions he was kept under. "Without humor, I would have lost. I would have failed," he said.

Norman Cousins, in his *Anatomy of an Illness*, claims that humor saved his life. He watched old Marx Brothers movies from his hospital bed. Cousins maintains that humor controls pain and speeds healing in four ways: by distracting attention, by reducing tension, by changing expectations, and by increasing the production of endorphins, the body's natural painkillers.

Humor helps us connect to life and each other. Laughter shortens the distance between people. It's a chance to drop your tension, your anger, your stress. It renews energy, builds acceptance when we meet new people, and helps us trust each other.

There is a close relationship between humor and creativity. They both require imagination. In children there is a measurable correlation between intelligence and sense of humor. Smart people laugh.

You Can Measure Wisdom by the Drop in Ill Temper

A friend of mine used humor to survive her mastectomy. She was a young woman, an actress, and unmarried. The loss of a breast and the threat of cancer were deep hurts. I was waiting for her outside the recovery area when they wheeled her by on the way to her room.

I leaned over to see how she was. She was groggy still. I asked her, "How are you feeling?" She answered, "All I have now is 'idge.'" "What do you mean by 'idge'?" I questioned. "They took the 'cleve'," she replied. She had spent her time in the recovery room cooking up a joke for the rest of us.

Humor is laughing at yourself or with others. It is based on caring and empathy, a sense of our foibles. It is supportive joking that invites others to laugh and be part of the fun. It brings people closer and leads to a positive exchange of quips.

Making fun of others is not humor; it is usually a veiled attack. You may call it kidding or teasing, but it is based on a desire to dominate. This kind of exchange destroys confidence and embarrasses people through put-downs. I've written about one particular form in the section on criticism.

Negative comments, disguised as jokes, usually exclude someone (minorities, women, religious groups, for example), and the person who's the butt may not have a choice. He or she ends up the victim of the comment whether they want to be or not. Sarcasm often abuses, offends, and divides people and then the victimizer says, "Can't you take a joke?"

Nervous laughter is the feeling of not knowing what to do. You find it difficult to genuinely be present in life, even a conversation, so you just make noises at random. It's a cover for taking yourself so seriously that you cannot see a light side to anything. You may laugh at others' mistakes, even if they have hurt themselves, because you literally don't know what else to do.

When we are not at peace with ourselves it is difficult to empathize with another or joke about the absurdity of our choices. Try to create safety for yourself and others. Then you will understand that we're all in this together and genuine laughter helps.

What You Can Do

There are now specialists to teach us to laugh. It's easier if you're born into a family that views life with humor, but it's never too late to learn. The important first step is to decide that you want to be able to laugh more. If you find yourself saying, "Wait, there are things to be serious about," then you're in trouble. Yes there will always be things in our lives to be serious about—many more than we want or need. There is very little danger of laughing too much. Most of us let the opportunities for laughing pass us by. We worry too much about what is appropriate.

Relax, stretch out the tension before you try to stretch your sense of humor. Feeling comfortable makes it easier to see the humor around you. Start a collection of happy and humorous moments. They happen in every life if you can notice them. Sometimes they start out sad and a month later are hilarious. Can you recall any?

Get your friends to share their stories with you and borrow them. We all use each other's stories and jokes.

The next time something awful happens to you, see if you can find the humor, even if it's gallows humor. You rear-end someone on the freeway. After you've traded information and are getting ready to drive away, tell yourself that God cares so much about you she's sent this special message to slow you down. Relax before you pull back into the fast lane.

Clip funny stories out of newspapers and magazines until you perk up. Read the comics, joke books (even dumb ones), until you find something that tickles you. Let your friends pun around you. Go to hear comedians.

Adopt an attitude that lets you play. It's okay to be silly some of the time. You don't have to keep a tight hold on everything.

Laugh at yourself as much as possible—not with derision but with understanding of your humanity. At the end of a tough day find a humorous view, a way of seeing the absurdity of what we do to ourselves.

Give others the opportunity to laugh whenever possible, even if it's about you. They can laugh with you, not at you. Share the silly mistakes you make, and exorcize them with a giggle.

Watch out for people without a sense of humor. Stay away from them if you can. Seek out people who are funny, whose spirit you admire. It's catching.

Write something funny for your grave stone:

"I told you I was sick."

"Don't forget, I'm still your mother and I know what you're doing."

"This is what I expected, but not so soon."

Don't squelch other people's humor even if it's terrible. It's okay to boo.

Don't worry that you may not be serious enough.

Never say, "Wipe that smile off your face."

Try to take life easy; there will be many things to be serious about.

"Angels can fly because they take themselves lightly."

—*Jean Cocteau*

42. A Little More Bliss, Please

There is still something missing. You are not sure what, but you have the feeling that there is more to life. You are happy you can laugh, but you don't have it all. "I have a nice house, a nice husband, a good job; the kids are okay, and I'm reasonably attractive. I have it all by the usual measures. Why do I feel so dissatisfied?"

The issue may not be having it all by the usual measures. The issue is to have it all by the unique measures that resonate within you. You need to use your values, rather than those of the public, the media, or the marketplace. Chances are, you don't even know what "having it all" really means for you. You have had neither the time nor the inclination to set out a set of values and priorities that fit you.

Who do you know or who have you heard about that has it all? Make a list.

Would you trade places with any of them? How picky are you? Would you just choose certain parts of their bodies or their lives but refuse to trade straight across? Do you find parts of your own life compare favorably?

It was easier to find models when we had fewer options. When we knew less about life we imagined that some people "have it made," and we envied them. Now we put value on our own individuality.

List out what *you* would have if you had it all.

What would you like to overhear people saying about you? Quick, they're talking about you just around the corner.

What do you want? Write down the first three things that come to mind.

What is in the way? What are the barriers?

What is truly important to you?

The hardest part of getting the feeling that you have it all is knowing what you really want. Put some energy into finding out.

Spend time paying attention to what resonates within you. Stay flexible, because what you want will change over a year and over a lifetime. Life is a process of constant stretching and reevaluating.

Find your balance; clarify your values; put enough bliss into your life; and reach out for passion.

Having it all includes bliss. Some people are afraid of the term, it seems a little too soft for them. They are not sure what it means. Bliss hits are the little oohs that shiver in you when certain things happen. They are short, a wave of pleasure, a sudden awareness of joy. They wash over you in unexpected moments.

Most of us would describe a part of happiness as the increasing of these moments of joy. Some of us consciously put them in our life but forget to do it often enough. Some of us think that they should be surprises, things that just happen. I'm a fan of building as much bliss into your life as you want.

What You Can Do

It is easy to do if you know what gives you that kind of thrill. Make a list of what turns you on. Include only things you don't need another person for. If you get stuck before you've listed twenty, then think back to when you were ten. A lot of the best bliss hits were developed in our childhood, and we've lost track of them. Write down all those little things that give you a thrill, a tingle, or a feeling of peace or happiness. Here's my list:

Music. Mozart or Merle Haggard. You can always change a mood by adding music. You can wait for your spouse or roommate to come home so you can tell someone what a rough day you had, or you can put on music and dance.

Water. I was raised around irrigation ditches. Just putting my hands in water feels good. I've dug ponds in my backyard to stand in, dabble in, or lie next to. You can also sit in a tub or create a fountain so you can hear the sound.

Growing things. It's an optimistic act: chickens, plants, fish, dogs, cats, worms, mold, anything with life in it.

Flowers. Why not buy one for myself? Tulips in February are luxurious and wonderful!

Smells. Put herbs or lemon oil into steaming water. Buy potpourri, or make your own. Burn scented candles. Buy perfume. Anything that smells good to me is a turn on.

Letting go. Remember the "blobette" from the stress section? Let it all hang out.

Dreaming. Imagine other possibilities, new gardens, new books, new places.

Travel. Go anywhere fifty miles from home. I love peeking into other cultures, lives, and designs. Travelling further becomes a passion.

Hotel rooms. I shut the door behind me, check out room service, my own bathroom, a television, and flop on the bed.

Exotic catalogs. Review the wonders of the world over tea.

Bits of elegance. Who wants furs or jewels when you can have big linen napkins? I was raised when your mother would buy three hundred tiny paper napkins for twenty-seven cents.

Gray days. You can wrap them around you like comforters and become a philosopher.

Solitude. Listen to be quiet within.

Touching. Massage, facials, hugs, and snuggles are all touching. Cats and dogs are great, but stuffed animals do work. I have, after great resistance bought the *Wind in the Willows* crowd (Toad of Toad Hall, Ratty, Mr. Mole, and Badger). I have occasional naps on a couch where they gather.

Chats. Have little conversations with strangers with no purpose except to connect.

Champagne. I bought a recorker so I can enjoy a bottle over an entire week and not think it's a waste to open it just for me.

The Market. In Seattle we have a wonderful public market full of life, fish, arts, and vegetables. Twenty minutes there restores me even on a stressed day.

Dragonflies. When I was a little girl, one summer we spent two weeks in a cabin at Newman Lake outside of Spokane. I would float on my back in the water feeling free and weightless. Iridescent blue dragonflies would land on me, and I was thrilled.

The year after we dug the pond I was lying next to it and another blue dragonfly landed on me. I hadn't seen one in many years. I knew it had flown to me all the way from Newman Lake. I felt a powerful thrill; it ran through my body like an orgasm. I ran into the house and told my husband what had happened. He looked at me, smiled, and said, "Jennifer, you are so easy to please." Easy to thrill? You bet. If you're not easy to thrill, it doesn't happen often enough.

Here are some things my friends added to the list:

- herb teas
- comfortable shoes
- Irish music
- gravel roads
- chocolate
- thunderstorms
- funny cards
- calls from friends
- sushi
- Earl Grey tea
- yellow roses
- the smell of cottonwoods
- fresh tortillas
- putting up my feet
- movies
- children's choirs
- cats
- drives in the country
- "Battle Hymn of the Republic"

How easily available are these things to you? How many of them depend upon someone else making a decision? How many of them depend only upon your deciding that you deserve them? Get out your calendar, and reserve some times for you to have the experiences or do the things on your list that give thrill you. Make a sign for your door, mirror, or dashboard that reminds you that you have the choice to be "up" or not.

Now that the connection with yourself is stronger and you are aware of your own tingle, start looking at the other parts of passion: community, world, and Spirit.

What are the things in your community that give you the same feeling? How in control of these are you?

- working with children
- hugging strangers
- connecting people to resources
- picking up litter (a real self-righteous thrill)
- school pageants
- singing with others (whether "The Battle Hymn of the Republic" or Christmas carols)
- cheering on runners in a marathon

Once you have mastered personal balance, happiness, a sense of your own worth, bliss, and a clear set of values, passion is next.

Remember

Don't assume other people can provide it all if you can just get them to. They may want to, but they will always define bliss in their way and by their values, and it will never feel quite right.

Don't count on luck, magic, the lottery, or something to drop from heaven. We ourselves create bliss.

Let go of measuring it all by the yardstick of another person. It can only be measured within you by your connections and the carrying through of your own values.

Let go of wanting things that are clearly not within anyone's power.

There is no love that rewards with more consistency than the love one has for the world.

43. Sources of Passion

Passion requires many of the themes that recur throughout this book: bliss, humor, self, community, spirit. As we go deeper the feelings intensify, the language changes. The shift now is all the way to the hunger we feel for passion. We think we know what it is; we want it deep in our bones; but there is ambivalence. Passion takes us to the limits of our knowledge and intuition.

There are many definitions of passion. The only one that counts is yours. What turns you on? What makes you tingle, thrill? What leads to heavy breathing for you? Your passion is extraordinarily powerful because it is unique.

> No one chooses to
> possess the whole
> world if he has first
> to become someone
> else.—Aristotle

Passion is a universal life force. You can breathe it in on cool nights and bright mornings. You can feel it flowing through your body as a ripple of remembered pleasure.

Passion is that wild, thrilled sense of being rewarded beyond all expectation, beyond deserving.

It is a sensation described as a chill, shudder, tingling, or tickling, often accompanied by goosebumps, a lump in the throat, or weeping.

Passion is energy, subtle, varied, and as pure as the life moving through you.

Passion requires sustained attention. It is the secret of self-discipline. To achieve its intensity, you must sacrifice scope. That is hard for those who skate on the surface wanting "it all."

NOW IT'S YOUR TURN (close your eyes, take a deep breath, imagine): What does passion feel like for me?

Find out what turns you on. Men often have access to a broad range of passions because of their longer tenure in the complete world. Women usually think of passion in relation to men or to another person who is a love object. We are less likely than men to see passion within ourselves. Women over thirty five know you don't get passion from men. Many women under thirty-five think you do. Now, there are thrills and wonderful sensations available in loving and making love with men but not lifetime, twenty-four-hour-a-day passion. That comes from your relationship to yourself, your world, your community, and to the Spirit, however you define it.

The basic sources of passion have not changed much over the centuries. The difficulty has always been the ability to tap into them intensely. Some people seem able to from birth, and others learn over time. For most of us the important element is the choice of passions. They must resonate within.

What all these have in common is commitment, time spent, faith, intimacy, understanding. Passion emanates from our connections to life and the intensity we are willing to give them.

Try to slow down a little as you read the list that follows, and allow your memory to tap into ones that may have touched you.

Environment

Whether it is scenery that moves you by its beauty or grandeur, your own garden, or the intimacy of the botanist, there is passion outside our doors. There are those who experience tiny orgasms when climbing in the Himalayas or holding a dahlia on a gray morning. Japanese gardens, English gardens, the wilderness, oceans, dragonflies, sunrises—the possibilities are endless.

Science

Science has the lure of intimacy. Seeking information and ultimately understanding can ripple through the levels of your mind and overflow into your body. When two ideas come together in your brain and you break through to new understanding, it is an orgasm. That's why people study late at night in attics of universities. They are hungry for the thrill that is hidden in the connections between their unique thoughts and those of others. The opportunities for testing and stretching are endless.

Travel

Knowing and remembering the world—the feel, the smell, the climate, the sound of all the possibilities for life—is passion again. A feast for the senses, a challenge for the mind, character and heart, that's what travel is. There is passion in a casual drive through small towns or an adventure in the Amazon. It is the thrill of connecting to the planet.

Wait a minute! I want sexual passion, real orgasms, not all these alternatives!

Many women think of passion in only a direct sexual sense even when life experience provides only rare moments. We cling to the early romantic notion of moments of pure passion with the one and only love: *Cinderella, Romeo and Juliet,* novels that end with the first major clinch, lots of anticipation and minimal payoff, a painful illusion. Stop and think how much actual passion (versus anticipation) you've ever got from a relationship. It's wonderful when it's available. Enjoy, pursue; but remember all the other sources of passion, or you may feel that somehow you didn't get what you wanted or thought was possible.

Relationships

Knowing, and being known, over a lifetime is a source of passion: friends, children, colleagues, relatives, people we share our history with. It is possible to build all the elements of passion—intensity, understanding, faith, intimacy, love, commitment, time—in a friendship.

Music

The deeper you hear, the more notes in your memory, the stronger the passion. The ability to hear the oboe, the cello, the French horn is passion. Music moves us, whether it's classical or country and western. I have cried with joy listening to Mozart and Bach, been thrilled by the Beatles, and felt the pure sexuality of Ernest Tubb singing "Waltz Across Texas." You know the music that touches you deeply, why isn't it playing?

Animals

Raising animals has some of the same thrills as raising children, but it's a lot easier. If you were raised on a farm or you're in love with a standard poodle you know of these passions. Koi, rabbits, horses, birds, cats—the possibilities are endless. It's the chance to participate in another life in an intimate fashion. There is unique pleasure in finding animals in their own habitat: singing whales, beautiful fish, graceful swans, incredible giraffes, sleek panthers, glorious lions, marvelous moose, need I go on? What is your level of pleasure at an unexpected encounter with an animal in the woods?

Farming

There is much news about the plight of farmers but little about their passion. You may resonate to the thrill of growing a few vegetables, but think of generations of families touched by wind, rain, earth, and sun. Living close to and intimately tied to the earth is a unique lifestyle. For many farmers that way of life is the primary love, and practical considerations are a distant second. That is why they don't want to give it up.

Writing

There is passion in putting words together, whether poetry or prose: creating something new out of old, worn parts, delighting in finding the one that fits, that carries the emotion. The words of a single language impose limits on passion, but the possible combinations of words in languages gives it back. A single phrase can change a life.

Sports

Sports is a difficult source of passion for some women because for so long we had limited access. It will be easier for our daughters, and it is easy now for men: the thrill of using your own body and watching the passion of others, slipping through the water as you learn to swim, or watching Joan Benoit complete the first women's Olympic marathon.

I learned about the real passion in sports from my husband and his brother. They used to go out in the backyard and throw a baseball until they literally burned their hands through the leather gloves they wore. They would come back into the house flushed, happy, clearly thrilled. I didn't understand until their father died. He was a man of very few possessions and left only a few cardboard boxes of belongings. One box was filled with all the baseball score cards, neatly filled out, for every game his two sons had ever played in from grade school until they both moved to another state after college. He had kept these cards as one of his most treasured possessions; that's passion.

Arts and Crafts

Whether you do it yourself with needles and thread, clay, paint, or some other medium or become intimate with the works of others, art has all the elements of passion. What touches you? What paintings make you return again and again to try and understand the heart and eye behind the canvas? Stained glass windows, paperweights, carpets, flower arrangements, tapestries, sculpture, mobiles, origami, hand-blown glass, photographs, neon—the list is endless, which is one of the passions of art. There are an infinite number of perceptions of the world and its beauty.

Business

Women used to ask their husbands in business, "Do you love me or your work best?" It was a dangerous question; some men were tempted to lie, because the answer was business. It has some of the same elements as raising children. You put together a concept, test it, develop it, build it, and in a way it is all yours. You are the first one to get there in the morning, when it is still quiet. You know what's in the drawers and files. You may be the last to leave, turning the key in the door and feeling a sense of completion. As more and more women create their own businesses, we will not only have another source of passion but we will understand that passion in men.

Children

One of the most obvious of all our passions is children. There is intimacy, faith, intensity, understanding, and time in abundance. Our passion for our children is almost overwhelming. There is nothing we do that is more important than caring for the next generation. It is a deep and abiding bond.

Mechanics

Cars are connected to men, as technology has been for a long time. This is another one of those passions I did not understand until I learned it from men: the ability to put disparate parts together and end up with a machine, parts that when connected move, generate an energy that is new.

I learned about the passion in cars from my son. When he was fourteen, he decided to build a car. He was barely passing in school, difficult to live with, occasionally stoned, but he wanted to take over the garage. Neither his father nor I had any interest in cars or mechanics, we were barely tolerant.

Our son Devon got a job as a busboy at a fancy French restaurant to earn the money for parts. I used to sneak into the adjacent cocktail lounge just so I could see him cleaned up, in a bow tie and cummerbund with his long hair tied back neatly.

One day he came home with two axles and a frame—no car body, just a frame. It took him two years to build an immense car. It was a Camaro with a supercharger coming out of the hood, a gray fur interior, and a credit card ignition. I didn't believe it would even start. I'm barely able to change batteries.

He announced one Sunday afternoon that he was going to drive the car out of the garage. I was worried, thinking it would be a dismal failure and he would be hurt. He went out and gathered the neighbors, many of whom knew more about the progress of this vehicle than I did. Then he rolled up the garage door, slipped into the driver's seat, put the card in the ignition, and varoom!!! It started with a roar and lunged out into the driveway, and everyone cheered. I understood the passion of cars. Through my tears I realized the intensity, the joy, of putting all those parts together into a whole that moves and hums.

Spirituality

I hesitate to write about the passion of spirituality. For many of us it is the most difficult and the most powerful. Faith can be a life force. Spiritual passion can be a way of life. Throughout the centuries men and women have turned their lives over to their belief in another world or a higher power. The quest is a passion for some, the afterlife for others, the faith itself for many.

It is the ultimate issue of the meaning of it all: nirvana, enlightenment, satori, communion, and all the other ways of describing the breakthrough into truth and ecstasy.

There are many sources of passion beyond these, within each of us. Take a moment to go inside and add to your list. If you don't know what your passions are, you'll forget to choose them. If you don't have any now, it's time to find out why.

What Gets in the Way

The hunger for passion is there in all of us. The problem is tapping into it. If you don't pay attention to this hunger in your life, you will sooner or later run into a brick wall and wonder if your fire's gone out. Understanding our place in history helps us to find out what get's in the way of passion.

Culture

Passion used to be survival, the thrill of bedding down knowing you would awake with enough food and shelter to live another day. Throughout most of our economic history we were marginal hunters and gatherers. We still carry those passions with us when we jog, camp, hike, or backpack in the wilderness.

Today many of us have been released from the constant effort to survive. We seem to have replaced it with constant activity but not with other sources of passion. Where once we were too tired from working, we are now too tired from trying to do everything. The result is confusion and ambivalence. We ask questions that don't make sense and seem greedy to those still trying to find enough to eat.

Underlying these questions is a basic shift in our culture from having to being. For most of our history we were concerned with basics—food, shelter, safety. Until this century few people lived well as we now define it. Most people in the world still have limited floor space and far less control of the quality of their political and social life.

The old quest centered around creating safety by getting more. A full pantry, a house with a fence around it, a car that started, and a guaranteed wage were passions in a sense. Once we became safer, as the middle classes developed, the priorities shifted.

In the fifties women developed a passion for cleanliness and literally thrilled at clean floors and bright laundry. "You can eat off my floor." Keeping all the stuff we'd acquired clean and stored became the next level of safety. In the sixties the "hippies" tried to change the definition of safety, moving away from material goods and out into mind expansion, communal living, and spirituality. Peace became more important than cleanliness.

The quest in the seventies was for self-awareness: creating safety through self-knowledge. Now in the eighties more and more of us are trying to combine all four: material goods, mind expansion, self-awareness, and peace. Passion and intimacy will be the pursuits of the nineties.

But somehow passion became harder to come by as we became more detached from real survival. Passion shifted gears. Passion took time, intensity, commitment, trust, faith, understanding, and we were exulting in control.

Arrgh! For those of us just learning to buy and store it is frustrating to be asked new questions. We can master the survival skills for having, but we don't have many for being.

We have created an illusion of safety around things, and it is very difficult to let go of control (traditional safety) long enough to let our life force flow again—to feel.

We are changing. Bits and pieces of passion may come from the collection of objects, but few find true commitment in the holding of inanimate objects. Most of us want to feel a pulse in what we love and connect to. We just don't know how.

Understanding your family, and your culture, will help.

Fear

It's not easy to opt for passion when it seems like a choice between all open or all closed. Safety and passion don't seem connected or connectable. Some women describe orgasm as the feeling of going over a cliff or dropping into an abyss, a frightening image filled with excitement, sort of like hang gliding just before you hit. With orgasms we forget there's a built-in parachute.

Have you ever laughed until you cried? You feel yourself about to lose control and then stop yourself before you become hysterical. What's wrong with a little hysterical pleasure? In our culture, lots. Women, in particular, end up with a mixed message about pleasure and control that can be very difficult to sort out, no matter how safe the circumstances.

Passion and anxiety feel the same physiologically, that is, heightened awareness, but psychologically one is negative and the other is positive. Some women report that the feeling of passion is negative, and they like to avoid getting upset. They choose a life of quiet frustration and repression.

The feeling of hysteria combines elements of passion and anxiety, but the most common example of the combination is in a love affair with someone. It can be hard to tell the difference. The adrenalin rush is the same, but one is a defense response, and the other is anticipation. Women have been raised with such high anxiety about their worth that just the relief of it is enough to pass as real passion. He finally calls, he comes home, even if it's late. You finally get married.

Many of the messages in our culture encourage women to mistake anxiety for passion: romance novels where only great peril results in true love, the rules about calling boys in high school; the message to wait, to be passive, all lead to anxiety in relationships. The so-called Cinderella complex, is waiting for life to happen to you rather than making it happen the way you want. Can you imagine how Cinderella felt hanging around the house all day wondering if either a prince or a fairy godmother would show up? You could end up waiting a long time.

Anxiety	Passion
I wonder about my value.	I feel valuable.
Will this last?	It will go on forever.
I don't trust him.	I trust me.
I'm not safe.	I'm safe.
Will he take care of me?	I can take care of myself.

Take a step away from anxiety and toward passion by creating the safest possible situation for yourself around something you love. Start small, with music, for example. Pick a piece of music you love, and create a safe place to listen to it. Try to anticipate distractions: noise, not being the right temperature, hunger, needing to use the toilet, interruptions, the wrong environment, guilt about doing something for yourself. Get these under reasonable control (remember, headphones can help create an island of peace amidst chaos), take ten deep breaths, and let yourself enjoy. Bring the music into your body in whatever way works for you. Fill up with it, tingle to it, and snuggle into the pleasure.

Control

Many of us resist even the suggestion that we practice passion. We want control. Control equals safety. Passion is messy, and besides, we don't like other people suggesting things to us. Check your past. Was there a time in your life when you had very little control and got hurt? Some of us spend a lifetime protecting ourselves from parents we've been safe from for years.

How safe are you really? What could hurt you in the midst of passion and pleasure? What's the worst possible thing that could happen? Someone would see me or hear me? I would open up some part of myself that I have carefully kept closed? It might hurt? I might not feel anything even though I want to? Passion requires risks, because it requires you to let all of your life energy flow.

We are all afraid of what we don't know about ourselves. We are afraid of where our sexual energy will take us if we don't exert control. We doubt (again) our ability to make choices and still feel free. Discipline and passion work very well together. The discipline is necessary, as it is in work, to create the intensity.

Passion does have the power to reveal, create, and transform. There is nothing safe or stable about it. Finding the child within, feeling the message from a world we once deeply knew but have long since forgotten breaks the separation between your true and false self. It is sometimes painful, because we reconnect with parts of ourselves and in that sense relive that pain that led us, when children, to disconnect from self.

Trust the intuitive, let go of a little of the control you hold over your life and memories. You are safe.

Check yourself for perfectionism. Passion is messy, whether you are painting or making love. Is that okay with you? When did you last finger-paint, make mud pies, or otherwise revel in a little disorder?

Self-value

Harp, harp, you do deserve it. Read about self-esteem, and work on it. What possible purpose can it serve for you to feel anything less than wonderful? Watch out for the theory of retribution that sometimes sneaks into our consciousness, the feeling that if I feel this good I must be in trouble.

Many of us were raised on the retribution theory of life, the idea that if you're having a good time valuing your life, something is sure to go wrong to reestablish balance. You're driving home from work after just completing a project. You feel exhilarated, alive, full of pleasure when suddenly another message creeps in: If I feel this good, something bad must have happened. The house is on fire; the child is hurt; the dog got hit by a car. We will literally create a downer to restore our sense of balance.

Think of all the messages we give when people are on a roll.

"They'll get theirs."
"It won't last."
"Who does she think she is?"
"Enjoy it while you can" (sigh).
"Anyone having that much fun is not too bright."

Retribution is a religious myth that grew out of our lack of understanding of the universe. When we couldn't explain the sun, storms, and rain we created gods with personalities like ours so we would feel safer. As long as we placated the sun god the crops would be fine. We assumed the gods would want what we wanted, so we gave them a portion of the crops and the occasional virgin in hopes they would let us have the rest. The idea of sacrifice was born: not the ideal of sacrifice for a good purpose but sacrifice for an illusion.

This idea of sacrifice and suffering has stayed with us. It's a lot like original sin; you are guilty no matter what. In many religions people physically beat themselves so their god won't be tempted to do it to them at a less convenient time. We will hurt or deprive ourselves as a balancer, a protection against the laws of the universe that we created.

You are the product of centuries of cultural limits whether they are religious or not. Virginity cults, battered children and wives, sexual violence and abuse, passions labeled as sins, threats of the consequences of touching yourself all conspire to create a powerful fear of passion. Women have been exploited for the destructive passions of others. It will take self-knowledge and an understanding of your past to clear the barrier of retribution.

Competition

A full sense of passion in your life does have some real dangers that hold many of us back. Envy is one danger. It is sad but very true that the energy you exude will upset, irritate, and sometimes hurt others. They will feel a loss by comparison. Your passion reminds them of their lack of passion. It's as if you were questioning their worth and their choices.

Most people will let it go, but others, even close friends and relatives, will sabotage you. They may not even know why. Gossip will follow you around; negative things will be revealed and, if you are a public figure, published. It will take a sure sense of self and an understanding of the pain of others to hold on to your positive feelings. Reread the section on competition, and try to keep known hurters out of your life.

Being Out of Touch

One of the most difficult barriers to passionate feelings is just being out of touch with ourselves: too many years of disconnecting from our body and our feelings, too much sugar, alcohol, caffeine, and repression.

We have become experts at blocking our natural emotions or discounting our intuition. You were taught as a child to be unaware, to conform and please everyone but yourself. Sometimes we carry those lessons too far. We cannot separate survival skills learned as children from pleasures safe for adults.

You may not want to feel responsible for passion. It is better to be coerced, to be "taken" by someone else. Then, somehow the pleasure is an accident we didn't plan. That's how a lot of women get pregnant when they don't really want to. Drugs are another avenue to passion that give us the feeling that somehow we don't have a choice, our body takes off without us.

We are all tempted to skate on the surface. We're skilled at keeping passion out of our lives. It's a tremendous loss. We use time, priorities, energy, preoccupation, to keep people and life at bay. What you risk is your fundamental relationship to yourself, because passion is a measure of the depth you will allow in your character and your life.

What You Can Do

Body. Check the section on body image, and prepare to take better care of yourself. Take wonderful baths; do aroma therapy with lotion; exercise until you tingle again; dress in natural fabrics and colors that help you glow. The right sweatshirt is better than an expensive suit that you don't connect with. Get a massage or a facial, have other hands treat you well too. Take frequent stress breaks just by breathing or stretching.

- meditate
- breath deeply
- exercise
- play
- dance
- touch
- make love
- feel textures
- squeeze and let go

Mind. Ask yourself regularly, What do I want? Answer. Remind yourself that you are lovable and capable. Dream, travel, connect to the world you live in on every level. Check all the sources of passion I've listed plus your own. Stretch your mind and heart.

- get bliss hits
- daydreams
- imagine
- make affirmations
- time alone
- keep a journal
- love the child within
- forgive
- find the humor

Spirit. Put some time and energy into the growth of your spiritual self. I could not begin to help you define God or the forces that you sense are in the universe. I can only tell you that for most of us it is the greatest of all sources of lifetime passion. It is our connection to the universe. There is no difference between sexual and spiritual passion, they are both part of your life force.

- create visions
- study religion
- offer prayers
- travel the world
- give to your community
- cherish solitude

No one else can do it for you. If you want it all—peace, intensity, excitement, heavy breathing, commitment, intimacy, and love—you must do it yourself. True, intense, lifetime, daily passion comes only from your relationship to yourself, to the world and to the Spirit.

We move ahead by going deeper.

Open up, a little at a time. Be gentle. Treat yourself and others with utmost kindness. No one else can do it for you. There is no passion in being someone else.

Yours is the hand you will hold the longest.

In Case You Want More Help

Addiction

Alcoholics Anonymous. New York: A.A. World Services, 1976.

Appel, Willa. *Cults in America: Programmed for Paradise*. New York: Holt, Rinehart, and Winston, 1985.

Drews, Toby. *Getting Them Sober: A Guide for Those Living with Alcoholism*. Vols. 1 and 2. South Plainfield, NJ: Bridge Publishing, Inc., 1980.

Gravitz, Herbert, and Julie Bowden. *Guide to Recovery: Book for Adult Children of Alcoholics*. Holmes Beach, FL: Learning Publications, Inc., 1986.

Halpern, Howard. *How to Break Your Addiction to a Person*. New York: Bantam Books, 1982.

Norwood, Robin. *Women Who Love Too Much*. New York: Pocket Books, 1986.

Peele, Stanton, and Archie Brodsky. *Love and Addiction*. New York: New American Library, 1987.

Seixas, Judith. *Living with a Parent Who Drinks Too Much*. New York: Greenwillow Books, 1979.

Steiner, Claude. *Games Alcoholics Play*. New York: Ballantine Books, 1977.

Woititz, Janet. *Adult Children of Alcoholics*. Pompano Beach, FL: Health Communications, 1983.

Adult Children

Bloomfield, Harold H. *Making Peace with Your Children*. New York: Random House, 1983.

Davis, Bruce, and Genny Wright Davis. *The Magical Child Within You*. Berkeley, CA: Celestial Arts, 1985.

Halpern, Howard. *Cutting Loose: An Adult Guide to Coming to Terms with Your Parents*. New York: Bantam Books, 1978.

Hoffman, Bob. *No One Is to Blame—Getting a Loving Divorce from Mom and Dad*. Palo Alto: Science and Behavior, 1979.

Leonard, Linda Schierse. *The Wounded Woman: Healing the Father-Daughter Relationship*. Athens: Ohio University Press, 1982.

Age

Anderson, Barbara Gallatin. *The Aging Game: Success, Sanity, and Sex After Sixty*. New York: McGraw-Hill, 1981.

Brammer, Lawrence M. *Joys and Challenges of Middle Age*. Chicago: Nelson-Hill, 1982.

Levinson, Daniel. *The Season of Man's Life*. New York: Ballantine Books, 1979.

Sheehy, Gail. *Pathfinders*. New York: William Morrow and Co., Inc., 1981.

Tomb, David A. *Growing Old: A Handbook for You and Your Aging Parent*. New York: Viking Penguin, Inc., 1984.

Anger

Augsburger, David. *Caring Enough to Confront*. Scottsdale, PA: Herald Press, 1980.

Lerner, Harriet G. *The Dance of Anger: A Woman's Guide to Changing the Patterns of Intimate Relationships*. New York: Harper & Row Publishers, Inc., 1985.

Rubin, Theodore. *The Angry Book*. New York: Macmillan Publishing Co., Inc., 1970.

Tarvis, Carol. *Anger: The Misunderstood Emotion*. New York: Simon and Schuster, 1982.

Weisinger, Hendrie D. *Dr. Weisinger's Anger Workout Book*. New York: William Morrow and Co., Inc., 1985.

Anxiety (Worry)

Agras, Stewart. *Panic: Facing Fears, Phobias, and Anxiety*. New York: W.H. Freeman, 1985.

Beck, Aaron. *Anxiety Disorders and Phobias: A Cognitive Perspective*. New York: Basic Books, 1985.

De Rosis, Helena. *Women and Anxiety*. New York: Dell Books, 1981.

Friedman, Martha. *Overcoming the Fear of Success*. New York: Warner Books, 1982.

Greist, J. H. *The Anxiety and Its Treatment: Help is Available*. Boston: American Psychiatric Press, 1986.

Kratochwill, Thomas, and R. J. Morris. *Treating Children's Fears and Phobias*. Elmsford: Pergamon Press, 1983.

May, Rollo. *The Meaning of Anxiety*. New York: Pocket Books, 1979.

Neuman, Frederic. *Fighting Fear: An Eight-Week Guide to Treating Your Own Phobias*. New York: MacMillan Publishing Co., Inc., 1985.

Weekes, Claire. *Hope and Help for Your Nerves*. New York: Bantam Books, 1978.

Assertiveness

Alberti, Robert E., and Michael L. Emmons. *Your Perfect Right: A Guide to Assertive Living*. Evanston: Impact Publications Catalogue, 1986.

Fensterheim, Herbert, and Jean Baer. *Don't Say Yes When You Want to Say No*. New York: Dell Publishing Company, Inc., 1975.

Body Image

Birkinshaw, Elsye. *Think Slim—Be Slim*. Santa Barbara, CA: Woodbridge Press Publishing Company, 1981.

Orbach, Susie. *Fat Is a Feminist Issue: The Anti-Diet Guide to Permanent Weight Loss*. New York: Berkley Publishing Company, 1987.

Breaking Up

Colgrove, Melba; Harold Bloomfield; and Peter McWilliams. *How to Survive the Loss of a Love*. New York: Bantam Books, 1977.

IN CASE YOU WANT MORE HELP

Change

O'Connell, April, and Jacqueline Whitmore. *Choice and Change: The Psychology of Adjustment, Growth, and Creativity.* Englewood Cliffs, NJ: Prentice-Hall, Inc., 1985.

Rusk, Tom, and Randy Read. *I Want to Change but I Don't Know How!* Los Angeles: Price, Stern, and Sloan Publishers, Inc., 1986.

Criticism

Elgin, Suzette Haden. *The Gentle Art of Verbal Self-Defense.* Englewood Cliffs, NJ: Prentice-Hall, Inc., 1980.

James, Jennifer. *The Slug Manual: The Rise and Fall of Criticism.* Seattle: Bronwen Press, 1984.

Weisinger, Hendrie, and Norman M. Lobsenz. *Nobody's Perfect: How to Give Criticism and Get Results.* New York: Warner Books, 1981.

Crying

Frey, William H., and Muriel Langseth. *Crying: The Mystery of Tears.* New York: Harper & Row Publishers, Inc., 1985.

Death

Grollman, Earl. *Living When a Loved One Has Died.* Boston: Beacon Press, 1987.

Kübler-Ross, Elizabeth. *Death: The Final Stage of Growth.* New York: Simon and Schuster, 1986.

Kübler-Ross, Elizabeth. *Living with Death and Dying.* New York: Macmillan Publishing Co., Inc., 1982.

Leshan, Eda. *Learning to Say Goodbye: When a Parent Dies.* New York: Macmillan Publishing Co., Inc., 1976.

Stein, Sara Bennett. *About Dying.* New York: Walker and Company, 1984.

Viorst, Judith. *The Tenth Good Thing about Barney.* New York: Macmillan Publishing Co., Inc., 1975.

Depression

Beck, Aaron T. *Depression: Causes and Treatment.* Philadelphia: University of Pennsylvania, 1972.

Burns, David. *Feeling Good: The New Mood Therapy.* New York: William Morrow and Co., Inc., 1980.

Derosis, Helen, and Victoria Pellegrino. *The Book of Hope: How Women Can Overcome Depression.* New York: Bantam Books, 1977.

Fieve, Ronald. *Moodswing: The Third Revolution in Psychiatry.* New York: Bantam Books, 1976.

Gold, Mark. *The Good News about Depression: Cures and Treatments in the New Age of Psychiatry.* New York: Random House, 1987.

Greist, John H., and James W. Jefferson. *Depression and Its Treatment.* New York: Warner Books, 1985.

McCoy, Kathleen. *Coping with Teenager Depression.* New York: New American Library, 1985.

Quinnett, Paul G. *Suicide: The Forever Decision: A Book for Those Thinking about Suicide and for Those Who Know, Love or Counsel Them.* New York: Continuum Publishing Co., 1987.

Divorce

Gardner, Richard A. *The Boys and Girls Book about Divorce.* New York: Bantam Books, 1971.

Gardner, Richard A. *The Parent's Book about Divorce.* New York: Bantam Books, 1979.

Ricci, Isolina. *Mom's House, Dad's House; Making Shared Custody Work.* New York: Macmillan Publishing Co., Inc., 1980.

Energy

Kriegel, Robert, and Marilyn Harris Kriegel. *The C Zone: Peak Performance Under Pressure.* New York: Doubleday and Company, Inc., 1985.

Exercise

Hittleman, Richard. *Yoga: Twenty-eight Day Exercise Plan.* New York: Bantam Books, 1973.

Forgiveness

Augsburger, David. *Caring Enough to Forgive: Caring Enough Not to Forgive.* Scottsdale, PA: Herald Press, 1981.

Huxley, Laura. *You Are Not the Target.* New York: Avon Publications, 1984.

Jampolsky, Gerald. *Love Is Letting Go of Fear.* New York: Bantam Books, 1982.

Smedes, Lewis. *Forgive and Forget: Healing the Hurts We Don't Deserve.* San Francisco: Harper & Row Publishers, Inc., 1984.

Friendship

Augsburger, David. *Caring Enough to Confront.* Scottsdale, PA: Herald Press, 1980.

Bach, George, and Ronald Deutsch. *Stop—You're Driving Me Crazy.* New York: Berkley Publications, 1985.

Margolies, Eva. *The Best of Friends, The Worst of Enemies: Women's Hidden Power Over Women.* New York: Doubleday and Company, Inc., 1985.

McGinnis, Alan Loy. *Friendship Factor.* Minneapolis: Augsburg Publishing House, 1979.

Shain, Merle. *When Lovers Are Friends.* New York: Bantam Books, 1980.

Gossip

Bok, Sissela. *Secrets: On the Ethics of Concealment and Revelation.* New York: Random House, 1984.

Holbrooke, Blythe. *Gossip: How to Get It Before It Gets You and Other Suggestions for Social Survival.* New York: St. Martin's Press, 1983.

Grief

Colgrove, Melba; Harold Bloomfield; and Peter McWilliams. *How to Survive the Loss of a Love.* New York: Bantam Books, 1977.

Jewett, Claudia L. *Helping Children Cope with Separation and Loss*. Cambridge: Harvard Common Press, 1982.

Kübler-Ross, Elizabeth, and M. Warshaw. *To Live Until We Say Goodbye*. Englewood Cliffs, NJ: Prentice-Hall, Inc., 1978.

Miller, William A. *When Going to Pieces Holds You Together*. Minneapolis: Augsburg Publishing House, 1976.

Phillips, Debora, and Robert Judd. *How to Fall Out of Love*. New York: Warner Books, 1982.

Schiff, Harriet Sarnoff. *The Bereaved Parent*. New York: Penguin Books, 1978.

Stearns, Ann K. *Living Through Personal Crisis*. Chicago: Thomas Moore Press, 1984.

Thomas, Susan. *What to Do, Know and Expect When a Loved One Dies*. Seattle: Type + Plus, 1984.

Viorst, Judith. *Necessary Losses*. New York: Simon and Schuster, 1986.

Guilt

Hansel, Tim. *When I Relax I Feel Guilty*. Elgin, IL: David C. Cook Publishing Co., 1979.

Jampolsky, Gerald. *Goodbye to Guilt: Releasing Fear through Forgiveness*. New York: Bantam Books, 1985.

Health

Cousins, Norman. *Anatomy of an Illness: As Perceived by the Patient*. New York: Bantam Books, 1979.

Epstein, Gloria. *Help Yourself to Chronic Pain Relief: The Patient's Point of View*. Seattle: Manchester Group, 1981.

Moss, Richard. *How Shall I Live: Transforming Surgery or Any Health Crisis into Greater Aliveness*. Berkeley: Celestial Arts, 1985.

Help in Crisis

Burns, David. *Feeling Good: The New Mood Therapy*. New York: William Morrow and Co., Inc., 1980.

Cousins, Norman. *Human Options: An Autobiographical Notebook*. New York: W.W. Norton and Company, Inc., 1981.

Miller, William A. *When Going to Pieces Holds You Together*. Minneapolis: Augsburg Publishing Company, 1976.

Pelletier, Kenneth R. *Mind As Healer, Mind As Slayer: A Holistic Approach to Preventing Stress Disorders*. New York: Dell Books, 1977.

Intimacy

Barbach, Lonnie. *For Yourself: The Fulfillment of Female Sexuality: A Guide to Orgasmic Response*. New York: New American Library, 1976.

Barbach, Lonnie, and Linda Levine. *Shared Intimacies: Women's Sexual Experience*. New York: Bantam Books, 1981.

Leonard, George. *The End of Sex*. Boston: Tarcher/Mifflin Co., 1983.

Masters, William H. and Virginia E. Johnson. *The Pleasure Bond: A New Look at Sexuality and Commitment*. Denver: Little Publishing, 1975.

Meshorer, Marc and Judith. *Ultimate Pleasure: The Secrets of Easily Orgasmic Women*. New York: St. Martin's Press, 1986.
Woititz, Janet. *The Struggle for Intimacy*. Pompano Beach, FL: Health Communications, 1985.

Jealousy

Clanton, Gordon, and Lynn F. Smith. *Jealousy*. Frederick: University Publications of America, 1987.
Ephron, Nora. *Heartburn*. New York: Knopf, 1983.
Friday, Nancy. *Jealousy*. New York: Bantam Books, 1987.

Lesbian

Martin, Del, and Phyllis Lyon. *Lesbian/Woman*. New York: Bantam Books, 1972.

Lifework

Bolles, Richard N. *The Quick Job Hunting Map*. Berkeley, CA: Ten Speed Press, 1982.
Bolles, Richard N. *What Color Is Your Parachute?* Berkeley: Ten Speed Press, 1988.
Jackson, Tom, and Davidyn Mayleas. *The Hidden Job Market for the Eighties*. New York: Time Books, 1981.

Men

Bateman, Py, and Bill Mahoney. *Macho? What Do Girls Really Want?* Scarborough, NY: Youth Education Systems, Inc. Forthcoming.
Druck, Ken and James C. Simmons, *The Secrets Men Keep*. New York: Ballantine Books, 1987.
Friday, Nancy. *Men in Love: Male Sexual Fantasies: The Triumph of Love Over Rage*. New York: Dell Books, 1980.
Goldberg, Herb. *Hazards of Being Male: Surviving the Myth of Masculine Privilege*. New York: New American Library, 1977.
Shain, Merle. *Some Men Are More Perfect Than Others*. New York: Bantam Books, 1980.
Singer, June. *Androgyny: The Opposites Within*. Boston: Sigo Press, 1987.
Zilbergeld, Bernie, and John Ullman. *Male Sexuality: A Guide to Sexual Fulfillment*. New York: Bantam Books, 1978.

Parenting

Blume, Judy. *Letters to Judy: What Your Kids Wish They Could Tell You*. New York: Putnam Publishing Group, 1986.
Briggs, Dorothy. *Your Child's Self-Esteem: The Key to His Life*. New York: Doubleday and Company, Inc., 1970.
Chess, Stella. *Your Child Is a Person: A Psychological Approach to Parenthood without Guilt*. New York: Penguin Publishing Company, 1977.
Crary, Elizabeth. *Without Spanking or Spoiling: A Practical Approach to Toddler and Preschool Guidance*. Seattle: Parenting Press, 1979.
Dinkmeyer, Don, and Gary D. McKay. *The Parent's Handbook: Systematic Training for Effective Parenting*. New York: Random House, 1982.

Dreikurs, Rudolf, and Loren Grey. *A Parent's Guide to Child Discipline*. New York: Dutton Publishing, 1970.

Faber, Adele, and Elaine Mazlish. *How to Talk So Kids Listen and Listen So Kids Will Talk*. New York: Avon Books, 1985.

Freeman, Lory. *It's My Body*. Seattle: Parenting Press, 1983.

Reid, John. *Living with Teenagers: A Survival Manual for Adults*. Everett, WA: Ampersand Publishing, 1983.

Roosevelt, Ruth, and Jeanette Lofar. *Living in Step*. New York: McGraw-Hill, 1977.

Swan, Helen, and Victoria Houston. *Alone After School: A Self-Care Guide for Latchkey Children and Their Parents*. Englewood Cliffs, NJ: Prentice-Hall, 1985.

Thevenin, Tine. *The Family Bed*. Garden City Park, NJ: Avery Publishing Group, Inc., 1987.

Whelan, Elizabeth. *A Baby? Maybe: A Guide to Making the Most Fateful Decision of Your Life*. New York: New Bobbs Publishing Company, 1980.

York, Phyllis and David. *Tough Love*. Sellersville: Community Service Foundation, Inc., 1980.

Passion

Anderson, Nancy. *Work with Passion*. New York: Carroll and Graf, 1984.

Keen, Sam. *The Passionate Life: Stages of Loving*. New York: Harper & Row Publishers, Inc., 1983.

Personal Growth

Bloomfield, Harold H., and Robert B. Kory. *Inner Joy*. New York: Jove Publications, 1985.

Braiker, Harriet B. *The Type E Woman*. New York: Dodd, Mead, and Company, 1986.

Briggs, Dorothy. *Embracing Life: Growing through Love and Loss*. New York: Doubleday and Company, Inc., 1985.

Buscaglia, Leo. *Love*. New York: Fawcett Crest Books, 1977.

Davis, Bruce, and Genny Wright Davis. *The Magical Child Within You*. Berkeley, CA: Celestial Arts, 1985.

James, Jennifer. *Success Is the Quality of Your Journey*. New York: Newmarket Press, 1987.

James, Jennifer. *Windows*. New York: Newmarket Press, 1987.

Jampolsky, Gerald. *Love Is Letting Go of Fear*. New York: Bantam Books, 1982.

Jampolsky, Gerald. *Teach Only Love: The Seven Principles of Attitudinal Healing*. New York: Bantam Books, 1983.

Levine, Stephen. *Who Dies: An Investigation of Conscious Living and Conscious Dying*. New York: Doubleday and Company, 1982.

Miller, Alice. *Thou Shalt Not Be Aware: Society's Betrayal of the Child*. New York: New American Library, 1986.

Newman, Mildred, and Bernard Berkowitz. *How to Take Charge of Your Life*. New York: Bantam Books, 1978.

O'Connor, Elizabeth. *Our Many Selves*. New York: Harper & Row Publishers, Inc., 1971.

Pines, Ayala. *Burnout: From Tedium to Personal Growth*. New York: Free Press, 1981.

Rubin, Theodore. *Compassion and Self-Hate*. New York: Ballantine Books, 1971.

Rusk, Tom, and Randy Read. *I Want to Change but I Don't Know How*. Los Angeles: Price, Stern, and Sloan Publishers, 1986.

Viorst, Judith. *Necessary Losses*. New York: Simon and Schuster, 1986.

Viscott, David. *Risking*. New York: Pocket Books, 1977.

Perspective

Cousins, Norman. *Anatomy of an Illness: As Perceived by the Patient*. New York: Bantam Books, 1981.

Halas, Celia, and Roberta Matteson. *I've Done So Well—Why Do I Feel So Bad?* New York: Ballantine Books, 1987.

Harvey, Joan C., and Cynthia Katz. *If I'm So Successful Why Do I Feel Like a Fake?: The Imposter Phenomenon*. New York: Pocket Books, 1986.

James, Jennifer. *Success Is the Quality of Your Journey*. New York: Newmarket Press, 1987.

James, Jennifer. *Windows*. New York: Newmarket Press, 1987.

Relationships

Bach, George R., and Ronald M. Deutsch. *Stop—You're Driving Me Crazy*. New York: Berkeley Publishing, 1979.

Brandt, David. *Is That All There Is?* New York: Pocket Books, 1984.

Huffines, Launa. *Connecting*. New York: Harper & Row Publishers, Inc., 1986.

Krantzler, Mel. *Learning to Love Again*. New York: Harper & Row Publishers, Inc., 1977.

Lederer, William, and Don Jackson. *The Mirages of Marriage*. New York: W.W. Norton and Company, 1968.

Leonard, Linda Schierse. *The Wounded Woman: Healing the Father-Daughter Relationship*. Athens: Ohio University Press, 1982.

Mandel, Bob. *Two Hearts Are Better Than One*. Berkeley, CA: Celestial Arts, 1986.

Peele, Stanton, and Archie Brodsky. *Love and Addiction*. New York: Taplinger, 1975.

Scheid, Robert. *Beyond the Love Game*. Berkeley, CA: Celestial Arts, 1980.

Shain, Merle. *Some Men Are More Perfect Than Others*. New York: Bantam Books, 1980.

Shain, Merle. *When Lovers Are Friends*. New York: Bantam Books, 1980.

Sheehy, Gail. *Spirit of Survival*. New York: William Morrow and Co., Inc., 1980.

Visher, John and Emily. *How to Win As a Stepfamily*. New York: Dembner Books, 1982.

Romance

Grice, Julia. *How to Find Romance After Forty*. New York: M. Evans and Company, 1985.

Raphael, Sally Jesse, and M. J. Abadie. *Finding Love: Practical Advice for Men and Women*. New York: Arbor House, 1984.

Self-Esteem

Briggs, Dorothy. *Celebrate Yourself: Enhancing Your Own Self-Esteem*. New York: Doubleday and Company, 1986.

Briggs, Dorothy. *Your Child's Self-Esteem: The Key to His Life*. New York: Doubleday and Company, 1970.

Clarke, Jean Illsey. *Self-Esteem: A Family Affair*. New York: Harper & Row, 1980.

Friedman, Martha. *Overcoming the Fear of Success*. New York: Warner Books, 1982.

James, Jennifer. *Life Is a Game of Choice*. Seattle: Bronwen Press, 1986.

Newman, Mildred, and Bernard Berkowitz. *How to Be Your Own Best Friend*. New York: Ballantine Books, 1984.

Rubin, Theodore. *Compassion and Self-Hate*. New York: Ballantine Books, 1976.

Sex

Barbach, Lonnie. *For Yourself: The Fulfillment of Female Sexuality*. New York: Doubleday and Company, 1975.

Barbach, Lonnie. *For Each Other: Sharing Sexual Intimacy*. New York: Doubleday and Company, 1982.

Barbach, Lonnie, and Linda Levine. *Shared Intimacies*. New York: Bantam Books, 1981.

Fay, Jennifer, and Billie Jo Flerchinger. *Top Secret: A Discussion Guide*. Santa Cruz, CA: Network Publications, 1985.

Goldberg, Herb. *Hazards of Being Male: Surviving the Myth of Masculine Privilege*. New York: New American Library, 1977.

Leonard, George. *The End of Sex*. Boston: Tarcher/Mifflin Company, 1983.

McCarthy, Barry, and Emily McCarthy. *Sexual Awareness*. New York: Carroll and Graf, 1984.

O'Connor, Dagmar. *How to Make Love to the Same Person for the Rest of Your Life and Still Love It*. New York: Doubleday and Company, 1985.

Singer, June. *Androgyny: The Opposites Within*. Boston: Sigo Press, 1987.

Zilbergeld, Bernie. *Male Sexuality: A Guide to Sexual Fulfillment*. New York: Bantam Books, 1978.

Single

Hellman, Lillian. *Pentimento: A Book of Portraits*. Denver: Little Publishing Company, 1973.

Johnson, Stephen. *First Person Singular: Living the Good Life Alone*. New York: New American Library, 1978.

Spirit

Bach, Richard. *Illusions: The Adventures of a Reluctant Messiah*. New York: Dell Publishing Company, 1977.

Buscaglia, Leo. *Living, Loving, and Learning*. New York: Fawcett, 1983.

Cousins, Norman. *Human Option*. New York: W.W. Norton and Company, 1981.

Ferguson, Marilyn. *The Aquarian Conspiracy*. Boston: Tarcher/Mifflin Company, 1980.

Fields, Rick; with Peggy Taylor; Rex Weyler; Rick Ingrasci. *Chop Wood, Carry Water: A Guide to Finding Spiritual Fulfillment in Everyday Life.* Boston: Tarcher/Mifflin Company, 1984.

Gawain, Shakti. *Living in the Light.* Mill Valley, CA: Whatever Publishing, 1986.

Jampolsky, Gerald. *Love Is Letting Go of Fear.* Berkeley, CA: Celestial Arts, 1979.

Kopp, Sheldon. *If You Meet the Buddha on the Road, Kill Him.* New York: Bantam Books, 1976.

Peck, M. Scott. *The Road Less Traveled.* New York: Simon and Schuster, 1985.

Stress

Atkinson, Holly. *Women and Fatigue: Effective Solutions to This Very Real Problem.* New York: Putnam Publishing Group, 1986.

Braiker, Harriet B. *The Type E Woman.* New York: Dodd, Mead, and Company, 1986.

Garfield, Charles. *Peak Performers: Strategies and Insights of America's Most Productive People.* New York: William Morrow and Company, 1986.

Osborn, Carol. *Enough Is Enough.* New York: Putnam Publishing, 1986.

Pines, Ayala. *Burnout: From Tedium to Personal Growth.* New York: Free Press, 1981.

Selye, Hans. *The Stress of Life.* New York: McGraw-Hill, 1978.

Violence

Davis, Diane. *Something Is Wrong at My House.* Seattle: Parenting Press, 1985.

Fay, Jennifer, and Billie Jo Flerchinger. *Top Secret: A Discussion Guide.* Santa Cruz, CA: Network Publications, 1984.

NiCarthy, Ginny. *Getting Free.* Seattle: Seal Press, 1986.

NiCarthy, Ginny. *The Ones Who Got Away: Women Who Left Abusive Partners.* Seattle: Seal Press, 1987.

NiCarthy, Ginny; Karen Merriam; and Sandra Coffman. *Talking It Out: A Guide for Abused Women.* Seattle: Seal Press, 1984.

Sanders, Margo C., and Patricia DeVargas-Walker. *Child Abuse: Empowering Victims to Become Survivors.* Vancouver: Network Graphics, 1987.

Shainess, Natalie. *Sweet Suffering: Woman As Victim.* New York: Bobbs-Merrill Company, Inc., 1984.

Women and Culture

French, Marilyn. *The Women's Room.* New York: Jove Publications, 1987.

Friedan, Betty. *The Feminine Mystique.* New York: W.W. Norton and Company, 1983.

Friedan, Betty. *The Second Stage.* New York: Summit Books, 1982.

Friedl, Ernestine. *Women and Men: An Anthropologist's View.* New York: Holt, Rinehart, and Winston, 1984.

Gilligan, Carol. *In a Different Voice: Psychological Theory and Women's Development.* Boston: Harvard University Press, 1982.

Leonard, Linda Schierse. *The Wounded Woman: Healing the Father-Daughter Relationship.* Athens: Ohio University Press, 1982.

Noble, Kathleen. "The Dilemma of the Gifted Woman." *Psychology of Women Quarterly* 11 (Sept. 1987): 367–378.

Norwood, Robin. *Women Who Love Too Much*. New York: Pocket Books, 1985.

Schaef, Anne. *Women's Reality: An Emerging Female System in the White Male Society*. New York: Harper & Row Publishers, Inc., 1986.

Shainess, Natalie. *Sweet Suffering: Woman As Victim*. New York: Bobbs-Merrill Company, Inc., 1984.

Steinem, Gloria. *Outrageous Acts and Everyday Rebellions*. New York: Holt, Rinehart, and Winston, 1983.

Walker, Alice. *The Color Purple*. San Diego: Harcourt Brace Jovanovich, 1982.

Index